ARSC Guide to Audio Preservation

Sam Brylawski, Maya Lerman, Robin Pike, Kathlin Smith, editors

ASSOCIATION FOR RECORDED SOUND COLLECTIONS | ARS

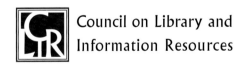
Council on Library and Information Resources

National Recording Preservation Board
OF THE LIBRARY OF CONGRESS

ISBN 978-1-932326-50-5
CLIR Publication No. 164

Copublished by:

Association for Recorded
Sound Collections
c/o Nathan Georgitis, Knight Library
1299 University of Oregon
Eugene, OR 97403
Website at http://arsc-audio.org

Council on Library and
Information Resources
1707 L Street NW, Suite 650
Washington, DC 20036
Website at http://www.clir.org

The Library of Congress
101 Independence Avenue, SE
Washington, DC 20540
Website at http://www.loc.gov

Commissioned for and sponsored by the National Recording Preservation Board of the Library of Congress.

Publication inquiries should be directed to Kathlin Smith at the Council on Library and Information Resources (CLIR).

Additional copies are available for $30 each. Orders may be placed through CLIR's website at http://www.clir.org/pubs/reports/pub164.

The paper in this publication meets the minimum requirements of the American National Standard
for Information Sciences—Permanence of Paper for Printed Library Materials ANSI Z39.48-1984.

Cover design: Kim Smith

Library of Congress Control Number: 2015940108

CONTENTS

Foreword vi
Message from ARSC viii
Acknowledgments x
About this Guide xi

CHAPTER 1: Preserving Audio, *Curtis Peoples and Marsha Maguire* 1
    1.1   Recorded Sound at Risk 2
    1.2   Preservation Efforts to Date 4
    1.3   The Role of Your Institution 8
    1.4   Organization of the Guide 9
    1.5   Conclusion 12
    References 12

CHAPTER 2: Audio Formats: Characteristics and Deterioration, *Harrison Behl* 14
    2.1   Cylinder Formats 15
    2.2   Grooved Disc Formats 17
    2.3   Magnetic Formats 22
    2.4   Optical Disc Formats 28
    2.5   Unusual Formats 31
    2.6   Digital Audio File Formats 32
    2.7   Conclusion 34
    References 35

CHAPTER 3: Appraisals and Priorities, *Maya Lerman* 37
    3.1   Developing a Selection/Collection Development Policy 38
    3.2   Deciding Whether to Acquire a Collection 39
    3.3   Making the Preservation Reformatting Decision 42
    3.4   Tools to Help Make Evaluations 44
    3.5   Other Considerations Affecting Preservation Priorities 45
    3.6   Evaluation for Taxes 48
    3.7   Conclusion 50
    References 50

CHAPTER 4: Care and Maintenance, *Carla Arton* 52
    4.1   Handling 52
    4.2   Assessing Condition 54
    4.3   Cleaning 58
    4.4   Housing 62
    4.5   Storage 65

4.6   Arrangement...68
4.7   Climate Control 69
4.8   Transportation 70
4.9   Playback 71
4.10 Conclusion...74
References 75

CHAPTER 5: Description of Audio Recordings, *Marsha Maguire* 77
5.1   Metadata and Tools for Collection Management........................79
5.2   Exposing Metadata for Public Discovery..............................86
5.3   Choosing Among Metadata Standards 87
5.4   Library Metadata: Standards and Tools 89
5.5   Archival Description: Standards and Tools 94
5.6   Dublin Core Initiative Metadata: Standards and Tools 103
5.7   Conclusion...104
References..105

CHAPTER 6: Preservation Reformatting, *William Chase* 110
6.1   Conversion to Digital Files 111
6.2   Metadata for Reformatting..112
6.3   Digitization: In-House and Vendor Outsourcing........................119
6.4   Funding for Preservation Initiatives 124
References 125

CHAPTER 7: What to Do After Digitization, *Chris Lacinak*.......................127
7.1   Digital Preservation and Access: Process and Practice...................128
7.2   Storage Infrastructure 140
7.3   Conclusion...148
References 149

CHAPTER 8: Audio Preservation: The Legal Context, *Brandon Butler* 152
8.1   Copyright 152
8.2   Special Issues..160
8.3   Control and Responsibility for Downstream Use of Works 164
8.4   Donor Agreements 165
References 166

CHAPTER 9: Disaster Prevention, Preparedness, and Response,
Kara Van Malssen 168
9.1   Disaster Prevention and Mitigation...................................169
9.2   Disaster Planning...174
9.3   First Response Steps...178
9.4   Case Study 183
9.5   Conclusion...192
References 192

APPENDIX A: Fair Use and Sound Recordings: Lessons from Community Practice, *Brandon Butler and Peter Jaszi* 194

APPENDIX B: Glossary 223

Contributors and Editors 231

Index 234

FOREWORD

Today's librarians, archivists, and collectors face a minefield of preservation challenges, none more daunting than the goal of saving our richly diverse recorded
sound heritage. Many factors contribute to the massive scope of the problem: lack
of funding, constant change from new tools and evolving technology, and insufficient training of custodians often more prepared for print material conservation.
Most tellingly, our enjoyment of these recordings has regrettably far exceeded our
commitment to preserve them.

What all these dissimilar recordings together represent is an audio DNA of our culture: how we experience entertainment; how our national mores have continually
evolved; how creativity and passion expressed through the arts have helped push
us to new heights and social progress; and, finally, how they have united us as a
nation even with a population as diverse as the sounds that emanate from formats
large and small.

America's cultural heritage has been expressed through many creative outlets, and
the Library of Congress has active ongoing preservation programs in almost all of
them, including recorded sound. The Library's abiding interest in recordings starts
with the nearly three million sound items found in its collections, given safe harbor
for all time through the extensive conservation projects undertaken at its Packard
Campus for Audio Visual Conservation, and made available to the American public
via access initiatives such as the National Jukebox. These are supplemented at the
Library by the cutting-edge research on audio materials done at our Preservation,
Research and Testing Division, as well as the many grants and partnerships coordinated through the National Digital Information Infrastructure and Preservation
Program.

Through passage of the National Recording Preservation Act of 2000, Congress
recognized the importance of preserving our nation's magnificent audio materials.
This landmark legislation mandated preparation of a study to provide a snapshot
of the problem, to be followed by a comprehensive national preservation program.
The recorded sound community rose to the challenge issued by Congress. With
help from its National Recording Preservation Board and colleagues throughout
the commercial and nonprofit fields, the Library publicly released the study in
August 2010, followed by the national plan in February 2013. This extensive planning process diagnosed problems and proposed a broad range of recommended
solutions. But as we all know, it is easy to make suggestions, and far more difficult
to follow through on them. Now our field has begun the lengthy task of implementing the dozens of recommendations found in the plan.

The Library and Board will serve as facilitators and guide successful completion of the plan. Simply put, ensuring the preservation of our vast recorded sound heritage is far beyond the capacity of even the best-financed single institution and requires extensive resources. These include an effective spirit of cooperation to buttress a coordinated national strategy featuring creative public-private partnerships and actions.

I am pleased to report we are off to a good start. This guide, the result of a model collaboration of many organizations and individuals, constitutes a tangible—and highly promising—first step. It will assist the many non-specialists who have audio in their collections with a basic, readable primer, illustrating ways to preserve these vital, yet vulnerable, items.

Sound recordings comprise an evocative time capsule brimming with many of the most important cultural artifacts entrusted to archives and libraries. In conserving this heritage, preservation begins from the ground up, and this guide helps lay the seeds for that effective grassroots campaign. Solving this enormous task will require vast, creative, and decentralized efforts, fitting given that those terms aptly describe the essence of our captivating recorded sound heritage.

J. Mark Sweeney
Associate Librarian for Library Services
Library of Congress

MESSAGE FROM ARSC

The Association for Recorded Sound Collections (ARSC) is pleased to join with the Council on Library and Information Resources (CLIR) and the Library of Congress in presenting this guide to managing the conservation and preservation of audio collections. ARSC is a nonprofit organization dedicated to the preservation and study of sound recordings of all kinds, regardless of genre, format, or date. Founded in 1966, we bring together individuals and institutions with a wide variety of personal and professional relationships to collections of recorded sound. Our membership includes not only librarians, archivists, and curators from many of the world's largest and most significant institutional repositories of audiovisual heritage, but also engineers, private collectors, musicologists, historians, discographers, musicians, producers, dealers, reviewers, and broadcasters. What we all share in common is a passion for sound recordings and a commitment to preserving them—a challenge which our diversity of perspectives and areas of expertise makes us uniquely well-equipped to address. In addition to our annual conference, our publication of the semiannual *ARSC Journal*, and other ongoing projects of our own, we also recognize and fund outside scholarship, publication, and preservation activities in relevant fields through several awards and grants programs. We are proud to build on our tradition of promoting the well-informed stewardship of recorded sound with the publication of this guidebook.

ARSC's involvement with this guide began in 2007 when CLIR provided support to a group of ARSC members to meet and develop an outline of the contents of a general guide to audio preservation. In 2013, a group of members reconvened under the leadership of ARSC's Education and Training Committee to update the content outline and recruit expert authors to contribute to the guide. Nearly every author who wrote for the guide is a member of ARSC. As a group, they represent more than 200 years of experience working with contemporary and historical sound recordings and related preservation issues.

The mission of ARSC's Education and Training Committee is to address the education and training needs of ARSC members and the larger recorded sound community by providing workshops on sound archiving and preservation, discographic dissemination, bibliographic standards, digitization of sound libraries, copyright, and other related topics. The committee has been providing workshops to ARSC members and the public since our first symposium on "Basic Care and Management of Sound Recordings" in 2000. We are committed to providing information on the preservation and study of sound recordings to a larger audience, and we now provide opportunities to those who cannot attend in person by offering our workshops online.

Our special thanks are due to Sam Brylawski, Maya Lerman, and Robin Pike, the chairs of the Audio Preservation Guide Subcommittee, as well as to the guide's authors, who together comprise an impressive team of authorities in the audio preservation field. We also want to express our gratitude to CLIR—especially co-editor Kathlin Smith and President Chuck Henry—and the National Recording Preservation Board of the Library of Congress, for their essential contributions to making this guide a reality.

If you share ARSC's dedication to keeping our legacy of recorded sound alive—and since you're reading this, you probably do—we cordially invite you to join us. Please visit arsc-audio.org for details.

Patrick Feaster
President

Aaron Bittel
Karen Fishman
Chairs, Education & Training Committee

ACKNOWLEDGMENTS

Publication of this guide would not have been possible without enormous contributions from many people. Each of the chapter authors contributed expertise, time, talent, and patience to make this work possible. The guide could not have been created without the commitments of the three institutions that have supported it through its development: the Library of Congress, the Council on Library and Information Resources, and the Association for Recorded Sound Collections. The editors of the guide take full responsibility for any errors or omissions found in the work.

Special thanks are due to Brian Leney of CLIR and Kim Smith, the two individuals responsible for the guide's layout and cover design; and to Carla Arton, Harrison Behl, Sam Brylawski, and David Seubert for their help in taking photographs used in this guide.

FROM THE ASSOCIATION FOR RECORDED SOUND COLLECTIONS

Patrick Feaster, *president*
ARSC Copyright Committee and Fair Use Committee, Tim Brooks, *chair*
ARSC Education and Training Committee, Aaron Bittel and Karen Fishman, *chairs*

FROM THE COUNCIL ON LIBRARY AND INFORMATION RESOURCES

Lizzi Albert Adam Leader-Smith Christa Williford

FROM THE LIBRARY OF CONGRESS

Matthew Barton David Jackson Hope O'Keeffe
Gene DeAnna Steve Leggett Donna Ross
Alan Gevinson Gregory Lukow Mark Sweeney
Bryan Hoffa Larry S. Miller Emily Vartanian
Caitlin Hunter Cary O'Dell

ADVISORS AND REVIEWERS

Jeanette Berard Richard Green David Seubert
Phil Bloch Joshua Harris Douglas L. Siegler
George Blood John Lyon Gail Sonnemann
Connie Brooks Gail Martin Louise Spear
Brandon Burke Alec McLane Thomas Walker
Susannah Cleveland Barbara Need Steve Weiss
Adrian Consentini Brenda Nelson-Strauss

LIBRARY OF CONGRESS NATIONAL RECORDING PRESERVATION BOARD

We thank the University of California Santa Barbara, Northeast Document Conservation Center, and Creative Technology Ltd., for permitting use of their photographs.

ABOUT THIS GUIDE

The guide aims to help public and private institutions, as well as individual collectors, that have sound recordings in their collections but lack the professional expertise in one or more areas to preserve them. The chapters that follow cover audio conservation and preservation, recorded sound formats and their associated risks, appraisal, related copyright issues, and disaster preparedness. The guide also offers advice on making informed decisions about digitization, as well as strategies for managing digital content.

The guide is an introduction to audio preservation principles and practices. Users of the guide will each have varying degrees of expertise, and varying goals and priorities. Readers may find certain chapters more relevant to their immediate needs than others. The guide is designed so that chapters may be read and understood individually or sequentially through the entire volume. The inspiration for this book is *The Film Preservation Guide*, created by the National Film Preservation Foundation. We are grateful to the foundation for providing this model and the high standards it represents.

For more detailed information and technical guidance than is included in this volume, there are excellent resources, many of which are cited in the pages ahead. As an introduction to audio preservation, this guide can only touch on certain technical topics, including the requirements for doing preservation reformatting in-house. The first resource to consult for more detailed technical information about audio preservation is the now-definitive guide to reformatting, *Guidelines on the Production and Preservation of Digital Audio Objects*, published by the International Association of Sound and Audiovisual Archives.

Digital preservation of audio is an evolving field, and best practices evolve as new technologies and tools are developed. To keep abreast of new developments, we encourage you to take advantage of the web pages, resources, discussion list (ARSClist), and tools offered by ARSC, the National Digital Information Infrastructure and Preservation Program, Library of Congress National Recording Preservation Board, CLIR, and the web pages of vendors such as AVPreserve and Richard L. Hess.

As the Library of Congress National Audio Preservation Plan emphasizes, our success in preserving audio recordings will depend on collaboration. Our audio heritage is collective. It is held not by a few large organizations, but by hundreds, if not thousands, of institutions, large and small, and by individuals, all of whom bear the responsibility for ensuring that today's, as well as yesterday's, recordings are available for generations. If institutions and individual collectors work to implement best practices to every extent possible, we can meet the challenge. We hope that this guide will further the effort so that recordings so important to our lives today will enrich the lives of others tomorrow, and hundreds of years from now.

Sam Brylawski
Maya Lerman
Robin Pike
Kathlin Smith

CHAPTER 1

Preserving Audio

By Curtis Peoples and Marsha Maguire

In the fall of 2014, a group of ethnographers and audio specialists at the Library of Congress gathered to hear some very early and quite fragile wax cylinder recordings played back on a modern cylinder player developed and built in France in 1998. The cylinders, recordings of Passamaquoddy Indians Noel Josephs and Peter Selmore singing and telling stories, are of immense historical significance. Recorded in 1890 by Jesse Walter Fewkes, they are the first ethnographic field recordings made. Because the modern machine, called an Archéophone, can capture far more detail and clarity in playback than original phonographs could, those present were able to hear remarks by Fewkes that were previously inaudible. Of hearing the new transcriptions of the old cylinders, ethnomusicologist Judith Gray of the American Folklife Center remarked, "I was … jumping up and down in glee at the sheer presence of the Passamaquoddy singer, Noel Josephs. Despite the cylinder noise, it felt like this was a real person and that he was essentially in the room with us."

As cultural and historical treasures, the original Fewkes wax cylinders have been given the best possible care for 125 years. The cylinders were duplicated several decades earlier on 10-inch analog reel-to-reel preservation tapes, using the best technology then available. Now, with improved technology, we can recover previously indecipherable sound from the original recordings and preserve the voice of a Native American from eastern Maine with surprising clarity and immediacy. Thanks to careful and thorough conservation practices and the expert use of sophisticated technology, listeners in the twenty-first century may transcend time and space, and be in the presence of a performer in the nineteenth century.

Saving the sounds of human culture for those who come after us is a powerful reason to preserve audio. Ethnographic recordings document the spoken word, music, stories, and songs of cultures around the world and at different points in time. Recordings enable linguists to study the grammar and vocabularies of thousands of living and extinct languages and dialects; in addition, they allow for the detection of accents, intonations, and inflections that could not be accurately described before the invention of audio recording devices in the second half of the nineteenth century.

History is also represented in sound recordings. Repositories and individual collectors hold recorded radio broadcasts of historic events, news, and public affairs programs. They may include sports broadcasts, wartime recordings, speeches of presidents and ministers, and recollections of working people and family members. Preserved audio recordings make it possible to compare recordings of authors and poets reading their own works with interpretations of those works by great actors; to hear productions of great theatrical works and comedic performances, from the vaudeville era to the present; and to learn the techniques of performers who may no longer be living or who live on the other side of the planet.

People have used audio recorders to capture the sounds of birds and animals, the noises generated by naturally occurring events (such as rainstorms and landslides) in different locations and times, and the environmental sounds of everyday human life (such as street scenes, playground sounds, machine sounds, and indoor environments). Sound editors have created and altered sounds in designing audio effects that add realism and emotional force to radio, film, and television.

Recorded sound also entertains us and it enriches our daily routines. Twenty-first century lives are experienced within a persistent landscape of sound. We listen to standard and webcast radio, compile and share playlists, and take advantage of the portability of digital audio by listening to music, podcasts, and audio books on digital audio players and mobile phones while we walk, exercise, and commute. Earphones and portable players and receivers make our interactions with audio profoundly personal and ubiquitous.

The reasons we make, use, and value sound recordings are endless.

Because recorded sound is so pervasive in modern life, we may not realize how susceptible it is to deterioration and loss.

1.1 RECORDED SOUND AT RISK

Because recorded sound is so pervasive in modern life, we may not realize how susceptible it is to deterioration and loss. Since the end of the nineteenth century, technological innovations have enabled people to record sound with greater ease and fidelity. Experts have experimented with and improved techniques of recording and playback, and developed new audio media, or carriers. As a result, there are many audio formats in personal and institutional collections throughout the world. Although some formats are more durable than others, all are at risk. For analog sound carriers, levels of risk vary according to their physical composition, storage conditions over time, and access to playback equipment and the knowledge to use it. The availability of proper storage space, functioning playback equipment, and expertise in working with obsolete formats diminishes with each passing year.

Although legacy analog recordings pose daunting preservation challenges, contemporary digital formats and carriers are also at risk. Hard drives and servers crash; bits are lost; and carriers such as compact discs suffer warping, scratches, light and heat damage, and aluminum oxidation (laser rot). In addition, digital files created with one version of audio editing software may be unreadable by later releases of the same software.

Compounding these challenges are those inherent within the future of recorded sound distribution and consumption. Throughout the 125-year history of the record business, convenience has often prevailed in the marketplace over audio fidelity quality. Many people believe that the sonic capabilities of cylinder recordings 100 years ago were higher than those of 78-rpm discs made at the time. Yet flat discs, easier to store and able to provide two selections instead of one, became the format of choice. For a brief period before the introduction of compact discs, audio-cassettes outsold LP discs, largely because they could be played in automobiles and in small portable players. More recently, the easy access and portability of compressed audio files, such as MP3s, has placed compact discs in eclipse. Each year, more listeners take advantage of free and subscription streaming services and do not acquire physical recordings at all. Yet, streams and consumer audio file formats, such as MP3, AAC (iTunes), and Windows Media Audio (WMA), are "lossy" files, compressed derivative files that are of much lower fidelity than the master file from which they are derived, or the audio quality of a compact disc. Some companies are attempting to offer high-quality audio files for sale, but it is not yet known whether there is a viable market for these recordings.

Consequently, the obstacles to preserving contemporary recordings are two-pronged. If compressed files are the only versions made available to the public, we have no assurances that anyone is maintaining the higher fidelity originals. At the same time, if the streaming business model prevails over sales of physical objects, how can libraries, archives, and collectors ensure that recordings are preserved at all?

The growth of streaming threatens the preservation of historical recordings as well. Long-playing vinyl discs (LPs) are among the most stable formats found in an audio collection when they are stored properly. However, they can wear easily from playback. If archives and libraries cannot replace their worn LPs with physical copies or digital files of equally high sound quality, LPs will compete for reformatting resources with audio formats at even greater risk of deterioration than LPs. The immense volume of digital audio on the Internet, the ephemeral nature of online resources, and the effort and expense required to preserve audio create a situation in which losses of our audio legacy could become catastrophic.[1]

---

[1] The threats to recorded sound are described in great detail in *The State of Recorded Sound Preservation in the United States: A National Legacy at Risk in the Digital Age* (Council on Library and Information Resources and Library of Congress 2010).

1.2 PRESERVATION EFFORTS TO DATE

From the 1950s to the 1980s, open-reel quarter inch tape was the preferred medium of professionals. Never perceived as being permanent, tape was considered to be—and probably was at the time—the best affordable medium available for long-term preservation. All the while, it was hoped that modern science and technology would develop a permanent medium. That never occurred, and worse, by the early 1990s, many preservation master tapes were found to be unplayable because they suffered from "sticky shed syndrome" (hydrolysis), in which the binder that holds the magnetic particles breaks down. Meanwhile, digital recording was on the ascent. In the late 1980s and early 1990s, both digital audio tape (DAT) and the recordable compact disc (CD-R) were thought to have promise as preservation media, but they have proved to be unreliable for archival purposes. As a result, the original recordings that were reformatted for preservation have often outlasted the reformatted versions.

FROM MEDIUM TO STRATEGY

The future of sound preservation is not dependent on a physical format, but, rather, on a strategy.

Technology did ultimately provide a solution, however. With the growth of digital audio and the development of preservation storage systems, engineers and archivists have come to understand that the future of sound preservation is not dependent on a physical format, but, rather, on a strategy—an ongoing process of selection, digitization, system management, and migration to new formats. This has led audio preservationists to distinguish, for the first time, between the sound itself and the medium on which it is carried. Preserving the audio essence entails refreshing high-quality, uncompressed digital sound files regularly and migrating the sound essence to new digital formats over time.[2] By the early years of the twenty-first century, this approach to audio preservation had become common practice.

Despite this basic, if recent, agreement among professionals about the overall approach to audio preservation, we are now in a critical period of transition. The existing infrastructures and resources required to support these strategic processes are inadequate. We lack basic knowledge of the quantity and condition of sound recordings held both publicly and privately. Financial resources, technical expertise, and advocacy for audio preservation are inadequate, and we have not yet developed ways in which both large and small institutions can share the workload. The sheer volume of recorded audio is such that our best efforts may not be able to save every recording worth saving. To meet the challenge, efforts must be made regionally and nationally to promote collaboration in recorded sound preservation (Council on Library and Information Resources and Library of Congress 2010).

---

[2] *Essence*, in the context of digital preservation, refers to core content—e.g., audio, text, still and moving images—without regard to the original physical format.

FIRST STEPS TOWARD AN EFFECTIVE NATIONAL COLLABORATION

In 2000, the U.S. Congress passed the National Recording Preservation Act (Public Law No. 106-474). The legislation affirmed the nation's collective interest in preserving sound recordings for posterity and promoting greater public awareness of the issues involved. The law established the Library of Congress National Recording Preservation Board. The board, the Library of Congress, and partners have fulfilled several of the mandates assigned to it under the 2000 Preservation Act. The legislation has established the National Recording Registry, an annual list of 25 U.S. recordings selected for preservation because of their cultural, historical, or aesthetic significance, and conducted five critical studies on specific issues affecting sound recording preservation and access. In 2010, *The State of Recorded Sound Preservation in the United States: A National Legacy at Risk in the Digital Age* was released. The report outlines the challenges to long-term audio preservation in the United States and urges national coordination of public and private sector efforts to address those challenges (Council on Library and Information Resources and Library of Congress 2010).

The Library of Congress has fulfilled the congressional directive to develop a national, coordinated preservation program with the 2012 publication of *The Library of Congress National Recording Preservation Plan*. Developed by experts representing different aspects of preservation and access, the plan offers 32 specific recommendations covering national infrastructure, preservation implementation, education, copyright reform and public access to sound recordings, and planning for long-term sustainability of audio preservation (Council on Library and Information Resources and Library of Congress 2012). Work on several recommendations of the Recording Plan is under way. The Library of Congress National Digital Information Preservation Program (NDIIPP) has commissioned several useful resources and tools relating to audio preservation and provides much useful information on its website.[3] Other U.S. government agencies also actively support digital preservation initiatives. Both the National Endowment for the Humanities and the Institute of Museum and Library Services have funded important audio preservation projects.

CONTRIBUTIONS BY ACADEMIC INSTITUTIONS AND PROFESSIONAL ORGANIZATIONS

Audio experts at major academic and research institutions in the United States have undertaken work, both in preserving recordings and in developing guidelines, tools, and models that other institutions can use. The following are just a few of these efforts:

- A joint project of the Indiana University Archives of Traditional Music and the Archive of World Music at Harvard University culminated in the 2007 publication of *Sound Directions: Best Practices for Audio Preservation* (Casey and Gordon 2007).

[3] http://www.digitalpreservation.gov.

- Freely available online tools for collection assessment and prioritization are available from Indiana University (Casey 2007), Columbia University (Columbia University Libraries 2005), the University of Illinois (forthcoming), and New York University (2013).
- In 2008, Indiana University conducted a media preservation survey of sound recordings across the Bloomington campus (Casey 2009); the survey led to the preparation of planning and prioritization reports and, ultimately, to the 2014 launch of a campuswide digitization operation.

Professional organizations in the United States and elsewhere have also contributed the expertise of their members through projects and publications. Organizations that have developed standards, guidelines, projects,

Audio Formats History

This is a brief chronology of the introduction of recorded sound formats commonly found in libraries, sound archives, and private collections. As with nearly all technological developments, there are broad periods of overlap. Audio formats rarely, if ever, either gained prominence or became obsolete instantly. For instance, discs began to outsell cylinders after 1910, but Edison continued to manufacture cylinders for home use until 1929. Wax cylinders were used for dictation into the 1950s. Lacquer instantaneous discs remained in use as a recording medium as late as 1970.

A comprehensive timeline of all technological developments related to recorded sound has been developed by Steve Schoenherr (2005).

The Acoustic Era

1889
The North American Phonograph Company introduces brown wax cylinders. Intended primarily for office dictation, they gain use for entertainment and home recording. Thomas A. Edison's National Phonograph Company begins selling cylinders commercially in 1896.

1893
Emile Berliner's U.S. Gramophone Co. begins sales of mass-produced flat disc recordings for home entertainment. Discs could not be "homemade."

1900–1902
Moulded (i.e., mass-produced) cylinders are introduced.

1912
Edison introduces "Diamond Discs," vertically modulated flat discs.

The Electrical Era

1925
Major record companies begin using microphones and electrical amplifiers in recording and playback processes, which results in recordings of higher fidelity. Nevertheless, recordings are still cut directly to wax blanks that cannot be edited. Therefore, a mistake during a performance may render the disc useless. It is in this era, too, that disc recording speeds are standardized to 78 rpm (revolutions per minute).

Late 1920s
Instantaneous recording on blank aluminum discs provides a means to make custom single recordings. They are used to record radio broadcasts, personal "home" recordings, ethnographic field recordings, and many other genres. With the introduction of lacquer-coated discs and the portable Presto brand recorder in 1934 and 1935, tens of thousands of discs are made every year until the late 1940s, when magnetic tape supplants the medium.

1940
Wire magnetic recorders intended for commercial use are demonstrated. They are used by the U.S. government during World War II and are marketed to the public after the war.

1948
Widespread commercial use of magnetic tape begins in the United States. The open reel format is used to prerecord radio programs, and magnetic tape eventually replaces discs as the medium for making a commercial recording master. Because tape can be easily edited and

training programs, and much more to advance the work of audiovisual preservation and access include the following:

- Association for Recorded Sound Collections (ARSC)
- Audio Engineering Society (AES)
- Council on Library and Information Resources (CLIR)
- Association of Moving Image Archivists (AMIA)
- International Association of Sound and Audiovisual Archives (IASA)
- United Nations Education, Scientific, and Cultural Organization (UNESCO)
- European Broadcasting Union
- PrestoCentre organization of archivists, researchers, technologists, and producers

History, continued

used for multitrack recording, it has a significant impact on the content of recordings.

1948
Polyvinyl chloride compounds begin to supplant shellac compounds in the manufacturing of commercial records. Discs made of vinyl compounds were first introduced in the early 1930s.

1948
Columbia Records introduces a long-playing disc that uses a narrow (micro) groove and revolves at 33⅓ rpm, enabling a recording on one side to be as long as 20 minutes or more. It is called an LP, or album, the latter name deriving from earlier 78-rpm disc sets.

1949
RCA Victor introduces a long-playing 7-inch disc that plays at 45 rpm as competition to Columbia's LP. By the mid-1950s, LPs dominate the market for long-form recordings, and 45s supplant 78s.

1958
Stereophonic LP discs are introduced.

1964
The Phillips Compact Cassette tape cartridge is first sold in the United States.

1966
The first Dolby tape noise reduction system is introduced.

1972
Pulse code modulation (PCM) adapters that enable digital audio to be recorded on videotape stock are introduced. Broad commercial use begins in 1978.

1980
The Sony Walkman portable cassette player is introduced in the United States.

The Digital Era

1982–1983
Digitally recorded compact discs (CDs) and players are introduced to the consumer market.

1986–1987
The digital audio tape (DAT or R-DAT) is introduced. Intended to replace analog cassettes in the consumer market, it is not a success. However, it is widely used for professional recording.

1990
The recordable compact disc (CD-R) is introduced.

1997–1998
The downloadable Winamp player for MP3 files is released, and the proliferation of MP3 audio files follows. MP3, short for MPEG-1/2 Audio Layer III, is a lossy compressed audio file format that creates audio files small enough to be distributed over the Internet easily.

2003
Apple, Inc. opens its online iTunes store. The success of the retailer helps to alleviate music business losses from piracy, but diminishes sales of the long-form (compact disc-length) recordings.

2011
Sales of recordings as physical formats and digital files decrease while free and subscription music streaming services gain in popularity.

1.3 THE ROLE OF YOUR INSTITUTION

Despite the significant, even transformational, accomplishments in audio preservation by large research libraries and professional organizations, their combined resources are inadequate to meet a preservation challenge of the magnitude we face today. Efforts of institutions both large and small, as well as the work of private collectors, will be needed to make a meaningful dent in the enormous volume of significant recordings that have not yet been digitized for preservation. Medium-sized and smaller libraries, archives, local history repositories, museums, local cultural organizations, corporations, and individuals hold tens of thousands of local and regional radio broadcasts, ethnographic recordings, recorded sounds of local musical styles and performers, environmental recordings, and many more types of sound captured on analog and digital media.

Depending on the mission and subject focus of your institution, your collections may include commercial sound recordings (both rare and common), recordings that are unique or unpublished, or both. Media for commercial recordings, which are generated for mass consumption, range from cylinders and early discs to today's wide array of available digital formats. It may be difficult for a nonspecialist to determine whether a commercially distributed recording in relatively good condition is rare and worth preserving, but many resources are available that can help. These include printed and online discographies, collector websites and portals, price guides, audio magazines and newsletters, and online auction results.

Unpublished recordings hold historical, sociocultural, aesthetic, and personal or family content that may well be irreplaceable. Included in this category of material are field recordings; oral histories; audio "letters" and homemade recordings of personal narratives and family voices and events; recorded music, drama, and other performances not intended for commercial release; local studio master tapes; radio broadcasts and podcasts; and work tapes and other unedited or partly edited pre-release or pre-broadcast recordings. Archives tend to give unpublished recordings priority for attention over commercial recordings. Their content may be unique; they are often made on the least stable of recording formats; and many were recorded under less-than-ideal conditions by amateur recordists. Any one of these circumstances might argue for preservation priority.

If we are to preserve our audio legacy, all institutions with significant recordings must be part of the effort. Given the budgetary and staffing limitations that all cultural heritage institutions face, what can your institution do to preserve and make accessible the sound recordings in your care? This manual is intended to address that question.

1.4 ORGANIZATION OF THE GUIDE

As you read through this guide, you will become familiar with the major audio formats and innovations of the past 130 years. You will learn about

- Basic concepts and terminology used in audio archiving and engineering
- Various types of recordings, their preservation risks, and ways to appraise their value for acquisition and preservation purposes
- Recommended organization, playback, handling, and storage techniques
- Inventorying an audio collection and providing metadata that will facilitate the discovery of audio resources
- Legal and ethical issues relating to access and use
- Preparations necessary for outsourced or in-house digitization and curation of digital audio systems after initial reformatting
- Development of disaster management plans

Chapter 2 addresses audio formats commonly found in recorded sound collections, along with the types of deterioration to which they are most susceptible. More in-depth discussion on collection development and establishing preservation priorities is provided in chapter 3.

Basic identification, care and maintenance, appraisal, and metadata are covered in chapters 4 and 5.

Beginning with chapter 6, responsibilities are discussed that might require specialized knowledge of audio-related technology, intellectual property issues, and long-term planning.

Because audio reformatting itself, especially the transfer of legacy analog formats to preservation-quality digital audio files, requires particular skills and training, outsourcing to an audio engineer or company may be the best option for institutions lacking specialized equipment and staff. You will need to choose a vendor, prepare a vendor request for proposal (RFP), and possibly get funding to cover the costs of preservation reformatting. Chapter 6 provides useful information in all these areas.

Digital audio files, whether obtained through an institution's regular acquisition processes or as the result of analog-to-digital reformatting, present their own serious preservation problems and require a different skill set for effective long-term preservation. Chapter 7 discusses the requirements for a system to preserve digital content (both born-digital and reformatted analog), and for sustaining the system over the long term.

The issues associated with outsourcing digital file storage, a distinct possibility for institutions lacking the resources to undertake management of a local repository, are also addressed in chapter 7.

Institutions and professionals working to preserve and provide access to audio works need to understand the basic outlines of copyright law. Chapter 8 summarizes copyright and special issues relating to recorded sound. Appendix A of the guide explores ways in which the doctrine of Fair Use applies to sound recording preservation and access.

Some Basic Principles of Acoustics

To understand audio and to analyze and interpret recordings, it is necessary to have some basic knowledge of acoustics—the properties of sound. Sound is an acoustic phenomenon. It is vibrations that travel through a medium, like air, and can be heard by the ear. The pressure rises and falls in a regular pattern and is propagated outward. When we refer to audio or audio signals, we generally are referring to an electrical or mechanical representation of sound.

Through acoustics, we can learn how sound is created, how sound travels, and how sound is perceived: production, propagation, and perception, respectively. When sound travels through the air and water, it travels in longitudinal waveforms. Longitudinal waveforms occur when the medium is being displaced in the same direction in which the wave propagates. Longitudinal sound waves travel through the air as mechanical pressure waves in cycles of compression and rarefaction, as shown in Figure 1.1. This can be illustrated by pushing and pulling a Slinky back and forth.

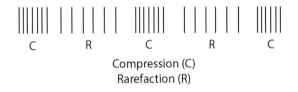

Compression (C)
Rarefaction (R)

Fig. 1.1: An example of compression and rarefaction

When sound travels through a solid, it travels in transverse waveforms. In transverse waveforms, the displacement of the medium is perpendicular to the direction in which the wave propagates. Using the example of the Slinky again, visualize the Slinky being shaken up and down.

Acoustic principles can be demonstrated through mathematical curve representations, such as a sine wave. The sine wave in Figure 1.2 shows frequency (cycles per second) and correlates to pitch. Pitch is the sensation of how high or low a sound is perceived. High sounds are associated with treble; low sounds, with bass. An example of pitch is the musical note A above middle C, sometimes called "Concert A." The International Organization for Standardization (ISO) has specified Concert A as oscillating at 440 Hz, or 440 cycles per second. Amplitude correlates to loudness, which is a subjective measurement of a sound wave's strength or weakness. An objective measurement of sound strength is sound pressure level (SPL) and is measured in decibels (dB). SPL is related to the intensity and volume of a sound.

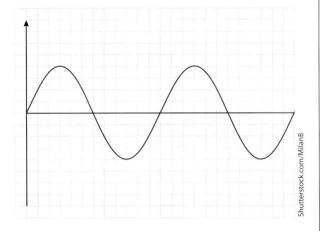

Fig. 1.2: Sine wave

When working with audio, you need to consider some acoustic principles in the physical space of the work environment. A good work environment should have room clarity, uniformity, and freedom from echo and noise. Parallel surfaces in rooms create problems with sound quality, such as standing waves. A standing wave is created when a reflected wave interferes with the incident wave creating nodes (zero amplitude or "dead spot") and anti-nodes (maximum amplitude). Therefore, it is a good idea to use acoustic treatments to improve your room's overall sound quality. Sound absorption materials, bass traps, and diffuser panels can often help with parallel surfaces, echo, and other common problems.

Familiarity with acoustic principles will also help you understand the digitization of audio. Digitization of audio is accomplished with an analog-to-digital (A/D) convertor. Pulse code modulation (PCM) is the most common method of encoding digital audio, but not the only one. Digitization is the process of taking continuous signals (the analog domain) and changing them into discrete signals (the digital domain). Digital audio is based on sampling rate and bit depth. The sampling rate is how many times per second a continuous signal is sampled, and thus may also be expressed in Hertz (samples per second).

There is a correlation between sampling rate and frequency. According to the Nyquist-Shannon Sampling Theorem, the sampling rate must be at least two times the highest frequency being recorded to avoid aliasing, an undesirable condition where the reconstructed sound wave appears to be lower-frequency than the original sound. The highest audible frequency is about 20,000 Hz, so the sampling rate must be at a minimum of 40,000 Hz.

When samples are taken, the amplitude at that moment in time must be converted to integers in binary representation (quantization). The number of bits used for each sample, called the bit depth, determines the precision with which you can represent the sample amplitudes. A higher bit depth will have more clarity, less noise, and a wider dynamic range. The fact that integers are used forces the samples to be measured in a finite number of discrete levels, as shown in Figure 1.3. A sample's amplitude must be rounded to the nearest of the allowable discrete levels, which introduces error in the digitization process. This is called quantization error. A higher bit depth allows for the capture of more accurate data. 16-bit/44.1-kHz is the Red Book standard[1] for audio CDs. However, improvements in technology now allow for greater bit depths and sampling rates, such as 24-bit/96-kHz. Higher bit depths and sampling rates help to maintain audio integrity when processing digital sound files.

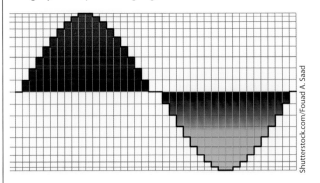

Fig. 1.3: Digital representation of a sine wave. Analog-to-digital conversion of sound entails "sampling" the sound a certain number of times a second and encoding it as bits. The number of bits used to represent each sample is referred to as "bit depth." The number of columns might represent the sampling rate, and the number of rows the bit depth. Keep in mind that this figure cannot be a literal representation. The specifications of sound represented in an audio compact disc are 44,100 samples a second and a depth of 16 bits.

Working with either analog or digital audio involves consideration of many topics, including dynamic range. Measured in decibels, dynamic range is the range of the largest to smallest amplitudes that can be accurately reproduced (i.e., the quietest to the loudest). The dynamic range of human hearing is roughly 140 dB. In analog and digital audio carriers, the dynamic range is less than that. For example, a CD has a dynamic range of 90 dB, and that of analog tapes varies from about 40 dB to 60 dB.

A great amount of audio today is distributed in the form of MP3 files and other compressed file formats. Audio data compression is a technique in which software and audio codecs decrease bandwidth and file size storage space. Data compression can be lossless (no loss of audio quality) or lossy (loss of audio quality). Free Lossless Audio Codec (FLAC) is a lossless format for audio data compression. MPEG-1 or MPEG-2 Audio Layer III (MP3) is a lossy format that relies on psychoacoustics (the science of the perception of sound) to compensate for the loss of information. By psychoacoustic, we mean perceptual coding, which aims to store only those data that are detectable by the human ear and does this with an effect known as masking. Masking could be described as a tendency in the listener to give precedence to certain sounds ahead of others, according to the context in which they occur. By assigning fewer bits to audio perceived as redundant, it is possible to achieve drastically reduced file sizes by simply discarding the imperceptible and irrelevant data captured in a PCM recording. Lossy compressed digital audio is unsuitable as a preservation format. There is broad agreement among professionals that long-term archival storage files should be uncompressed Broadcast Wave Format (BWF) files. However, an MP3 file may be adequate for public access, such as online streaming. See Figure 1.4 for a compressed audio data comparison. Clearly, there is a significant reduction in data in the compressed MP3 when it is compared with the uncompressed WAVE file.

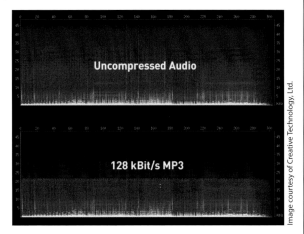

Fig. 1.4: Spectral view of audio data compression

Although this sidebar touches only briefly on acoustic principles and digital audio, a basic understanding of sound and acoustics can help identify problems you may encounter when working with audio materials.

---

[1] "Red Book" is the name of the set of technical specifications for an audio compact disc. The specifications were released in 1980 by the Philips and Sony corporations, and have been modified slightly since.

Disaster planning and response are the topics of chapter 9. The chapter outlines basic elements of disaster prevention, preparedness, and recovery for audio collections and includes a disaster recovery case study.

1.5 CONCLUSION

Preserving sound recordings and making them easy to find and hear is challenging and expensive. Perhaps that is why many audio collections have been boxed up and relegated to the dark corners of institutions to be dealt with "later." But there is no time left; this work cannot be postponed. As documented in *The State of Recorded Sound Preservation in the United States* and other studies published by CLIR since the passage of the National Recording Preservation Act of 2000, a distressingly large percentage of the recordings we are making now, as well as those we hold in trust from the past 130 years, are already gone or soon will be.

Librarians and archivists most often work with print materials and may not have the skills and resources needed for audio preservation. They may feel overwhelmed when they first encounter collections of old tapes, lacquer discs, or hard drives containing hundreds of digital audio files. This manual is intended to impart the knowledge, basic skills, and most importantly, the confidence to care for sound recordings over time.

We can accomplish much by collaborating with other institutions, professional organizations, and local and regional consortia to develop ideas; share selection and preservation responsibilities; share content when possible; educate and train librarians, archivists, and personal collectors across the United States; and develop or improve standards, local and national policies, and scalable preservation and access technologies. We cannot, and should not, save every recording. However, through collaboration and contributions from individuals and institutions of all sizes, we can select and preserve a significant amount of important audio content.

The great technological minds who invented recorded sound, and perfected it over the years to the point that a listener feels she is in the room with a performer who sang into a recording device 125 years ago, left us a gift. That gift—the sounds of human endeavor and the natural world–is one we must safeguard for future generations of listeners.

REFERENCES

All URLs are current as of May 1, 2015

Archéophone home page. Available at http://www.archeophone.org/windex.php.

Casey, Mike. 2007. *The Field Audio Collection Evaluation Tool (FACET). Format Characteristics and Preservation Problems, Version 1.0.* Trustees of Indiana University. Available at http://www.dlib.indiana.edu/projects/sound-directions/facet/facet_formats.pdf.

Casey, Mike. 2009. *Indiana University Bloomington Media Preservation Survey: A Report*. Available at http://www.indiana.edu/~medpres/documents/iub_media_preservation_survey_FINALwww.pdf.

Casey, Mike, and Bruce Gordon. 2007. *Sound Directions. Best Practices for Audio Preservation*. Trustees of Indiana University and President and Fellows of Harvard University. Available at http://www.dlib.indiana.edu/projects/sounddirections/papersPresent/sd_bp_07.pdf.

Columbia University Libraries. 2005. *Survey Instrument for Audio & Moving Image Collections*. The survey instrument and the instruction manual are available for download at http://library.columbia.edu/services/preservation/audiosurvey.html.

Council on Library and Information Resources and Library of Congress. 2010. *The State of Recorded Sound Preservation in the United States: A National Legacy at Risk in the Digital Age*. Commissioned for and sponsored by the National Recording Preservation Board of the Library of Congress. Washington, D.C.: Council on Library and Information Resources and the Library of Congress. Available in print or PDF format at http://www.clir.org/pubs/reports/pub148.

Council on Library and Information Resources and Library of Congress. 2012. *The Library of Congress National Recording Preservation Plan*. Sponsored by the National Recording Preservation Board of the Library of Congress. Washington, D.C.: Council on Library and Information Resources and the Library of Congress. Available in print or PDF format at http://www.clir.org/pubs/reports/pub156.

New York University. 2013. *Visual & Playback Inspection Rating System* (ViPIRS). Microsoft Access database for magnetic open reel tape and cassettes. Last updated October 2013. Available at http://library.nyu.edu/preservation/movingimage/vipirshome.html.

Schoenherr, Steve. 2005 (rev. July 6). Recording Technology History. Audio Engineering Society. Available at http://www.aes.org/aeshc/docs/recording.technology.history/notes.html.

University of Illinois. Forthcoming 2015. *Preservation Self-Assessment Program* (PSAP). Information available at http://psap.library.illinois.edu/.

CHAPTER 2

Audio Formats: Characteristics and Deterioration

By Harrison Behl

The breakneck pace of invention and innovation in audio technology has led to remarkable developments in recording and the variety of recordings available to us. Those interested in exploring and preserving the rich history of recorded sound must navigate a complex technological landscape, full of dead-end paths of proprietary secrets and littered with strange items that do not readily identify themselves or announce their contents. Digital file formats, which exist independent of specific physical media, have many problems in common with analog media, such as the need to maintain the integrity of the audio they represent and compatibility with playback systems (i.e., software in the case of digital audio) that change over time. However, digital file formats also present new preservation challenges, such as the need for reliable storage, discoverability, and retrieval in a complex networked information ecosystem. Both physical and digital media require preservation planning to sustain them into the future.

Understanding the various phases of sound recording development and the resulting formats is important to audio preservation planning for several reasons. First, all sound recordings are mediated through a playback device, so sound recording carriers must be decoded via the proper device or codec to be heard. Second, preservation requires knowledge of what the recording is made of, what types of deterioration might be expected, and how damage can be limited or repaired. Third, additional insights into the history of the content of a recording can be gleaned from understanding the history of its recording format. In some cases, accurate identification of a format can provide at least approximate dates for undated materials. And finally, understanding the components of the major groups of formats is necessary to successfully plan and carry out preservation activities.

The images and charts in this chapter organize physical audio carriers according to their form and function. Many formats were intended only for the dissemination of sound recordings, while others, either intentionally or inadvertently, allowed for recording and rerecording. Although this chapter focuses on formats specifically related to sound recording, nearly every format that has been developed to store moving images has at some point also been used to carry sound recordings.

2.1 CYLINDER FORMATS

At a glance:

- There are three main material types: brown wax, molded wax, and celluloid.
- Antique phonographs can be used only with the type of cylinder for which they were originally manufactured.
- Wax cylinders are very fragile and subject to mold. Store in a cool and dry environment.
- Rare or important cylinders should not be played on historical equipment.
- Cylinders have vertical-cut grooves.

Cylinder recordings were the first commercially viable sound recordings available. Beginning with Thomas A. Edison's tinfoil cylinder in 1877, cylinder development varied widely in materials, construction, playback speeds, and playback devices. Early cylinders were colloquially known as "wax" cylinders (although actually made of metal soaps). The stylus transcribed the sound wave into the wax by changing the depth of the groove that was incised. Referred to as the vertical-cut or hill-and-dale groove method, this technique was used for all cylinder recordings. The recording time available on a cylinder is determined by a combination of the cylinder's length, diameter, speed of rotation, and the density of the recording, which is measured in threads per inch (tpi). Recordings were made directly on the early brown wax cylinders. Methods for mass production were limited and often resulted in poor quality records.

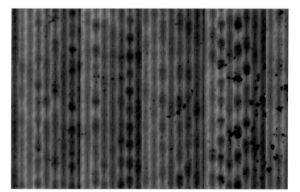

Vertical cut grooves

By 1888, the wax cylinder was the nascent industry standard. In 1902, Edison developed a process for molding cylinders that could increase production without sacrificing sound quality; he labeled these "Gold-Moulded" recordings (Seubert and Pollaczek 2005). Molded cylinders were originally made of material similar to that used for the brown wax cylinders, but later, celluloid and plaster were used. Recordings on cylinders were made at a variety of speeds, between 120 and 160 revolutions per minute (rpm) depending on when they were recorded, what company recorded them, or what machine was used to record a cylinder at home.

Brown wax cylinder

Material composition	A metal soap composed of stearic acid and aluminum powder
Primary dates of production	1888–1902
Recording characteristics	Direct recorded, or pantographically (mechanically) duplicated Vertical-cut groove Speed that varies from 120 to 160 rpm 100 tpi
Notes on playback	Most of these cylinders are considered rare. Research cylinders carefully and, if possible, consult with someone knowledgeable in cylinder history and preservation technology before attempting playback.
Deterioration	Fingerprints on playback surfaces leave behind organic compounds that not only attract dust and dirt, but also encourage microorganism damage. Wax cylinders are also fragile and can be easily broken through improper handling.

Molded ("Gold-Moulded") and [black] Amberol cylinders

Material composition	Metal soaps (lead stearate) with lampblack (carbon) with additional hardening agents
Primary dates of production	1902–1912
Recording characteristics	Mass-produced via molding process Vertical-cut groove Speed standardized at 160 rpm Gold-Moulded: 100 tpi Amberol: 200 tpi
Notes on playback	Gold-Moulded and Amberol cylinders are not cross-compatible because of the different number of threads per inch. An original machine built to play one of the formats cannot be used to play the other.
Deterioration	Fingerprints on playback surfaces leave behind organic compounds that not only attract dust and dirt, but also encourage microorganism damage. Molded cylinders are as fragile as brown wax cylinders, but they are far more common.

Blue Amberol / US Everlasting, Indestructible cylinder

Material composition	Plaster core with celluloid (in Blue Amberols, nitrocellulose) plastic playback surface layer
Primary dates of production	1912–1929
Recording characteristics	Mass-produced via molding process Vertical-cut groove Speed standardized at 160 rpm 200 tpi most common
Notes on playback	Edison Blue Amberol cylinders are compatible with black Amberol playback equipment.
Deterioration	The plaster and cardboard cores can absorb water through hydrolysis and expand (Welch 1972), which can make it difficult to fit the cylinder to the mandrel for playback. Nitrocellulose is a flammable substance. Although the spontaneous combustion of a cylinder is virtually unheard of, a concentrated collection of nitrocellulose compressed media can cause a fire to burn more intensely.

2.2 GROOVED DISC FORMATS

At a glance:

- Most feature a lateral-cut groove.
- Most are pressed/molded copies.
- Discs recorded before the mid-1920s varied significantly in speed; the approximate speed was 78 rpm.
- 78-rpm discs are "coarse," or "standard," groove. The width of the groove is approximately three times as wide as those found on long-playing discs.
- Long-playing discs (LPs) and 45-rpm discs are microgroove.
- Shellac is rigid and does not flex. The playback surface is dull or matte.
- Vinyl records will flex slightly when held by the outer edges. The playback surface is glossy or reflective.
- The most fragile commonly encountered audio format is the lacquer disc.
- Lacquer discs were sold as blanks. Recording characteristics can vary based on the cutting equipment used to produce them, which was not standardized.
- Lacquer discs very often carry unique content.

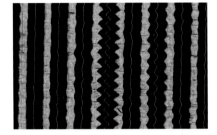

Lateral cut grooves

The earliest Berliner discs of the 1890s were composed of vulcanized rubber and were made from etched zinc masters. However, a composite material consisting of shellac (composed of a resin secreted from the lac beetle, and other substances) became the predominant material for mass-produced or stamped analog discs during the acoustic era (ca. 1890s–1925). Less information exists about the exact composition of shellac discs than of any other disc format. Ingredients varied widely by manufacturer and often by batch (Nguyen et al. 2011). Companies attempted to optimize both sound quality and economy of production, which led to frequent experimentation. Recycled masonry was sometimes used for filler material, in addition to organic cellulose, such as sawdust or remaindered discs from previous pressings (St. Laurent 1997).

A side-by-side comparison of a 12-inch 78-rpm disc and a 12-inch LP shows the matte surface of shellac and the reflectivity of vinyl discs.

Shellac is a thermosetting polymer, meaning that the application of heat during the molding process causes a chemical reaction that hardens the polymer. This curing process continues throughout the life of the finished product, at a very gradual rate. Shellac shrinks as it cures and becomes increasingly brittle. Most lateral-cut acoustic discs were formed by molding a single layer of homogenous shellac compound.

Shellac 78-rpm disc

Shellac 78-rpm disc (10")   *Shellac 78-rpm disc (12")*

Material composition	Composite of shellac and additives, such as recycled masonry, sawdust. Exact composition difficult to determine (Nguyen et al. 2011).
Primary dates of production	1890–1950
Recording characteristics	Mass-produced via stamping Lateral-cut groove (primarily) Recorded without electronic amplification until 1925
Notes on playback	Shellac records were played with a fine steel needle or a fiber needle (such as bamboo) that was intended for a single play; repeated use diminished sound quality and increased the risk of groove wear (Gracyk 2006). Historical equipment can be valuable for interpretation and provides a window into the experience of early recordings, but should not be used on recordings in archival collections. Contemporary preservation-grade phonographs and a wide range of styli are available for preservation recording engineers.
Deterioration	Shellac discs are a robust and relatively stable format. However, because of the variety in their composition, it is difficult to know for certain how shellac-based discs as a format will fare over time (Nguyen et al. 2011). Shellac discs become more brittle over time, particularly if stored without sufficient temperature and humidity controls (St. Laurent 1997). The organic cellulosic material present in most discs is susceptible to fungal growth, especially if conditions are humid or if the discs are exposed to water and not quickly dried. Exposure to water can also cause networks of fine cracks on the playback surface, a condition referred to as crazing.

Edison Diamond Disc

Edison Diamond Disc with paper label   *Edison embossed label*

Material composition	Condensite (an early synthetic plastic) playback surface laminated to a cellulose core of paper or very fine wood particles (St. Laurent 1997)
Primary dates of production	1912–1929
Recording characteristics	Vertical-cut groove Speed around 80 rpm
Notes on playback	Diamond discs are not compatible with most turntables for lateral-cut discs.
Deterioration	Risks of delamination, swelling of cellulose core, and fungal growth arise when diamond discs are exposed to water or prolonged high humidity.

Vinyl discs

Vinyl disc, 45-rpm 7-inch

Vinyl disc, black 12-inch 33⅓ LP

16-inch transcription sleeve

16-inch transcription pressing

Dimensions	7, 10, 12, and 16 inches in diameter
Material composition	Polyvinyl chloride (thermoplastic polymer). Some companies produced polystyrene (thermoplastic polymer) 45-rpm singles (Dawson and Propes 2003).
Primary dates of production	1948–present
Recording characteristics	Commercial 45-rpm and 33⅓-rpm discs • Lateral-cut • Early discs monophonic, majority after 1965 are stereophonic • Microgroove Radio transcription discs • Usually 16 inches in diameter • Vertical- or lateral-cut, inside- or outside-start, coarse or microgroove
Notes on playback	Many record players were produced that could play multiple speeds, from 16 rpm through 78 rpm. The most common speeds were 33⅓ rpm and 45 rpm, and these are still produced for both preservation recording and casual use. A variety of playback styli and electrical pickup cartridges exist to accommodate the different groove widths between 78-rpm "coarse groove" and "microgroove" discs, as well as special styli based on groove geometry.
Deterioration	Vinyl discs are the most stable physical sound recording format developed to date; they can last 100 years in a controlled environment. However, heat and ultraviolet radiation both degrade the polymer. Vinyl softens and flows when exposed to excessive heat, which deforms the grooves. Polyvinyl chloride (PVC) releases hydrogen chloride as it thermodegrades. Stabilizers added to the compound during production arrest this process, but excessive heat, ultraviolet radiation, and humidity accelerate the degradation and deplete the available stabilizers. Dust and foreign matter, such as oils from fingers, can cause distortion and surface noise in playback; these deposits can promote fungal growth and damage the playback surface. Water can combine with the offgassing of hydrogen chloride to form hydrochloric acid in excessively hot conditions (St. Laurent 1997). Heat and pressure can also cause the discs to warp, which can adversely affect playback. Vinyl discs are relatively soft compared with shellac discs, and they are susceptible to mechanical damage, such as scratches. Consequently, they require much lighter downforce from the tonearm on a playback device than do shellac discs (Schüller 2008). Polystyrene 45-rpm discs are more brittle and prone to cracking than vinyl discs. Because polystyrene is softer than PVC, these discs are also more susceptible to mechanical damage caused by the playback needle gouging the surface as it plays.

ELECTRICAL ERA DISCS

Although the development of electrical amplification dramatically changed recording and reproduction, the consumer product changed more slowly. The 78-rpm speed was well established among consumers, and the shellac record remained the dominant consumer format until after 1950 (Schoenherr 2005).

Large 16-inch discs were recorded for use in an early form of talking motion picture, the Vitaphone system (Schoenherr 2005). This format was later adopted and used for recording radio broadcasts. Instantaneous discs—those manufactured to be played immediately after recording without any further processing—also replaced wax matrices in the studio by the late 1940s.

Columbia Records adopted the speed used by the Vitaphone system, 33⅓ rpm, and developed a tighter groove pattern for its 12-inch diameter LPs in 1948. Microgroove records have a groove density of 300-400 grooves per inch, in contrast to coarse groove records with a density of approximately 100 grooves per inch, and could accommodate approximately 22 minutes of recording on each side (IASA 2009).

RCA Victor introduced its competing 45-rpm 7-inch disc in 1949, which was also made of a plastic, either polystyrene or polyvinyl chloride (Stauderman 2004). RCA Victor and Columbia competed to establish their own product as the new standard to replace the 78-rpm disc, but by 1951, the competition ended in a draw with both companies producing the opposition's format. Record players were produced that could play both speeds, and adapters were made to render the different spindle hole diameters largely moot.

Layers and Deterioration

Physical formats that are composed of layers of different materials are particularly susceptible to deterioration. These formats include lacquer discs, magnetic tape, and compact discs, as well as other less common formats, such as the Edison Diamond Discs.

In the case of lacquer discs, the reaction of the rigid base material (metal or glass) to environmental conditions differs from the reaction of the flexible, fragile layer of cellulose plastic. The cellulose layer can shrink as it loses plasticizing oils, while the base remains the same size, As a result, cracking and crazing of the playback surface can occur.

Similarly, the binder layer of magnetic tape that contains the magnetic information can shrink or deform at a rate different from that of either the acetate or polyester tape base. This can cause the tape to curl in on itself, referred to as "cupping," and in the case of binder hydrolysis—"sticky shed syndrome"—the binder layer can slough away from the tape base.

For compact discs, the dangers are different but the effect is the same. The layers of lacquer and polycarbonate plastic are sealed together around the reflective metal layer and the dyed or stamped data layer. If the plastic and lacquer delaminate, oxygen can damage the reflective layer, which prevents the laser from reading the information.

LACQUER DISCS

Lacquer discs are the most commonly encountered type of instantaneous discs. The format replaced wax matrices used for recording and mastering in the mid-1930s and was the dominant format for making original, or master, recordings until they were supplanted by magnetic tape in the late 1940s. Lacquer discs are often referred to as acetate discs, or acetates, even though the term misstates the composition of the discs. Lacquer instantaneous discs are composed of a nitrocellulose lacquer layer applied to an aluminum, glass, or steel base. Discs made during World War II often have a glass base because of wartime rationing of aluminum, and these are extremely fragile. The thin lacquer layer on new discs was blank, without grooves. The material was soft enough to be inscribed with grooves by a cutting stylus and resilient enough to survive several playbacks.

Lacquer discs were used to record radio programs, field recordings, and other "live" events. Many companies offered transcription services in the 1930s that produced instantaneous discs on demand. Those made by radio networks and others for professional purposes were usually 16 inches in diameter. Discs recorded for personal purposes were likely to be of a smaller diameter, from 7 inches to 12 inches.

There are other types of instantaneous discs. Pure aluminum discs, 10 and 12 inches in diameter, were used for personal recording in the late 1920s and early 1930s. Cardboard discs, coated with an acetate layer and "pre-grooved," were used for "instant" recordings in homes, personal dictation, and "audio letters" to and from members of the armed forces from the 1940s to the 1960s.

Lacquer discs (also known as acetate discs)		
Dimensions	7, 8, 10, 12, and 16 inch in diameter	
Material composition	Rigid base (aluminum, glass, steel) with a thin layer of nitrocellulose plastic adhered to one or both sides of the base; most glass base discs have a metal spindle insert	
Primary dates of production	1936–1960	
	Instantaneous discs can sometimes be identified by the presence of three "drive pin" holes under the label, in addition to the hole for the spindle.	
Recording characteristics	Lacquer discs may be • Inside- or outside-start • Lateral- or vertical-cut grooves • Coarse grooves or microgrooves	• Speed of 16, 33⅓, or 78 rpm • Stereophonic or monophonic
Notes on playback	All lacquer discs are at risk of deterioration and are a preservation priority. Because of their unique content and fragility, they should be preserved by an experienced audio engineer whenever possible.	
Deterioration	The recording layer of all lacquer discs is susceptible to loss of plasticizer, which produces exudation of palmitic and stearic acid. It may flake, crack, and separate from the rigid base, resulting in loss of playback capability. The soft surface is easily marred by needle drops, gouges, and scratches. During the World War II era, glass replaced aluminum as the base in lacquer discs. Glass instantaneous discs become brittle and are subject to cracks and breakage. Their inherent fragility increases over time as the glass becomes more brittle. Nitrocellulose is a flammable substance. Although the spontaneous combustion of a lacquer disc is virtually unheard of, a concentrated collection of nitrocellulose compressed media can cause a fire to burn more intensely.	

2.3 MAGNETIC FORMATS

At a glance:

- Electromagnets encode the shape of a sound wave as magnetic pulses onto metal.
- A wide variety of recording configurations are possible.
- Numerous formats proliferated in the past, but many are rare today.
- Playback hardware obsolescence is a serious preservation concern for many formats.
- Compact cassettes are still manufactured and sold today; they are increasingly present in mixed media collections.

Magnetic recording of sound was demonstrated as a viable technology as early as 1898 by Valdemar Poulsen, but it came into wider use in the 1940s after the development of electrical amplification and improvements in fidelity (Casey and Gordon 2007; Milner 2009). Research into and production of magnetic recording methods occurred separately in Germany and in the United States in the 1930s. Once the translation of sound waves into electric pulses and the encoding of those pulses in the magnetic orientation of metal were practically demonstrated with wire recorders, experimentation continued to develop other ways of storing and reproducing sounds that could capture a wider range of sound at a higher fidelity, which led to the development of magnetic tape.

Wire recordings	
Dimensions	Wire: approximately 4 mm in diameter (Casey and Gordon 2007) Standard commercial reel: 2.75 inches in diameter, 0.5 inch wide Armour Model 50a (U.S. Navy): 3.75-inch reel diameter, 1.5 inches wide Possible for each reel to hold up to 7,200 feet
Material composition	Stainless steel alloy (earliest wires not stainless)
Primary dates of production	1939–1955 (experiments and small-scale manufacture since 1898)

Small spool wire

Recording characteristics	Large reels recorded at either 60 or 30 inches per second Smaller reels recorded at approximately 24 inches per second (Casey and Gordon 2007)
Notes on playback	Wire cannot be played using tape machines. The best course of action is to use a rebuilt original wire recorder or a specially designed modern machine for playback; the record/playback head is unique to this format. The components within an original machine are not ideal; they are of a lower quality than more contemporary instruments. Patching different amplifiers or components into an older machine can be difficult. Some preservation recording studios have the necessary equipment and experience. Wire recordings should be preserved by a professional (King n.d.).
Deterioration	Early non-stainless steel wires may be susceptible to corrosion and rust. The most serious deterioration is caused by wire breaking and becoming tangled, as the wire travels through the playback mechanisms at a high speed. Splices or repairs were achieved by tying the wire in a standard square knot and pulling it tight. Some early practitioners bonded wire ends together with a lit cigarette.

WIRE RECORDINGS

The earliest wire reels produced by Armour for the U.S. Navy used non-stainless steel. The vast majority of recording wire reels in the civilian commercial market were made from stainless steel. Because wire is made from a stable metal alloy, as opposed to a composite of different layers of material, or a complex compound, it is considered to be very stable (Casey and Gordon 2007).

MAGNETIC TAPE

The production of magnetic tape involves attaching a layer of fine ferromagnetic particles on a flexible substrate, such as paper, cellulose acetate, or polyester. The dynamic range and fidelity of tape were much improved over those of magnetic wires, and tape was far easier to edit.

The wide band of magnetic particles on a tape can be divided into numerous discrete lines of recording information called tracks. Accurate playback of a magnetic tape requires a machine whose electromagnetic pickup, known as the reproducer head, is capable of reading the track configuration present on the tape. There are magnetic tape track configuration viewers available that suspend ferromagnetic particles in a solution on top of a tape (usually contained in a housing) that will align themselves to reveal the structure of the arranged particles on a tape. These tools can be helpful in surveying a large or diverse collection of tapes to evaluate their playback characteristics.

Tape can be found in open reel, cartridge, and cassette forms. Open reel tape can be recorded at several different standard speeds, sometimes on the same reel. Cartridges have a single reel inside an enclosure. The tape is either wound onto a takeup reel inside the playback machine or wound back around the cartridge reel after passing through the tape transports and playback heads. Cassettes contain two reels and the tape is wound from one to the other during playback. The tracks on the tape are arranged so that the cassette can be flipped and played and the tape wound back on the first reel.

Tape quickly replaced lacquer discs in the recording industry and radio. Although consumer market cassette sales rivaled those of LPs in the early 1980s, cassettes were more commonly used for home recording and field recording. Maintaining the necessary equipment for archival preservation of magnetic tape is becoming increasingly difficult.

What is Dolby? Why it Matters

Dolby refers to a noise (tape hiss) reduction process that entails pre-recording high-frequency tones into magnetic tape. These tones are filtered back out on playback to eliminate tape hiss. Different protocols were developed: Dolby A, B, and C, for example. If no Dolby correction, or correction for the wrong Dolby protocol, is applied at playback, tape hiss will be increased or high frequencies that are part of the recording may be suppressed.

Open reel magnetic tape

Dimensions	Tape width: ¼ inch through 2 inches Reel diameter: 3 inches through 14 inches; 7-inch and 10-inch reels standard Standard play: 38 microns (1.5 mils) thick base tape Long play: 25.4 microns (1 mil) thick base tape • Double play: 12.7 microns (0.5 mils) thick base tape • Triple play: 12.7 microns (0.5 mils) or thinner base tape (Casey and Gordon 2007) • Total thickness of tape varies based on thickness of other layers
Material composition	Ferromagnetic particles suspended in a binder adhered to a substrate Paper used early on as a substrate Cellulose acetate tape used into the 1960s Acetate-backed tape replaced by polyester backing Polyvinyl chloride (PVC) also used (primarily in Germany) Lubricants, plasticizers, and binding agents often not identified Several stocks produced between 1970s and 1990s contained polyester-urethane used in the binder layer
Primary dates of production	1945–2000s (still used in niche markets)
Recording characteristics	Possible to record on open reel at several different standard speeds described in inches per second (ips). The three most common tape speeds are 15 ips, 7.5 ips, and 3.75 ips, though both faster and slower speed tapes are often encountered. • Option for recorder to select the recording speed and change speed at any point on many tape recorders • Passages possibly recorded at different speeds on one tape • In some instances, the length of recording time on a single tape extended by reduction in playback speed • No ready way to determine the track configuration of an open reel tape with the unassisted human eye
Notes on playback	In the best cases, the container that held the reel, or sometimes the reel itself, has helpful notes left behind by an engineer or hobbyist indicating track configuration, recording speed, and noise reduction implementation. In most cases, clues on the container, combined with educated guesses and trial and error by the tape's current caretaker, are necessary to determine the true nature of the recording. Identifying the track configuration and the Dolby processing scheme by ear is a bit more complicated. Machines to play and many supplies to care for and store open reel magnetic tape are no longer in production.
Deterioration	Paper-backed tapes are generally stable and hold on to their magnetic material. The main deterioration is to the paper itself, and it can suffer all the possible ailments common to paper (swelling and disintegration in water, fungal growth in humid environments, acidification, and embrittlement). Paper substrate can also tear or break under tension as it is wound. These breaks are often clean and easily repaired with splicing tape, provided that the tape overall has sufficient structural integrity. Cellulose acetate-backed tapes are susceptible to vinegar syndrome, in which the tape base releases acetic acid, begins to shrink, and becomes brittle. The magnetic layer does not shrink, and the difference in width between the two layers causes the tape to deform (cupping). Cellulose acetate also breaks cleanly when it fails and can be repaired by splicing tape without much information loss. If the base deformation is substantial, the magnetic layer can separate or begin shedding particles gradually. Playback should be stopped if pieces are flaking off or if heavy deposits are being left on the playback head or along the tape path. Polyester-backed tapes are relatively strong and chemically stable, though the polyethylene terephthalate (PET) can absorb water (Hess 2008). Thin tape (e.g., 0.5-mil open reel tape and cassette tape stock) will stretch or break and can easily be damaged by malfunctioning playback machines, especially during fast winds or rewinds. In some tape stock, the binder absorbs atmospheric water and loses integrity as a result. This is known as binder hydrolysis or "sticky shed syndrome." (More information on treatment of sticky shed syndrome is provided in chapter 4.) • Polyester tape stocks with polyester-urethane (PEU)-based binders appear to be the most susceptible (Breitung et al. 2013). • Binder hydrolysis weakens the bond between the substrate and the magnetic layer. • When sticky tapes are played, the magnetic layer can peel off, leaving heavy deposits along the tape path and blank substrate. • If this separation happens before the playback head, then the recorded material is lost and cannot be rescued. • If it occurs after the playback head, it will be the last pass for that tape. • Sticky tapes can be identified by a squealing or chirping sound as the tape is wound. • If squealing is heard, playback should be stopped to prevent further damage.

Cartridges (8-tracks), Compact cassette, Microcassette

8-track cartridge

Comparison of compact cassette, microcassette, and 8-track cartridge

Dimensions	**Cartridges:** made in a variety of sizes for use in radio production; 8-tracks were the most common consumer cartridge format: 5.25 inches x 4 inches x 1 inch, ¼ inch tape width
	Compact cassette: 4 inches by 2.5 inches x 0.343 inch, ⅛ inch tape width, 11–16 microns in thickness
	Microcassette: ⅛ inch tape width, less than 11 microns in thickness
Material composition	Ferromagnetic particles suspended in a binder layer adhered to polyester substrate, enclosed within a plastic housing.
Primary dates of production	**Cartridges:** 1963–1982
	Cassettes: 1962–present
Recording characteristics	**Cartridges:** 4-track cartridges usually have two programs, each recorded on 2 tracks; 8-tracks have four programs, each recorded on 2 tracks. Playback time is roughly similar to that of 12-inch LP records.
	Cassettes: stereo tapes recorded with 4 tracks, alternating directions. Tracks 1 and 2 correspond to side 1. When played or wound all the way to the end, the cassette was then removed and flipped horizontally; the tape would wind back onto the original reel, playing tracks 3 and 4 as side 2. Monophonic cassettes contain 2 tracks playing in opposite directions (see p. 27).
Notes on playback	Cartridge playback machines contained a single 2-track playback pickup that moved up and down to select the desired track pairs. Rewinding was not possible because the tape loop was wound onto itself. In both car and home playback systems, the playback heads could easily become misaligned, causing distortion and cross-talk between the channels. Successful playback depends on a well-built player in excellent condition, which can be difficult to find.
Deterioration	The inevitable loss of tape lubrication within cartridges can cause the tape to wind improperly or stick together when unwound during playback. The pinch roller in some cartridges was made of improperly cured rubber, which can allow the roller to become dented or misshapen, particularly if exposed to excessive heat. Both of these factors contribute to a risk of tape snarls and catastrophic malfunction.
	The portable design of cartridge and cassette tapes encourages listening in all environments, and this makes them especially susceptible to binder hydrolysis. Many cassettes have also spent a considerable amount of time in cars, repeatedly exposed to extremes of temperature and humidity, as well as dirt and debris. High-capacity tapes use very thin polyester tape and are at a high risk of deformation, especially when stored in hot and humid environments.

Disc and Tape Channels and Length

Careful visual examination of an analog audio carrier, such as a tape or a disc, provides clues to the playback hardware required to hear the recording and the approximate, or at least maximum, length of the recording held by the carrier. This information can be useful for both playing the recording properly and estimating the time required to reformat it if the carrier is to be preserved.

Visual information usually reveals a great deal of technical information about a disc. Examination of disc groove width, or label information, indicates a recommended playback speed. Labels note whether the recording is monaural, stereo, or quadraphonic. Size and groove format provide clues to the maximum playback time of a disc side.

It is more difficult to visually discern the playback speed, number of channels, and maximum program of most tapes. If an open reel tape is housed in its original box, the box will identify the full length of the tape. Handwritten notations on the box may indicate the speed at which the tape was recorded, the track configuration—whether monaural or stereo—and whether the tape has been recorded in one direction or two.

Nearly every open reel tape found in libraries, archives, and personal collections is ¼ inch in width. Wider tapes may be found in professional recording studios. The three most common open reel tape track, or channel, configurations are full-track monaural, half-track monaural, and quarter-track stereo. A full-track tape recording is meant to be played back in one direction only. Many home reel-to-reel tape recorders have tape heads that are designed to record and play back two (stereo) channels. Each of the two heads reads only one-quarter the width of the tape. Half- and quarter-track tapes must be turned over to play in the opposite direction.

The table on the following page provides a guide to these maximum lengths, in one direction. If the tape was recorded at half-track, or quarter-track, in both directions, double the time estimates.

The maximum recording length of cassette tapes is usually clearly printed on the tape cartridge, preceded by a "C." For instance, a cassette tape marked "C-30" has a maximum playback of about 30 minutes, 15 minutes per side. A C-90 cassette may be recorded for about 45 minutes on each side, or a total of 90 minutes. (The estimates presume a playing speed of 1⅞ inches per second, the speed at which almost every compact cassette recorder operates.) So, how does a reel that can play for 45 minutes look exactly like a reel that plays for only 15 minutes, even when played at the same speed? The answer is the difference in the thickness of the tape. The tape stock used on a C-90 cassette may be one-third the thickness of tape stock in a C-30 cassette. It is important to keep this in mind when determining priorities for preservation reformatting. The thinner the tape stock, the more easily it can stretch or become tangled in the mechanism of a player.

Although an examination by the naked eye cannot determine track, or channel, configuration, there are magnetic viewers that reveal the number of recorded tracks on an open reel tape. One manufacturer of such viewers is Arnold Magnetic Technologies.

Polyester or Acetate?
It is important to be able to distinguish open reels of polyester tape from those of acetate tape as the formulations deteriorate in different ways. Mistaking one for the other and mistreating it, such as by baking an acetate tape, can damage a recording irrevocably. The easiest way to tell acetate from polyester is to hold the reel up to a light source. If it is translucent, as seen with the reel on the right, it is acetate tape.

Diagrams and Chart for Determining Tape Length

Full track

Half-track monaural

Quarter-inch tape. Four-track stereo

Left track

Right track

Right track

Left track

Audiocassette (one-eighth-inch). Four-track stereo

Right track

Left track

Right track

Left track

Duration of open-reel tape in each direction

Speed	Length of tape				
	600 feet	1200 feet	1800 feet	2500 feet	3600 feet
3 ¾ ips	30 minutes	1 hour	90 minutes	2 hours	3 hours
7 ½ ips	15 minutes	30 minutes	45 minutes	1 hour	1 ½ hours
15 ips	7 ½ minutes	15 minutes	22 ½ minutes	30 minutes	45 minutes

A tool designed to calculate the length of ¼-inch open reel tape may be found at http://www.avpreserve.com/tools/open-reel-audio-duration-calculator/.

Digital Audio Tape (DAT)

Dimensions	2 ⅞ inches x 2 1/16 inches x 5/16 inch
Material composition	Polyester-based tape with pure metal particles suspended in a polyester urethane binder; reverse side of tape base often coated with graphite or similar lubricating material
Primary dates of production	1985–2005
Recording characteristics	Unlike other magnetic tape–based audio formats, which are recorded with a lateral scan (in which the tracks run parallel to the length of the tape), DATs are recorded with a helical scan (diagonally to the length of the tape) with a rotating head. Can record pulse code modulation (PCM) information with a bit depth of 12 at a sampling rate of 32 kHz or 16 bits with sampling rates of 32 kHz, 44.1kHz, or 48kHz (Eldridge 2010).
Notes on playback	DAT decks produced by different manufacturers vary in the way they encode data onto a tape, so DAT tape recorded on a Sony DAT machine may not be playable in a TASCAM DAT machine. The short life span and limited adoption of the technology makes the prospect of procuring and maintaining DAT decks a daunting undertaking. Because of the helical scan encoding, the alignment of the read/record heads must exactly match the alignment of the heads at the point of recording for information to be retrieved (Eldridge 2010).
Deterioration	The pure iron pigments used in the magnetic layer of DATs are susceptible to oxidation (rust). Binder hydrolysis in the polyester urethane binder has proven to be a prevalent issue with many DATs, causing complete loss of information. The high speeds produced by the rotating heads passing by the moving tape exacerbate damage to the information layer. After the error threshold is crossed, the information is irretrievable. These factors combine to make DATs a very high-risk format, recommended for immediate digital preservation by trained preservation engineers with high-quality equipment (Eldridge 2010).

2.4 OPTICAL DISC FORMATS

At a glance:

- The first commercially successful consumer digital audio format was the optical disc.
- Pressed compact discs (CDs) differ from recordable CDs in composition and durability.
- CD-R and rewritable CDs (CD-RW) have different physical construction and employ different recording mechanisms.
- Physical or chemical damage to either side of the disc can damage the playback layer.
- The life span of recordable discs is estimated at an average of 5 years.

Audio CDs were the first successful consumer digital audio format. Sony and Phillips created the Compact Discs Digital Audio (CD-DA) standard, also known as the Red Book standard. CDs encoded according to the Red Book standard can store a maximum of 79.8 minutes of audio. Digital audio information is expressed in binary (1/0) and encoded via microscopic indentations (pits) or the lack thereof (lands) in the top polycarbonate layer of a CD. An optical stylus laser reads the difference in reflectivity between the pits and the lands; the playback system then reproduces the encoded digital audio. The Red Book standard also details the manner in which the data are arranged into sectors and how bytes are apportioned to audio content, error detection, error correction, and other features, such as copy protection (Collins 1998). CDs can also be used to store data of any file type, independent of the CD-DA standard. Alternatively, one of a variety of other standards created for encoding computer application information and other specialized data types may be used (IASA 2009).

Pressed compact disc

Dimensions	4.7 inches in diameter x 0.047 inch thick
Material composition	Protective lacquer layer, metal data layer, polycarbonate plastic layer
Primary dates of production	1982–present

Pressed commercial CDs are identifiable by a printed label and the shiny silver appearance of the reverse side.

Recording characteristics	CD-DA can encode linear pulse code modulation (LPCM) at a bit depth of 16 bits and a sampling rate of 44.1 kHz.
Notes on playback	Prerecorded CDs are currently the most popular physical audio format, though consumption of audio seems to be moving away from physical formats. Machines to play back CDs may become difficult to obtain in the future, but this is not a current concern.
Deterioration	Both polycarbonate layers are susceptible to damage. Scratches and abrasions to the bottom layer can cause read errors and, if severe enough, can prevent successful playback. The top layer, where the information is actually stored, can be damaged by acidic inks from pens or markers used to label a CD, or from dyes and adhesives used to decorate and label the disc. Accelerated testing conducted at the Library of Congress has indicated that the reflective metallic layer can delaminate from the polycarbonate plastic when a disc cycles repeatedly through heat and cold (Shahani et al. n.d.).

Shutterstock.com/Africa Studio

Once believed to be impervious to damage caused by playback, scratched compact discs can be marred to the point of being unplayable. Common causes of scratches are the automatic load and eject features of CD players in automobiles.

CD-R (CD+R)

Dimensions	4.7 inches in diameter x 0.047 inch thick
Material composition	Protective lacquer layer, organic dye layer, gold or silver metal reflective layer, polycarbonate plastic layer
Primary dates of production	1988–present
	CD-Rs are often identifiable by the green-blue tint of their reflective sides and indications of how much of the format's capacity has been used by changes in tint.
Recording characteristics	Data recorded into the dye layer by a laser of much higher intensity than that used for playback
	Dye burned by the laser to encode the digital information through the differences in reflectivity of the burned and unburned areas (Bradley 2006).
	Possible to author discs as CD-DA or as data discs containing any number of digital file formats
Notes on playback	CD-Rs are recordable one time; once the information is burned into the dye layer it cannot be edited or erased. There are standards for CD-R discs to facilitate the interchange of discs between burners and readers. However, there are no standards covering the burners or readers themselves, and the disc standards do not take preservation or longevity into consideration.
	Several different burning and reading speeds were developed, and earlier discs or burners are not compatible with later, faster speeds. As a result, there is considerable variability in whether any given disc can be read by any given reader (Schüller 2008).
	Not all CD drives intended for CD-DA are capable of reading data CDs, though some playback equipment can handle nested directories of MPEG-3 files, for example.
Deterioration	The dye layer is sensitive to ultraviolet radiation; exposure to sunlight for several days can render them unreadable (Schüller 2008). As disc drives become less common, it could become more difficult to find suitable drives for reading CD-Rs, as well as to acquire suitable software to read the data formats that might be encoded on a disc.

CD-RW

Dimensions	4.7 inches in diameter x 0.047 inch thick
Material composition	Protective lacquer layer, metal alloy (germanium, antimony, tellurium) recording layer, aluminum reflective layer, polycarbonate plastic layer
Primary dates of production	1991–present
	The CD-RW format is usually self-identified on the label side. The reflective side of a CD-RW disc is usually lighter in tint than that of a CD-R.
Recording characteristics	Two lasers of different intensities used: one heats a point on the metal alloy layer to its melting point; the other heats a point to its crystallization point. The pattern of melted or amorphous points and crystallized points within the track vary in reflectivity and binary digits encoded.
Notes on playback	Rewritable discs can be written and rewritten a finite number of times.
Deterioration	The metal alloy data layer and aluminum reflective layer can both be damaged when exposed to oxygen through delamination (Byers 2003).

2.5 UNUSUAL FORMATS

There have been dozens of short-lived or narrowly focused formats. They represent a small fraction of the sound recording ecosystem, but they can show up in unexpected places. In addition to odd sound-specific formats, nearly every carrier and playback system designed for moving image content has also been adapted into an audio-only carrier that may not be compatible with video playback equipment.

Edison Dictaphone cylinder

AmerTape

Grooved dictation belt. Paper clips often found on dictation belts should always be removed.

Magnetic dictation belt

- **Edison Dictaphone:** 8-inch long cylinder format specifically designed for dictation. It varied in both speed and threads per inch (tpi) from Edison's other cylinders and requires different playback equipment.
- **Marconi Velvet Tone disc:** early attempt at flexible laminated lacquer discs. It was produced only in 1917.
- **AmerTape:** raised grooves embossed into clear 35mm film stock. This format was used primarily by the U.S. military during World War II.
- **Pathé Brothers vertical-cut discs:** imported French disc format. Discs look very similar to standard 78-rpm discs and were produced between 1905 and 1920.
- **Optical soundtrack:** sound waves reproduced in photographic emulsion as part of a 35mm film negative or print, 1931 to present.
- **Music box discs:** flat metal discs with punched holes that provide instructions for mechanical reproduction in a music box. They range in size from 8 inches to 16 inches and were produced from 1880s to present (niche markets).
- **Grooved dictation belt:** wide belt of acetate or polyester joined into a loop. Recording technique is the same as that for a lateral-cut disc. It could carry about 12 minutes of sound and was used for office dictation, 1947-1980.
- **Magnetic dictation belt:** wide belt of polyester sheet joined into a loop coated in ferromagnetic particles. Recording technique was the same as that for magnetic tape; it was used for office dictation, ca. 1960-1970.
- **Sony MiniDisc:** a magneto-optical format, approximately 2 ¾ inches x 2 ⅝ inches in size and marked prominently with "MD." These discs are more stable than some digital carriers but were never adopted widely. However, they gained some popularity with journalists, for interviews, and for use by theater sound designers. It will become increasingly difficult to obtain the hardware needed to play them back; players have not been manufactured since 2013.

2.6 DIGITAL AUDIO FILE FORMATS

At a glance:

- Digital file formats are independent of any specific physical carrier and are likely never to have a dedicated physical carrier.
- Most digital audio files are encoded representations of an analog sound wave.
- Codecs are required to decode the data in the file.
- Various compression strategies have been developed to reduce file size.

Digital audio was first incorporated into the professional production of sound recording around 1976, eventually replacing time-consuming tape editing, just as tape editing had replaced time-consuming disc mastering before that, and as mastering had replaced direct recording. Digital recording was seen as a way to attain even better control over sound reproduction. One big advantage was the ability to create exact copies and avoid the sound artifacts introduced in each generation of analog copying.

Digital recording and editing has now all but completely replaced its analog predecessors, even though analog consumer formats such as vinyl LPs are seeing a growing audience. But the new risks and benefits associated with digital formats require an approach very different from those that have applied to analog formats and physical formats as a whole.

In a digital file, the analog sound wave is analyzed every few microseconds, and a value is recorded at that point. Together, these discrete points represent the original continuous sound wave; the size of the value that can be recorded and the number of samples taken determine the accuracy of the representation. This method of digitally describing a sound wave is called pulse code modulation (PCM) and is the backbone of most digital audio files, although new methods are being used now in ultra–high-resolution projects. The files encoded onto CDs, one of the first consumer digital formats, have a 16-bit resolution, meaning that each sample point can have a 16-bit value, and a sampling rate of 44.1 kiloHertz (kHz).

As the speed and storage capacity of consumer computers increased and the Internet enabled file sharing across massive networks, digital files could be divorced from a physical carrier, disseminated, and played back without ever being fixed in a physical form. However, the ability and desire for such transmission came before the large files created with PCM could be easily exchanged in their raw state. To reduce the size of the files, various means of compression were developed and used to various degrees. Lossless compression employs mathematical compression to reduce the file size, usually by a factor of 2:1. A mathematical function is performed on a statistical representation of the data in the file to produce a smaller value than the original representation. When the compressed file is decoded, the function is reversed and the original values are reconstructed. Higher rates of compression can be achieved by using lossy compression, in which file size is reduced by eliminating information present in the source sound. The chart at right looks at several of the more widely adopted compressed and uncompressed audio formats.

File type	Open or proprietary	Type of compression	Description
WAVE Broadcast WAVE (BWF) Multi-channel Broadcast WAVE (MBWF)	Open	None	Originally developed by Microsoft Longest standing high-quality audio format Limitations: a lack of extensive metadata on the content of the file and a file size limit of 4 gigabytes (GB) • BWF addresses the lack of metadata by incorporating additional metadata fields (either as a "BEXT" or "iXML" chunk). • MBWF addresses the size limit by enabling the capture of up to 18 channels and functionally removing any limit to file size. A 24-bit, 96-kHz BWF is the current preferred format for master files. WAVE recommended by the International Association of Sound and Audiovisual Archives in its TC–04 publication (IASA 2009)
Audio Interchange File Format (AIFF)	Open	None	Originally developed by Apple and proprietary, but fully documented Pulse code modulation (PCM) data remain unchanged if converting between WAVE and AIFF Used in the Apple ecosystem in place of Free Lossless Audio Codec (FLAC)
Windows Media Audio (WMA) Lossless	Proprietary	None	Lossless version of Windows Media Audio proprietary format Details and specifications on the format not disseminated and the extent of its adoption is unknown
Free Lossless Audio Codec (FLAC)	Open	Lossless	Developed as an open source project and now maintained and updated by the Xiph.Org Foundation Uses mathematical compression to reduce file size Can restore information removed during compression at playback without any reduction in audio quality
Apple Lossless Audio Codec (ALAC)	Open as of 2011	Lossless	Originally a proprietary format for the Apple ecosystem
MPEG-1 Layer III (MP3) (Extended in MPEG-2)	Open	Lossy	Originally developed in 1993 by the Motion Picture Expert Group (MPEG) at the request of the International Standards Organization (ISO) MP3 the most commonly encountered consumer audio file format Enabled the growth and development of digital music distribution by dramatically reducing audio file size File specification capable of many compression rates • The compression is based on a psychoacoustic algorithm that attempts to eliminate data from the bitstream with the least effect on the perception of the sound quality. • Once the source file is encoded into MP3, the compression algorithm removes information from the file that cannot be recovered. Need for a small file footprint becoming less important for the dissemination of files, as high bandwidth Internet connections became more common Small file sizes well suited to portable music players, which often cannot reproduce high-resolution audio. They are often heard through headphones or earbuds that lack the capability of full frequency reproduction. Consequently, playback conditions offset the limitations of the format. Sound quality dependent on the amount of compression employed

(continued, next page)

File type	Open or proprietary	Type of compression	Description
AAC/MPEG-4 v.2	Open	Lossy	Default audio file format for the iTunes store
			Massively prevalent in the current digital ecosystem
			Considered to sound better than MP3 files of equivalent bitrate because of different compression algorithms
Ogg Vorbis	Open	Lossy	Open source format developed and maintained by the Xiph.Org Foundation
			Intended to facilitate audio transfers across medium bandwidth Internet connections
			Sound quality dependent on the amount of compression employed
Windows Media Audio (WMA)	Proprietary	Lossy	Widely adopted early format
			Although not open, specifications fully documented
			Sound quality dependent on amount of compression employed

2.7 CONCLUSION

While sound recordings may be classified into broad groups, curators of collections must be familiar with the various formats that fall into these groups. Knowledge of the periods during which they were used, understanding their composition, and being aware of the various ways in which they may deteriorate over time is necessary to manage a recording collection.

The history of sound recording technology, as with many consumer products, often emphasizes innovation and marketability over longevity or interoperability. It is fortunate that these forces have produced robust and resilient physical formats, such as the shellac 78-rpm disc and the vinyl record. Other formats, such as the compact cassette, will likely remain accessible beyond their commercial lifespan because of the sheer volume of cassettes and playback decks produced. Digital sound recording is in early stages compared to these earlier examples, and it is impossible to say what access to a WAVE file might look like one hundred years from now. It is encouraging that open, stable format standards have emerged and that market forces seem to be incentivizing interoperability.

There are many challenges to address, including maintaining the ability to access all formats and preserving all recordings of cultural value. The ability to meet these challenges is aided by understanding the context in which recordings were made, both the era during which they were created and the forms in which they were distributed. The meaning and value of our work are realized by our ability to reintroduce historical recordings to successive generations of listeners. Proactive attention, care, and planning are critical to the future viability and value of both analog and digital recordings, with or without physical manifestations.

REFERENCES

All URLs are current as of May 1, 2015

Bradley, Kevin. 2006. *Risks Associated with the Use of Recordable CDs and DVDs as Reliable Storage Media in Archival Collections: Strategies and Alternatives*. Memory of the World Programme, Sub-Committee on Technology. Paris: UNESCO. Available at http://unesdoc.unesco.org/images/0014/001477/147782e.pdf.

Breitung, Eric M., Samantha Skelton, Juan Rodriguez, Lu Zhang, Brianna Cassidy, Peter Alyea, Stephen L. Morgan. 2013. Non-destructive Identification of Polymeric Binder Degradation in Audio and Video Tapes. Research and Technical Studies Specialty Group Postprints. American Institute for Conservation of Historic and Artistic Works, 41st Annual Meeting, Indianapolis, IN, May 29–June 1, 2013. Available at http://www.conservation-us.org/docs/default-source/periodicals/rats-004-2013.pdf?sfvrsn=20.

Byers, Fred R. 2003. *Care and Handling of CDs and DVDs—A Guide for Librarians and Archivists*. Washington, D.C.: Council on Library and Information Resources and Gaithersburg, MD: National Institute of Standards and Technology. Available at http://www.clir.org/pubs/reports/reports/pub121/pub121.pdf.

Casey, Mike, and Bruce Gordon. 2007. *Sound Directions. Best Practices for Audio Preservation*. Trustees of Indiana University and President and Fellows of Harvard University. Available at http://www.dlib.indiana.edu/projects/sounddirections/papersPresent/sd_bp_07.pdf.

Collins, Mike. 1998. "Compact Disc Formats Explained." *Sound on Sound* (January). Available at http://www.soundonsound.com/sos/jan98/articles/cdformats.htm.

Dawson, Jim, and Steve Propes. 2003. *45 RPM: The History, Heroes and Villains of a Pop Music Revolution*. San Francisco, CA: Backbeat Books.

Eldridge, Susan. 2010. "Digital Audio Tapes: Their Preservation and Conversion." Smithsonian Institution Archives. Available at https://siarchives.si.edu/sites/default/files/pdfs/digitalAudioTapesPreservation2010_0.pdf.

Gracyk, Tim. 2006. Information about Victrola Needles. Tim's Phonograph and Old Records. Available at http://www.gracyk.com/needletips.shtml.

Hess, Richard L. 2008. "Tape Degradation Factors and Challenges in Predicting Tape Life." *ARSC Journal* 39(2): 240–274.

IASA (International Association of Sound and Audiovisual Archives) Technical Committee. 2009. *Guidelines on the Production and Preservation of Digital Audio Objects*, second edition. (IASA-TC04). Kevin Bradley, ed. Aarhus, Denmark: International Association of Sound and Audiovisual Archives. Available at http://www.iasa-web.org/tc04/audio-preservation.

King, Gretchen. n.d. *Magnetic Wire Recordings: A Manual Including Historical Background, Approaches to Transfer and Storage, and Solutions to Common Problems*. Available at https://web.archive.org/web/20080512230050/http://depts.washington.edu/ethmusic/wire1.html.

Milner, Greg. 2009. *Perfecting Sound Forever: An Aural History of Recorded Music.* New York: Faber and Faber Inc.

Nguyen, Thi-Phuong, Xavier Sené, Emilie Le Bourg, and Stéphane Bouvet. 2011. "Determining the Composition of 78-rpm Records: Challenge or Fantasy?" *ARSC Journal* 42(1). Available via https://www.questia.com/library/journal/1G1-258437042/determining-the-composition-of-78-rpm-records-challenge.

Schoenherr, Steve. 2005 (rev. July 6). Recording Technology History. Audio Engineering Society. Available at http://www.aes.org/aeshc/docs/recording.technology.history/notes.html.

Schüller, Dietrich. 2008. *Audio and Video Carriers. Recording Principles, Storage and Handling, Maintenance of Equipment, Format and Equipment Obsolescence.* Available at http://www.tape-online.net/docs/audio_and_video_carriers.pdf.

Seubert, David, and Noah Pollaczek. 2005. Cylinder Recordings: A Primer. University of California Santa Barbara Cylinder Preservation Project. Available at http://cylinders.library.ucsb.edu/history.php.

Shahani, Chandru J., Basil Manns, and Michele Youket. n.d. "Longevity of CD Media Research at the Library of Congress." Available at http://www.loc.gov/preservation/resources/rt/studyofCDlongevity.pdf.

St. Laurent, Gilles. 1997. "The Care of Grooved Recordings." Pp. 250–258 in *Audiovisual Archives: A Practical Reader*, edited by Helen P. Harrison. Paris: UNESCO. Available at http://unesdoc.unesco.org/images/0010/001096/109612eo.pdf.

Stauderman, Sarah. 2004. Pictorial Guide to Sound Recording Media. Pages 29-42 in Judith Matz, ed., *Sound Savings: Preserving Audio Collections*. Proceedings of a symposium sponsored by School of Information, Preservation and Conservation Studies, University of Texas at Austin; Library of Congress; National Recording Preservation Board; and Association of Research Libraries, Austin, Texas, July 24-26, 2003. Washington, D.C.: Association of Research Libraries. Available at http://www.arl.org/storage/documents/publications/sound-savings.pdf.

Welch, Walter L. 1972. "Preservation and Restoration of Authenticity in Sound Recordings." *Library Trends* 21(1): 83–100. Available at http://citeseerx.ist.psu.edu/viewdoc/download?doi=10.1.1.204.4345&rep=rep1&type=pdf.

CHAPTER 3

Appraisals and Priorities

By Maya Lerman

Collections seem inevitably to grow in size. Whether materials have been actively solicited, received as donations, or purchased, institutions often have more items in their care than they have resources to provide adequate processing, cataloging, and preservation. Recorded sound materials add a depth and richness not found in other formats, yet these materials have particular requirements for storage, handling, playback, and preservation. Born-digital collections bring special concerns related to formatting, metadata, storage, and management of files. The required elements of both physical and digital collections can be costly, making it especially important to carefully consider the content and size of collections added to your library or archives.

The professional management of a collection requires the development of criteria for selecting and preserving collections of sound recordings. A selection or collection development policy defines and sets priorities for the types of collections that are most appropriate and suitable for an organization to acquire and to preserve. The basis for these criteria should be the goals and objectives of the individual institution. Policies are especially important when considering new acquisitions or preserving sound recordings and making them accessible. All institutions face some degree of budget constraints that affect the amount of resources that can be devoted to these activities. Selection policies can help ensure that resources are allocated as effectively as possible. Equally important, they should guide an institution in building on its inherent strengths and in further developing its constituency and garnering support for its specialized activities.

The task of appraisal involves assessing the value to your institution of a collection or parts of a collection, judging it in conjunction with your institution's mission and goals, and carefully considering the responsibilities and inherent costs of ownership. Another decision point in managing an archive is setting priorities about what materials are digitized. The criteria that guide decisions about the acquisition of a collection are similar to those that guide decisions about what should be reformatted for preservation.

The most effective collection development policies evolve naturally from an institution's mission and goals.

The most effective collection development policies evolve naturally from an institution's mission and goals. This chapter offers basic guidance to institutions and organizations interested in developing or revising a collection development policy and to those who already have established general collection policies, but have less familiarity with decisions about recorded sound materials. It provides a checklist of topics to consider both when selecting recorded sound collections to acquire and when determining which materials should receive priority for preservation and digitization.

All Things to No One

At the core of making an acquisitions appraisal are the questions: Does this collection belong with us? If so, why? A likely outcome of acquiring every collection available to you is the great risk of neglecting the strengths in your existing collection. However tantalizing an offer of a collection might be, you should carefully consider whether the responsibilities for maintaining the new collection will weaken your ability to sustain your core collections. The selection considerations presented in this chapter provide guidance in making an acquisitions decision. Broader considerations include these related questions:

- Does the collection expand on an existing strength?
- Is the collection in line with the mission of my institution?
- Is there an existing constituency that will consult the collection? If not, will I be able to develop one?
- Does the collection duplicate another collection in my geographic area?

3.1 DEVELOPING A SELECTION/COLLECTION DEVELOPMENT POLICY

In developing or revising your selection/collection development policy, consider the following questions:

- Is your mission to document a specific historical subject, time period, or genre?
- What kinds of material do you collect, and are special formats given any priority in your institution?
- How are collections acquired: gift, purchase, or part of existing institutional policy?
- How would potential new collections fit within the existing collections?
- Who is your constituency, and how may your organization better serve them?

■ What kind of access do you offer? Do you provide resources for researchers who visit the archive, digitally preserve materials for access in a reading room, or offer remote online access?

The Sound Archives Ngā Taonga Kōrero (SANTK) in New Zealand has developed a selection, acquisition, and accession policy that exemplifies how setting priorities for selection reflects and further refines an organization's overall mission. SANTK's collecting priorities are radio broadcasts from New Zealand and documentation related to these broadcasts, as well as other historically significant recordings made in New Zealand. The policy outlines the archives' selection criteria and the ways in which staff measure the cultural value of materials and set priorities for what they collect. For example, recordings of historical events or of social history and folklore are important selection criteria, with priority given to materials made in or about New Zealand or New Zealanders. SANTK's policy also emphasizes the priority that its staff has assigned to unique or endangered materials not held by other institutions.

In the acquisition criteria portion of its selection policy, SANTK specifies that its staff may inspect the materials in a collection before acquiring them and that staff may be selective within a collection about which materials they acquire, based on their appraisal and the institution's selection policy. Staff members take into account travel and packing costs and assess the benefits of acquiring the collection against the potential impact on available storage space, staff processing time, and budget.

3.2 DECIDING WHETHER TO ACQUIRE A COLLECTION

The following points should be considered when making appraisal decisions to purchase a collection of sound recordings or to accept one as a gift:

■ Relevance to mission
■ Size of collection
■ Environmental and conservation requirements and condition
■ Total cost of retention
■ Documentation
■ Restrictions

RELEVANCE TO MISSION

A major consideration when determining what to collect or acquire, maintain, and ultimately digitally preserve is the materials' relevance to your organization's goals and mission. Because the maintenance and preservation of sound recordings require specific and often costly supplies, equipment, and expertise, it is important to evaluate their relevance and projected use in your archive (Paton 1997, 128–129). A curator at a town's historical society may know that the daughter of a former town mayor is looking to sell a collection of recordings of her father's speeches. The organization's collecting priorities include materials documenting the town's political life, so this collection likely has great relevance to the historical society's mission. The recordings could be of greater value to users than written transcripts, because they document a more complete picture of the mayor, including aspects of his voice and character, as well as how his audiences received him. The relevance, value, and projected use of this collection would make it a strong candidate for acquisition by the historical society.

SIZE OF COLLECTION

Before making appraisal decisions about a purchase or gift, an institution's staff should evaluate their storage space against the size of the collection to determine whether they can accommodate the space requirements of the collection (Harrison and Schuursma 1987). If the collection requires significant storage space, is its value and relevance to the institution worth this use of space? If the collection is born-digital, is there an adequate data storage system? Is selecting within the collection an option? There may be items within a collection that duplicate your existing holdings, or there may be materials of lower value to your institution. In some cases, it is possible to be selective and to acquire only portions of a collection.

It is recommended that masters or original analog formats be maintained because of the potential for improved audio transfer capabilities in the future and because of their historical value.

Digital storage could be a solution for saving space when recordings are reformatted copies of originals (dubs), or are on physical digital formats such as recordable compact discs (CD-Rs) and Digital Audio Tapes (DATs), which are not suitable formats for long-term preservation. Such storage options for born-digital or digitized materials would be in a digital repository or on a hard drive. However, it is still recommended that masters or original analog formats be maintained because of the potential for improved audio transfer capabilities in the future and because of their historical value (ARSC Technical Committee 2009). Does the collection being considered include primarily formats that would need to be maintained after they are digitized? Or, would digital preservation eliminate the need to continue to store the originals?

ENVIRONMENTAL AND CONSERVATION REQUIREMENTS AND CONDITION OF COLLECTION

Chapter 4 outlines the environmental and conservation requirements of recorded sound formats. Does your institution have the resources necessary for proper conservation conditions and housing for the sound recordings in the collection? A professional institution has an obligation to conserve and preserve the collection; the ability to provide adequate environmental and conservation conditions for the sound recordings for the long term is an important factor in deciding whether to acquire the collection. It is also important to evaluate the condition of the collection. Are most of the sound recordings in good condition, or are they fair to poor? Unless they are unique or difficult to obtain otherwise, discs that are severely scratched or worn may be of little value to an institution. If you are unfamiliar with the best way to determine the condition of sound recordings, it may be useful to find an experienced audio engineer, media preservationist, or consultant who can help evaluate the condition of the collection.

TOTAL COST OF RETENTION

The costs of retention encompass storage and conservation requirements, supplies, and equipment, as well as staff to process, catalog, and preserve the recordings. If the equipment and staffing requirements challenge your organization's means, it may be necessary to evaluate the relevance of the collection's content to your organization. If the collection will greatly enhance the institution's goals and support an important area of research, it is worth considering ways to stretch your institution's capabilities or adjust priorities. One manager of a major sound archive has recently argued that, in light of academic libraries' reliance on providing access to professional journals through online subscriptions, serial binding budgets should be reallocated to audiovisual conservation and preservation. This may include the purchase of equipment or outsourcing preservation reformatting of the collection.

If the equipment and staffing requirements challenge your organization's means, it may be necessary to evaluate the relevance of the collection's content to your organization. If the collection will greatly enhance the institution's goals and support an important area of research, it is worth considering ways to stretch your institution's capabilities or adjust priorities.

DOCUMENTATION

In the case of unpublished recordings, which are not by nature self-identified by record labels or boxes, accompanying documentation is nearly as important as the condition and quality of the recordings. A collection may come with an inventory that contains information about its contents, such as title, date, speaker/performer names, recording details, and timing. Information may also be typed or written on or within the containers of individual recordings. Record sleeves, tape boxes, and documentation within containers can all be sources of important information about the contents of the recordings (Paton 1997, 130). Born-digital collections should include documentation or metadata about provenance, content, and the characterization and quality of the digital files. Unfortunately, collections of unpublished recorded sound materials frequently contain little or no documentation about the recordings. Additional resources are required to play back, listen to, and document the contents of these recordings. When making appraisal decisions, high-quality documentation gives the archivist a sense of the contents and the value of the materials and influences the decision to acquire or digitally preserve a collection. Collection holders may also need to consult with subject matter experts to supplement the documentation and to determine the value and significance of a particular collection.

RESTRICTIONS

Copyright and donor-imposed restrictions can make it difficult to provide access to recorded sound collections so that the public can listen to, appreciate, and use them. Access restrictions can put collections at risk because they may create obstacles to their preservation as well. Institutions tend to give greater precedence to accepting materials for which wide access can be provided. Additional information about donor agreements may be found in chapter 8.

3.3 MAKING THE PRESERVATION REFORMATTING DECISION

As with acquisitions, many factors affect the determination of preservation reformatting priorities:

- Uniqueness
- Technical obsolescence
- Cultural and historical value
- Generation
- Format degradation

UNIQUENESS

An important consideration in making appraisal decisions is uniqueness. Recordings not commonly held by other libraries or archives are good candidates for the use of limited preservation funding. On the other hand, uniqueness alone does not necessarily warrant top priority for preservation (Waffen n.d., General Policy).

Commercial or published recordings are mass-produced for distribution or sale to the public; they include music, spoken word, sound effects, and "books on tape" that can appear on most sound formats (Paton 1997, 119). Because other institutions often have duplicates, commercial recordings may be of lesser value to an archive unless they have particular relevance to the archive's mission or collection focus. In considering whether to preserve commercial records donated as part of a manuscript collection, your institution may want to ask how important these recordings are to the body of work of the person or organization that owned them. For example, a politician's personal record collection of long-playing discs (LPs) may not be relevant to the reasons the collection was acquired. In these and other cases, it might be sufficient to inventory and deaccession the commercial materials.

It must be emphasized that being mass-produced is not a sufficient reason to judge a recording an unsuitable acquisition for a specialized archive or library. Most published recordings are now out-of-print or available only in a compressed digital format or as streams. The original formats are often the only versions that include liner notes and illustrations, as well as the high-quality audio fidelity.

Noncommercial or unpublished recordings are unique or published in limited quantities. They include recordings of events, field recordings, oral histories, and radio broadcasts. They can also refer to the masters or stampers used to create the commercial recordings (Paton 1997, 120). Noncommercial recordings are more likely to be unique, inaccessible, or undocumented elsewhere. When determining priorities among these materials, the staff should try to establish the relative rarity of the recordings, as well as their relevance to the institution's mission.

TECHNICAL OBSOLESCENCE

The potential for technical obsolescence of the hardware required to play back a recording should influence priorities and resources allocated for preservation (Casey 2007). Many audio formats, including more recent media such as MiniDiscs, face technical obsolescence in that the devices required for decoding them, parts for those devices, and repair expertise are scarce. More recent media formats that qualify for preservation under this criterion include audio recorded on Betamax videotapes and Digital Audio Tape (DAT) cassettes.

CULTURAL VALUE

The cultural and historical value of materials, especially as they relate to the institution's mission and users' interests, should be a driving consideration when making appraisal decisions. Great value could be placed on significant musical performances, speeches of high impact, and documentation of a historical event. Cultural and historical values are particularly subjective criteria and dependent on users. In addition, some materials are of high value because of their relevance to the institution. Patrons of a university archive may express particular interest in important institutional figures, such as past presidents, deans, or influential professors. If this is the case, a collection of speeches given by a former university president may have special cultural value and could attract use by the public.

GENERATION

It is important to determine whether the formats are original recordings or copies, and their generation. The term *generation* refers to the number of times a recording is removed from the original format. Many recordings have historically been copied, and sometimes recopied, onto other formats for preservation purposes (Paton 1997). Perhaps a master reel was dubbed to a cassette for access, or a lacquer disc was dubbed to open reel tape for preservation. The original source recording, or the copy closest to first generation, should be the copy reformatted in a preservation program.

Before making preservation decisions, it is important to take into account different versions of recordings. For example, in spite of their historical format, most Edison Blue Amberol wax cylinders are dubs of Edison Diamond Discs and are not of the best recording quality. In most cases, the same may be said of commercial cassettes. The content of most commercial cassettes made in the United States is identical to that of LPs of the same title. However, if played properly, LPs degrade at a significantly slower rate than cassettes and always have superior sound fidelity. Therefore, LPs are preferable to cassettes as a preservation source. Exceptions

The Impact of Duplicates

Collections of both unpublished and commercial recordings often include multiple copies of the same recording. Duplicate items take up shelf space, require staff processing time, and may waste preservation resources and impede disaster recovery efforts. A common type of duplicate unpublished recording is a cassette or open reel tape copy created for access purposes. Collection inventories, discussed in chapter 5, will help you to discover duplicates for deaccessioning and help identify the best copy of an item. This is especially important for preservation planning, as discussed in the section on generation at right. If maintaining multiple copies of recordings is part of your collection policy, it is good practice to store the copies in geographically separate locations.

exist; for example, some cassettes include "extra tracks" not found on comparable LPs. In addition, some cassette titles were not co-released as LPs. The latter case is especially common with Asian and African releases. Original copies are often more valued, so it is important to determine whether the original version or master is available to be used as the preservation copy.

FORMAT DEGRADATION

The condition of a recording can determine both whether it can be played back and whether its content is audible. When setting priorities for items to digitize, format degradation—or potential degradation—should be a major consideration. Certain sound formats are especially vulnerable because of their high rate of deterioration or potential for technical obsolescence. The length of time that content can be retrieved from these types of recordings may be limited (Casey 2007). This reality is a factor in setting priorities for preservation reformatting.

As evident from the descriptions of sound formats and their various types of deterioration found in chapter 2, evaluating the condition of recordings is critical in determining their potential risks. Some formats, such as lacquer discs, are inherently less stable than others and should be given priority for digitization. Recordings of high research value and at high risk of physical deterioration should be given priority for preservation reformatting when they are deemed to be unique or uncommon. Such recordings often attract external resources to support preservation as well.

Recordings of high research value and at high risk of physical deterioration should be given priority for preservation reformatting when they are deemed to be unique or uncommon.

3.4   TOOLS TO HELP MAKE EVALUATIONS

Several free, open source software tools are available to aid in assessing audio collections for the purpose of setting preservation priorities. They help the user identify media formats and present physical condition, point out those at special risk of deterioration, and assign points at the item or collection level based on visual observations. These factors are weighed against historical or research values assigned by the collection manager to give a holistic view and, therefore, help set preservation priorities for each collection.

- *The Field Audio Collection Evaluation Tool (FACET)*, developed by Mike Casey at Indiana University, is a software tool that helps institutions set preservation priorities about field collections based on their condition and level of deterioration. The software helps institutions gather data about the formats within a collection to weigh their preservation ranking against their research value.
- *Audio/Video Survey*, developed at the Columbia University Libraries, is a survey tool designed to help non-experts in audio and moving image materials determine preservation priorities based on volume of materials, physical condition, copyright restrictions, and research value. Users enter information about

items (can be minimal) into a Microsoft Access application, and the tool generates reports that help institutions rank collections for preservation based on their physical condition and research value.

- *Audiovisual Self-Assessment Tool (AvSAP)*, developed by the University of Illinois at Urbana-Champaign, is another survey tool that helps repositories make item-level and collection-level assessments to develop prioritized preservation plans. It does not require prior knowledge about audiovisual formats, and the software explains key preservation concepts as the user answers survey questions. Institutions can host the program on their own SQL server or can use the web-based version.
- *MediaSCORE and MediaRIVERS*, a collaboration between Indiana University and AVPreserve, are two open source software tools that help institutions analyze and assess risk and degradation factors of audiovisual formats, as well as their research value. The detailed analysis can provide the basis for making preservation decisions about collections. The software allows for collaborative data entry, while integrating quality assurance and consistency mechanisms.

3.5 OTHER CONSIDERATIONS AFFECTING PRESERVATION PRIORITIES

The considerations in setting preservation reformatting priorities that have been discussed in this chapter are widely accepted and commonly noted in professional literature. But in addition to these, many of which have scientific bases, there are more subjective considerations, often influenced by day-to-day circumstances. Demands on an institution from the public, from donors, and from administrators can equally influence appraisal decisions. For example, a donor may want to personally fund a project to digitize the donated collection by a certain date. Such circumstances can affect preservation priorities, but can sometimes lead to the donation of additional resources for your institution. The following factors are among the more subjective considerations:

- Current technical capabilities
- Donor conditions and agreements
- Access restrictions
- Frequency of use
- Quality of documentation
- Subject relationship of the content to the institution
- Availability of funding
- Publicity needs
- Timeliness

CURRENT TECHNICAL CAPABILITIES

When acquiring or selecting items for preservation within a recorded sound collection, it is important to evaluate your institution's current technical capabilities. A collection's content may be highly relevant to the institution's mission, but the resources required to preserve that content may not be at hand. Some questions to consider are: Do you have machines to play back the sound formats? Do you have engineers with knowledge in handling formats and playing them back? Do you have staff and time to inventory or catalog the recordings?[1] Some archives have given specific formats preservation priority because a staff member holds specialized expertise with the format. Chapter 6 outlines the required personnel, equipment, and time necessary for digitization. After evaluating your capabilities, you should determine whether your institution has the funding to purchase additional equipment or to hire additional staff. If the technical capabilities are outside your institution's means, chapter 6 provides guidance in selecting vendors for outsourcing audio digitization and in writing a vendor Request for Proposal (RFP).

DONOR CONDITIONS AND AGREEMENTS

The conditions of agreements made with donors may affect the preservation and use of the collection. A donor may stipulate in a gift agreement that the beneficiary of the collection catalog and digitally preserve the materials within a certain period of time. However, that may be unrealistic for some institutions, given technical capabilities and resources. Therefore, it is important to negotiate conditions with the donor that are realistic and beneficial to your institution and its users.

ACCESS RESTRICTIONS

Access restrictions limit an institution's ability to preserve recordings and the public's ability to use them, which lowers the value of a collection.

As mentioned earlier, copyright- or donor-imposed access restrictions can affect decisions about acquiring collections and about preservation reformatting. Access restrictions limit an institution's ability to preserve recordings and the public's ability to use them, which lowers the value of a collection. Funding agencies are often more willing to support a preservation project if the content will have the potential to reach a wide audience. Rights and donor agreements are discussed in greater detail in section 8.4 of this guide.

FREQUENCY OF USE

Materials that are requested frequently for listening and research often have a higher priority for preservation. User needs should influence appraisal decisions and affect priorities for improving the conservation, preservation, and access to the recordings. For instance, frequency of use may be reason to reformat for preservation content found on a commercial recording, even though the format, such as a vinyl disc, is one of the more stable types. Repeated playback can easily result in loss of audio quality of the original, even when the medium is otherwise relatively stable.

---

[1] See Casey 2007.

QUALITY OF DOCUMENTATION

As noted earlier, the quality of documentation can vary among collections and materials. A collection that has little or no documentation will be more difficult to catalog and will require significant time and resources to determine its contents and value. Conversely, it is easier to make curatorial decisions when you have an inventory, or extensive documentation, about the content, performers, and dates of the recordings in your collection. The level and quality of a collection's documentation should be evaluated prior to making preservation decisions and, ideally, before acquiring the collection.

SUBJECT RELATIONSHIP OF THE CONTENT TO THE INSTITUTION

A collection that is closely related to your institution's mission or a core constituency may be allocated a higher priority on this basis (see section 3.2). For example, a historical society that houses collections relating to and documenting the activities of a particular town or city would likely place a high value on recordings of town hall meetings, because they document the history of the town and its residents.

AVAILABILITY OF FUNDING

To preserve a sound recording collection, adequate funding must be available to cover the costs of storing, cataloging, and digitizing the collection. It is important to examine the economic situation of your institution over the next few years and the long-term access to and sustainability of resources from your city, state, and/or the federal government. Funding situations can change dramatically, affecting an institution's ability to do preservation work. Before making appraisal decisions, consider how much of your institution's funding can be devoted to preservation work and decide on the scale of the project accordingly. In addition, it is not unusual for the availability of special funding to determine preservation decisions. Examples of such situations are funds from a "Friends" organization to pay for the preservation reformatting of a local musical ensemble or funds from a local corporation to preserve oral histories of prominent people in its field of business.

PUBLICITY NEEDS

Institutions without stable funding sources may be influenced by the need for publicity to generate funding for preservation work. It can be worth placing a high priority on preserving high-profile collections to generate more awareness, use, and publicity about your institution and its materials. Increased publicity may lead to increased funding opportunities for your institution.

TIMELINESS

There may be upcoming events or anniversaries related to collections within your institution. Preserving and providing access to a collection to coordinate with these times can increase the public's awareness and use of the collection.

3.6 EVALUATION FOR TAXES

Another type of appraisal is that of the monetary value of a donated collection for the purposes of a tax deduction for the donor. In the United States, Internal Revenue Service (IRS) regulations prohibit a donor from using an evaluation created by the recipient (i.e., your library or archives) for the purpose of documenting the value of a gift for a charitable deduction. The donor is responsible for securing an appraisal of the fair market monetary value of the donated collection.

The IRS has special rules that apply when the value of "an item or group of similar items" donated to a nonprofit institution is worth more than $5,000. They include the following:

- The donor must obtain a "qualified appraisal" of the value of a donated collection, performed by a "qualified appraiser," when the materials donated in a given tax year have a fair market value greater than $5,000.
- The appraisal must be prepared not earlier than 60 days before the donation or later than the filing date of the donor's tax return claiming the deduction.
- IRS Form 8283, Section B, completed by both the qualified appraiser and a representative of the recipient of the collection, must accompany the donor's tax return.
- The fee paid for a qualified appraisal may not be based on a percentage of the appraised value of the collection.
- Appraisal fees are not tax-deductible as a charitable donation.
- In some instances, a charitable donation may be reclaimed (i.e., lost) if the institution to which it was donated sells, trades, or otherwise disposes of the property within three years of the contribution.
- Unique items that are self-created by the donor, such as unpublished recordings, works of art, or manuscripts, are not tax-deductible.
- In most cases, the amount of a donor's charitable deduction that may be taken in a given tax year may not exceed a certain percentage of the donor's adjusted gross income.

These rules do not constitute all of the IRS regulations and procedures that must be followed to claim a tax deduction for the gift of an item or a group of similar items in a donation. IRS Publication 561, *Determining the Value of Donated Property*, explains the regulations in detail, lists the information to be included in a qualified appraisal, outlines how fair market value may be determined, and includes the agency's definition of a "qualified appraiser." IRS Instructions for Form 8283 provides additional information.

Special care must be taken with all tax appraisals. Publication 561 states, "The weight given an appraisal depends on the completeness of the report, the qualifications of the appraiser, and the appraiser's demonstrated knowledge of the donated property. An appraisal must give all the facts on which to base an intelligent judgment of the value of the property."

The donor of a collection valued at less than $5,000 may choose to evaluate the collection without the assistance of a qualified appraiser. IRS Publication 561 notes,

> Publications available to help you determine the value of many kinds of collections include catalogs, dealers' price lists, and specialized hobby periodicals. When using one of these price guides, you must use the current edition at the date of contribution. However, these sources are not always reliable indicators of [fair market value] and should be supported by other evidence.
>
> For example, a dealer may sell an item for much less than is shown on a price list, particularly after the item has remained unsold for a long time. The price an item sold for in an auction may have been the result of a rigged sale or a mere bidding duel. The appraiser must analyze the reference material, and recognize and make adjustments for misleading entries. If you are donating a valuable collection, you should get an appraisal. If your donation appears to be of little value, you may be able to make a satisfactory valuation using reference materials available at a state, city, college, or museum library.

FOR DEPOSITS OF RECORDED SOUND COLLECTIONS

To spread the deductions over several years or to avoid having to hire a qualified appraiser, some donors prefer to place collections on formal deposit with an institution and convert portions of the collection to a gift annually. In this way, the donor can convert parts of the deposit to a gift in a number of phases over two or more years. If each annual gift is valued at less than $5,000, a formal appraisal is not required.

Under arrangements such as these, many institutions include financial disincentives to premature withdrawals of deposits by donors in the deposit/gift contract. If a deposit is withdrawn and not converted to a gift, donors must reimburse the institution for the actual expenses incurred for housing, storage, processing, or preservation of the collection on deposit. In addition, it is advisable for donors to make clear in the deposit agreement or under their will what happens to the deposited collection on their death.

FOR SALES OF RECORDED SOUND COLLECTIONS

Fair market value appraisals may also be useful in instances of sales of recorded sound collections. An institution or collection owner may commission an appraisal to ensure that the sale price is fair. When a collection offered for sale has substantially increased in value over that paid for the recordings (its "basis"), the seller is responsible for paying any applicable capital gains on the difference between the price paid for the collection and that received from its sale. When the sale is to a nonprofit institution, such as a library or archive, the seller and institution may negotiate a gift/ sale agreement in which one portion of the collection is sold and the other portion donated as a charitable gift.

For more information about charitable deductions in the United States, consult with a qualified tax advisor.

3.7 CONCLUSION

Library and archival sciences, as well as digital preservation, are constantly evolving fields. As in other fields, it is uncertain how technology will apply to and change current practice. Still, the lessons from this chapter will continue to be relevant. Time and budget constraints, relevance of collections to mission, conservation requirements, and access decisions will remain issues to confront management of any collection. At the same time, as institutions acquire more born-digital collections, it will be necessary to apply concepts of appraisal alongside those related to the management of digital assets.

Notwithstanding the inevitable advances in the science of conservation and new means and opportunities to make sound recordings accessible, collection managers will continue to use judgment and discretion concerning the building and maintaining of their collections. This chapter can serve as a guide to the issues and trade-offs involved in making their decisions.

REFERENCES

All URLs are current as of May 1, 2015.

ARSC Technical Committee. 2009. "Preservation of Archival Sound Recordings," version 1. Available at http://www.arsc-audio.org/pdf/ARSCTC_preservation.pdf.

Casey, Mike. 2007. *The Field Audio Collection Evaluation Tool: Format Characteristics and Preservation Problems Version 1.0*. Bloomington, IN: Indiana University. Available at http://www.dlib.indiana.edu/projects/sounddirections/facet/facet_formats.pdf.

Columbia University Libraries Audio/Video Survey: Survey Instrument for Audio & Moving Image Collections. Available at http://library.columbia.edu/content/libraryweb/services/preservation/audiosurvey.html.

Harrison, Helen P., and Rolf L. Schuursma. 1987. *The Archival Appraisal of Sound Recordings and Related Materials: A RAMP Study with Guidelines*. Paris: General Information Programme and UNISIST, United Nations Educational, Scientific, and Cultural Organization. Available at http://unesdoc.unesco.org/images/0007/000736/073606eo.pdf.

IASA (International Association of Sound and Audiovisual Archives) Technical Committee. 2009. *Guidelines on the Production and Preservation of Digital Audio Objects*, second edition. (IASA-TC04). Kevin Bradley, ed. Aarhus, Denmark: International Association of Sound and Audiovisual Archives. Available at http://www.iasa-web.org/tc04/audio-preservation.

Indiana University and AVPreserve. MediaSCORE and MediaRIVERS. Available at https://github.com/IUMDPI/MediaSCORE.

Internal Revenue Service. *Determining the Value of Donated Property* (Publication 561). Available at http://www.irs.gov/pub/irs-pdf/p561.pdf.

Internal Revenue Service. Instructions for Form 8283. Available at http://www.irs.gov/pub/irs-pdf/i8283.pdf.

New Zealand Archive of Film, Television and Sound Ngā Taonga Whitiāhua Me Ngā Taonga Kōrero. n.d. "Selection, Acquisition and Accession Policy." Available at http://www.soundarchives.co.nz/policies/selection_and_acquisition_policy.

Paton, Christopher Ann. 1997. "Appraisal of Sound Recordings for Textual Archivists." *Archival Issues: Journal of the Midwest Archives Conference* 22(2): 117–132.

University of Illinois at Urbana-Champaign, University Library. Audiovisual Self-Assessment Tool. Available at http://www.library.illinois.edu/prescons/projects_grants/grants/avsap/.

Waffen, Leslie. n.d. *The Art of Appraisal and Selection of Sound Recordings Archival Retention*. International Association of Sound and Audiovisual Archives. Available at http://www.iasa-web.org/selection/art-appraisal-and-selection-sound-recordings-archival-retention-leslie-waffen.

CHAPTER 4

Care and Maintenance

By Carla Arton

When an audio format is handled and played back correctly, cleaned and housed properly, and stored long-term in a low-temperature and low-humidity environment, the life of that recording is significantly prolonged.

This chapter addresses the care and maintenance of recorded sound formats. Caring for an audio format incorporates correct handling, assessment of condition, isolation of contaminated items, proper cleaning techniques, and appropriate housing choices with the aim of arresting deterioration or improving the overall condition of the item. Maintenance includes the correct storage and arrangement of items within a collection, the safe transport of those items on and off site, and the proper use and maintenance of playback equipment.

Despite our best intentions and efforts, not every action is completely safe; things sometimes just break, buildings leak, and machines malfunction. However, with a good knowledge of the care and maintenance needs of recorded sound items, most decomposition and damage can be significantly slowed or avoided completely.

Recorded sound formats are extremely susceptible to both physical and chemical damage and decay, but with proper handling and a basic understanding of conservation treatments, any format may be handled and inspected safely.

4.1 HANDLING

When handling audio formats there are two main objectives:

1. Provide full support to the item
2. Avoid touching the audio track or playback area

FORMAT-SPECIFIC HANDLING

Cylinders

Hold with either two fingers inserted inside or hold by the edges.

Discs (Grooved or Optical)

Either support the middle and edge of the disc or just the edges.

Damaged Discs

If a disc is cracked or flaking and needs to be inspected on both sides, place the disc between two boards and carefully flip it over so that the disc is completely supported throughout. Be mindful of flakes falling off lacquer discs.

Magnetic Wire

Hold the edges of the reel, touching only the head or tail ends of the wire. Wire tangles and breaks easily. The ends of a broken wire should be tied back together.

Dictation Belts

Avoid stretching or twisting belts. Remove paper clips or staples that might be attached to the belt.

Magnetic Tape– Open Reel

Hold similar to a disc, by the edges and supporting the middle hub. If the reel has been stored as a pancake, flanges must be installed (do not overtighten the screws). Avoid touching magnetic side of tape when possible.

Magnetic Tape– Cartridges

Avoid touching the exposed tape inside the cartridge. If possible, wind so that only leader is exposed.

It is best to hold an item by its edges, or by its cartridge, and, if needed, provide additional support to the middle, as with discs. Observe the item before picking it up for any damage that could potentially worsen if held, such as a crack in a disc.

4.2 ASSESSING CONDITION

It is important to know not only an item's content, but also the overall condition of a recording or collection of recordings when assigning processing and preservation priorities.[1] Some formats are more stable than others. For example, vinyl long-playing discs (LPs) and shellac discs are typically more chemically stable than lacquer discs or magnetic audio tape. However, if they show heavy physical damage, such as cracks or the presence of mold, they may warrant higher priority for conservation and preservation. More information on assigning processing and preservation priorities is provided in chapter 3.

When noting types of damage, a consistent tracking system and terminology should be used throughout the collection. Some damage types do not necessarily require a rating scale, but simply a confirmation of their presence, such as "sticky shed syndrome" or fingerprints.

Additionally, recordings exhibiting certain types of deterioration should be flagged for isolation and placed in a separate climate-controlled storage unit or space until they are stabilized and cleaned so as not to contaminate the rest of the collection. These include those with mold, dampness, broken pieces (e.g., of glass, shellac), pest contamination, and excessive dirt. Once you have cleaned and stabilized a recording, it is best to rehouse it in a new archival sleeve or box. If there is information on the original housing, you can transcribe, scan, or photocopy that information for cataloging and then dispose of the original housing to avoid further contamination.

> **Why Identify and Track Condition**
>
> - To determine preservation and processing priorities
> - To evaluate the effectiveness of your storage system
> - To isolate moldy, damp, broken, pest-contaminated, or excessively dirty items

TYPES OF DAMAGE

There are three main causes of damage and decay:

1. Mechanical
2. Handling
3. Environmental/chemical breakdown

Mechanical damage may occur during playback because of improper equipment setup, insufficient training of the operator, or mechanical failures. Items may become scratched, stretched, or broken. To limit this type of damage, playback machines should be regularly serviced and cleaned based on the frequency of their use, and staff should be trained on each machine before they operate it.

Handling damage may occur during inspection, cleaning, transfer, or transport. Items may become scratched, cracked, broken, or bent.

---

[1] This section addresses physical damage only, such as scratches or broken splices, as opposed to noise, such as ticks, pops, or dropout during audio playback. Problems with the audio should be noted by the transfer engineer during playback. A terminology guide for audio post production, including *wow*, *pops*, and *dropout*, can be found at Triggertone.com.

Although all formats naturally deteriorate over time, damage from environmental conditions or chemical breakdown may occur more quickly through prolonged exposure to or continuous fluctuations of extreme temperature and humidity, reactions to cleaning products or water exposure, and fungal growth. Poor housing, such as torn sleeves that leave discs exposed, may also subject media to environmental damage.

FORMAT-SPECIFIC DAMAGE

Each format is vulnerable to specific types of damage.

1. Grooved discs

Exudation: Palmitic acid, in the form of a white powder, may appear when the plasticizer in a lacquer disc starts to break down. Exudation is sometimes mistaken for mold.

Palmitic acid exudation on a lacquer disc

Laminate separation on a glass-based lacquer disc

Laminate separation: The peeling, cracking, crazing, or flaking of the laminate coating of a lacquer disc may generally be referred to as laminate separation.

Oxidation: Over time aluminum discs naturally undergo oxidation, which appears as whitish crusty or bumpy surface deposits. Oxidation may also appear on optical discs for different reasons.

2. Open reel audio tape

Poor tape pack tension: Audio tape becomes stretched, warped, and bent when the pack tension is too tight or too loose. Bent flanges may cause scraping of the tape edge when played back. Additionally, uneven winds make the tape more susceptible to temperature and humidity fluctuations, as well as dust, dirt, and mold. "Library winds" are recommended for all tapes before storage. A library wind is created when the tape is wound at a consistent speed, not fast-forward or rewind, creating a flat tape pack edge with even tension throughout. While ideal for long-term preservation, library winds are time-consuming to perform on large numbers of tapes.

Mold

Many sound recordings are susceptible to mold damage, especially tape and wax cylinders. Special care must be taken with items exhibiting mold. They should be segregated from other collections in a cool and dry environment, to prevent the mold from growing and spreading into other recordings. When cleaning collections with mold, wear a respirator, gloves, and goggles, and if a vacuum cleaner is used, be sure that it includes a HEPA filter.

Common Problems in Winding Open Reel Audio Tape

Tight
Spoking, cupping/curling

Loose
Cinching, windowing

Uneven
Scatter wind/popped strands; stepped pack/
pack slip

Spaghetti: A tape pancake—that is, an open reel tape without flanges—may become tangled like spaghetti if accidentally dropped or jostled in the box.

Broken splices: Weakened splicing tape or paper leader can result in broken splices that cause delays in transfer time and possible mechanical damage. Polyester leader should replace broken paper leader.

Sticky shed syndrome: Found in polyester-urethane (PEU)-based tapes, most often those with a back coating, sticky shed syndrome is typically characterized by stickiness, shedding, and squealing during playback. Tapes with this condition may also slow down during playback because the tape is sticking to itself or to the playback head. This condition develops when the binder holding the magnetic particles begins to deteriorate because of hydrolysis (moisture absorption) and lubricant loss. The binder and magnetic particles also build up on the playback equipment guides and playback head, causing high-frequency loss.

Sticky shed syndrome happens with a specific polyester stock manufactured in the mid-1970s onward and occurs when the tapes have been exposed to high humidity. These tapes can be baked at a low temperature before transfer to lessen the effects of sticky shed syndrome (see pp. 60–61 for further details on baking). Baking, however, should preferably be done only for preservation transfers, as each baking session will slightly damage the tape (Hess 2008, IASA 2014).

Vinegar syndrome: Cellulose acetate and paper-based tapes are more prone to binder hydrolysis when stored in humid locations and may give off a vinegar smell.[2] Plasticizer loss causes brittleness in cellulose acetate tapes.

---

[2] A more detailed explanation of audio tape deterioration can be found in IASA 2014, 17.

3. Cartridge audio tape

The most common damage to analog audiocassettes, digital audio tapes (DATs), and other cartridge-based tapes is a cracked or broken cartridge, or a loose or missing pressure pad. Mold, Soft Binder Syndrome[3], an uneven tape pack, and failure to fully wind the tape to the end of the recording can also cause damage. Leaving a tape in the middle of the recording can cause warping to the tape and physical damage from exposure to the elements in the open playing area of the cartridge.

Tip for storage: Always check to make sure the write protection tabs are set to lock or punched out so that the recording will not accidentally be recorded over when played back.

4. Optical discs

Damage to optical discs includes layer separation, corrosion or oxidation of the metallic layer, laser rot, diminished reflexivity, and organic solvent damage to the polycarbonate layer. Deterioration of optical media is often the result of manufacturing defects. Poor air quality has been cited as a cause of corrosion of the metallic layer of media. Storage in direct sunlight can cause failure of recordable optical discs (Byers 2003, California Audiovisual Preservation Project 2013).

Example of compact disc with laser rot, evident from its browning. This was caused by a manufacturing error where the polycarbonate coating was not sealed, leading to oxidation of the aluminum layer.

---

[3] Soft Binder Syndrome (SBS) is a broad term suggested by Richard Hess for any tape exhibiting stickiness, shedding, or squealing, regardless of its response to baking (Hess 2008).

4.3 CLEANING

An audio recording should be kept as clean as possible for long-term preservation. Although it may not be possible to clean every item as it is added to your collection, heavily damaged recordings, or recordings that have been isolated for such issues as mold or pest contamination, should be stabilized through cleaning or rehousing, or both, to avoid further contamination throughout the collection.

If you are unable to clean recordings at the initial condition assessment and processing, then you should clean them when they are pulled for listening or transfer. No recording should be placed on a playback machine without having been properly cleaned, as dust, dirt, and other damage (e.g., exudation with lacquer discs) can affect the sound of the recording and may cause further damage to the recording and the playback equipment.

Cleaning techniques and products used have varied greatly over the years, but there are a few basic points to consider before cleaning a recording. Cleaning should

- Not be abrasive
- Not react chemically with the playing surface
- Leave the recording dry and without residue

The goal of cleaning is to stabilize the medium and to remove any contamination that will impede the best possible playback, without introducing anything that will harm the artifact in the long run.

DRY CLEANING VERSUS WET CLEANING

Not every format should be cleaned with a solution. Sometimes dusting is all that is needed. Cracked shellac discs, for example, should be dry-cleaned, as the moisture from wet cleaning may cause the crack to spread. Also, the base or core of some audio formats, such as cardboard acetate discs or Blue Amberol cylinders, expands if wet-cleaned, thereby warping or destroying the playing area.

Wet cleaning can be a more effective technique for grooved media and for spot-cleaning other formats. Scrubbing and rinsing with a mild solvent, such as pure Tergitol diluted to 0.05 percent and deionized water,[4] helps loosen and remove dirt. Although disc-cleaning machines are more efficient with drying and dirt removal, cleaning by hand can also produce acceptable results.

When selecting a cleaning solution, check the ingredients and know the material composition of the recording. It is best to use cleaning solutions that have been tested and are in common use in institutional archives. Such products include Disc Doctor, L'Art Du Son Record Cleaning Fluid, Audio Intelligent Vinyl Solutions, Walker Audio Enzyme Cleaning

---

> ### Myths
>
> Collectors and professionals have used many types of cleaning methods on audio formats over the years without scientific studies to back them up; for example, they have used Windex as a cleaning solution, or they have played back discs wet for a supposed better transfer. When deciding which method of cleaning to use, always consider whether it will be abrasive, react chemically with the playing surface, or leave any residue. When in doubt ask a specialist.

---

[4] This is one of the cleaning solvents used by the Library of Congress. It is described in the online article, "Care, Handling, and Storage of Audio Visual Materials," at http://www.loc.gov/preservation/care/record.html.

Solution, LAST Power Cleaner, and SMART Record Cleaning Solutions. Most solvents commonly used for cleaning audio formats are mild; however, certain ingredients can be very harmful to individual formats. For example, an alcohol-based solvent should not be used to clean lacquer or shellac discs, as it will strip the lacquer from the base or dissolve the audio track.[5]

Playback machines and their individual guides and rollers may also require specific cleaning solvents. See section 4.9 for details.

FORMAT-SPECIFIC CLEANING

1. Cylinders
- Wax cylinders: Dry clean or wet clean with deionized water only.[6]
- Cellulose cylinders: Dry or wet clean with a solvent and deionized water.
- Dry or spot clean if cracked.

Tips:
— Never submerge cylinders in liquid.
— Clean only the grooves. Avoid the edge label.
— Never wet cylinders that have plaster cores.

2. Grooved discs
- Edison Diamond, cardboard, and discs with expanding bases:[7] Dry clean or spot clean with damp cloth using deionized water.
- Shellac, lacquer, and vinyl discs: Dry or wet clean with solvent and deionized water. Do not clean lacquers that are delaminating. Spot clean at most.
- Aluminum discs: Dry clean.

Tips:
— Cleaning machines with vacuum suction, such as a Keith Monks, VPI, or Lorictaft, may be used. Ultrasonic machines such as those made by Audio Desk or KLAUDIO may be an option for vinyl discs.
— Clean stylus before playing discs, brushing from back to front. This will extend the life of the stylus and limit groove wear on the disc. Specialized styli cleaners and brushes are available.

3. Wire recordings
- Dry clean only.

4. Dictation belts
- Magnetic belts: Dry clean only.

---

[5] See chapter 2 for details on the material makeup of each format.

[6] While this guide specifies deionized water because it is economical, other purified waters are also acceptable for rinsing.

[7] Edison Diamond Discs are early shellac discs made from a mixture of wood flour and shellac. If the disc gets wet, the wood flour will expand and ruin the recording. Amberol cylinders should not be cleaned with an alcohol-based solvent because the laminate is made of celluloid, which contains camphor, a chemical that reacts with alcohol. The surface becomes more brittle, and the recording is noisier when played back (Vinylville, n.d.).

- Grooved belts: Dry or wet clean with damp cloth and deionized water.

5. Open reel audio tape

- Wet clean any tape with excessive dirt, dust, or mold on the edge of the pack with a disposable wipe and *minimal* isopropyl alcohol.
- If resplicing, clean off residue from the old splice as thoroughly as possible before applying new professional splicing tape. Be careful, as excessive amounts of alcohol or rubbing will strip the iron oxide layer from the tape.
- If a tape is exhibiting sticky shed syndrome or binder hydrolysis and needs to be played relatively soon (within a month), consider baking it.
- Tapes should be baked only as a last resort for playback. Baking should be done in laboratory-grade ovens by trained professionals. Baking should consist of a low heat over an extended period of time, depending on the tape width and size. Acetate tapes, which are transparent when held up to the light, *should not be baked*. Polyester tapes are opaque and can be baked (see image on p. 26). Only bake tapes with metal flanges, as plastic reels may warp.
- Consult specialists before trying other techniques to combat binder hydrolysis, such as the use of a desiccant to remove moisture.

Tips:

— If multiple playback decks are available, consider removing the playback head on one and designate the deck for tape cleaning and library winds. Removing the playback head for library wind–designated machines helps prolong the life of the playback head.

Tapes being baked in an industrial oven. Note use of tape hub spacers between stacked reels.

In replacing the splice, the old adhesive is removed with isopropyl alcohol.

Tape Baking Facts for Sticky Shed Syndrome

- DO NOT BAKE ACETATE TAPES.
- The process is effective only temporarily.
- Long-term effects on tapes are unknown.
- Use a scientific incubator or laboratory grade oven.
- Do not bake a tape on a plastic reel.
- Temperature and time vary, depending on tape width and size.
- Baking should be carried out only by trained professionals.
- Baking does not fix all tapes with sticky shed syndrome.

Do not use acetone, benzene, or other harsh organic solvents on optical discs.

— Tape down loose ends to the outside of a flange. Be sure to use the "hold down tape" designed for this purpose; it is available from several audio supply stores.
— If removing old leader from the middle of a tape, be sure to replace it with the exact same length in case the tape served as an editing master.
— If time and resources allow, remove or replace paper leader, as it absorbs moisture and may become acidic. Any additional paper included in the original packaging should be removed as well to avoid acidity. See section 4.4 for more on accompanying documentation.

6. Cartridge and cassette audio tape

■ Dry or wet clean cartridge with a disposable wipe or cloth using *minimal* isopropyl alcohol.

Tips:
— Replace damaged cartridges.
— Replace pressure pads, if missing.
— Wind tape to end so only leader is exposed.
— Punch out write protection tabs (see image on p. 57).

7. Optical discs

■ Dry clean with a nonabrasive antistatic cloth in a radial motion straight from the inside of the disc to the outer edge. An air puffer may also be used to remove dust.
■ Wet clean sparingly with purified water, isopropyl, methanol, or other fast-evaporating solvents.
■ Do not use acetone, benzene, or other harsh organic solvents; they will permanently dissolve and damage the disc (Byers 2003, 18).

Tip:
— Avoid getting a paper label wet.

It is recommended that only specially designed "hold-down tape" be used to secure tape to the flange.

4.4 HOUSING

Audio formats should be housed in containers or sleeves that are sturdy, clean, and protective against environmental factors, such as dust, mold, fingerprints, scratches, water damage, or shocks.

When deciding whether to keep or replace original housing, consider the following questions:

- ■ Does the current housing expose the recording's playing area?
- ■ Is it torn, or is the spine weakened in any way?
- ■ Is it contaminated with mold, severe dirt, or pest droppings, or water damaged?

If the answer is yes to any of these questions, then housing should be replaced.

Original housing tends to be cardboard or paper-based with most formats (even some cassettes and CDs). Non-archival paper-based housing tends to break down and become acidic after a period of time. The off-gassing may damage the playing area of a recording and spread to other paper-based items in the storage area.

If keeping the original housing, be sure to remove any shrink wrap, rubber bands, or any other restrictive packaging. These will not break down in the same way or at the same rate as the recording or the housing itself and could possibly damage the items.

**Good, Better, and Best Approaches
to Housing Audio Recordings**

Good
- Isolate severely damaged, dirty, or moldy items. Stabilize, clean, and re-house in archival (i.e., acid-free) housing.
- Store remainder of items in original housing or new housing, if they arrived without housing.
- Keep all accompanying documentation with items.

Better
- Isolate severely damaged, dirty, or moldy items. Stabilize, clean, and re-house in archival housing.
- Process remainder of items in original housing, but replace with archival housing when accessed and cleaned.
- Provide separate archival storage for accompanying documentation. Maintain a record of the documentation that was originally with each recording.

Best
- Stabilize and clean all recordings and rehouse in archival housing when first acquired.
- Provide separate archival storage for accompanying documentation. Maintain a record of the documentation that was originally with each recording.

Note: Always record information found on original housing by inscribing it on the new housing (using pencil or archival pens), entering it into the item's catalog record, or creating a scan or photo of the housing.

FORMAT-SPECIFIC HOUSING

1. Cylinders

If a cylinder is to be housed in its original box, remove any cotton or padding, as it will pull moisture from the cylinder over time. Good cylinder housing supports the cylinder on its edge so that it is standing vertically without its sides touching the box. The commonly used Metal Edge box for standard-sized cylinders has archival cardboard with polyethylene foam interior posts. Additionally, a new container with a polycarbonate body, polyethylene lid, and silicone-based padding has recently been designed and approved for use at the Library of Congress.[8]

Left: original box with batting. Replacement of such boxes is recommended. Right: Metal Edge archival box with polyethylene interior posts; and the new ARSC-developed container with a polycarbonate body, a polyethylene lid, and silicone-based padding.

Large concert cylinders should have specially designed boxes.

2. Grooved discs

There are two methods for housing discs: (1) individual sleeves placed directly on a shelf, and (2) sleeves grouped in archival boxes on a shelf.

If discs are stored in a box, be sure that it can support the weight of multiple discs, is fully filled or includes a space filler, and allows easy removal of discs (Keller 2013, 16).

Archival paperboard sleeves with clear polyester covers, such as Mylar, are ideal for shellac, vinyl, or aluminum discs.

Commercial vinyl discs may be stored in their original sleeve, but should also be placed in a static-free high-density polyethylene (HDPE) liner to avoid print-through from the original sleeve.

A disc that is cracked or broken, or peeling in the case of lacquer discs, should be stored lying flat to prevent further damage. Archival broken disc housing can be arranged by using a large, flat, archival box of the proper size. Multiple broken discs may fit into one flat box if they are separated with archival cardboard, but be mindful of the pressure built up from the weight of several stacked discs.[9]

---

[8] The Association for Recorded Sound Collection's (ARSC) Technical Committee, in conjunction with the Library of Congress, has developed this container, with the intention of making it widely available as another archival housing option for cylinders (Keller 2013, 11 [p. 50 of pdf file]).

[9] The Library of Congress uses specially designed pizza-style flat boxes that have trays with circular inserts to prevent broken pieces from sliding out.

Vinyl disc in HDPE liner

Because broken disc housing can take up a large amount of space, it may make sense to reserve it for rare discs that may still be transferred by preservation specialists or specialized scanning equipment, such as IRENE 3D.[10]

3. Magnetic wire

Wire recordings should be stored on edge in acid-free archival boxes of the appropriate size with the wire wrapped evenly around its spool or contained in its original cartridge.

4. Dictation belts

Belts are traditionally stored in soft cardboard sleeves or cardboard ¼-inch tape boxes. Although flat storage creates a thump in the recording during playback, there is currently no standard archival storage option specifically designed to prevent the dictation belt from being flattened or warped.

5. Audio tape

All magnetic audio tapes should be stored in their original boxes or in archival boxes, vertically. Plastic containers provide the best protection from bumps, drops, and water leaks.

All audio tape should be wound and stored "tails-out," that is, with the tape of the program's beginning at the core of the reel and the end at its outer edge. Winding to tails ensures that any signal caused by a print-through of sounds from one layer of tape to the next will follow the recording signal, creating an echo effect. If stored wound to heads, the print-through signal precedes the recording signal, creating a pre-echo that is harder to listen to than an echo (3M 1994). (This rule, of course, cannot be applied to tapes that are recorded in two directions.)

Additionally, open reel magnetic tape should be prepared for storage with a library wind; flanges should not be warped, and the tape end should be attached to the flange with hold-down tape.

6. Optical discs

Optical discs should be stored in jewel cases in drawers or grouped in archival boxes.

LABELING

When new or old housing is labeled, it should always be done with the recordings removed from the container, as the pressure from the pen may imprint onto the audio underneath and possibly add noise during playback. If labeling original housing, we recommend the following:

- Use pencil or archival pen.
- Do not cover up important information or artwork with marker or shelving labels.

---

[10] IRENE is a system developed by the Lawrence Berkeley National Laboratory for the transfer of damaged or broken cylinders and discs using 2D/3D non-contact optical scanning technology.

- Consider placing disc sleeves in clear polyester sleeves and placing shelving labels on those sleeves. Be aware that adhesive may fail over time.
- Place labels on smooth container surfaces. Textured surfaces contribute to adhesive failing more quickly and labels falling off over time.

For optical disc labeling, writing should be done on the clear inner hub of the disc. Adhesive labels affect the magnetic layer and should not be used on long-term preservation copies or master recordings (Byers 2003, 22–23).

Label on clear inner hub

ACCOMPANYING DOCUMENTATION

In the documentation that accompanies sound recordings, there may be engineer notes, liner notes, letters, copy paper, photographs, transcripts, and the like. Although it may not make sense for you or your institution to separate documentation from each recording, you should be aware that offgassing from acidic cardboard or paper may affect the recording over time. If you decide to keep the items together, you may want to insert archival cardboard, tissue paper, or antistatic sleeves (for LPs) between the recording and the documentation.

4.5 STORAGE

Providing a clean, cool, dry, and level storage space with reliable temperature and humidity control is one of the most important factors for the long-term preservation of audio formats. You will want to provide the best storage option that your resources allow, and you should always factor in growth space. Grouping formats together by type and size is the best way to maximize collection storage space.

SHELVING

There are three main ways to store audio formats: (1) on metal or wood stationary shelving, (2) on metal compact shelving, and (3) in archival boxes on shelves.

When selecting shelving, you need to consider not only the space limitations of your storage area, but also the weight requirements of your formats. Metal shelving is recommended for sound recordings, because wooden shelving typically cannot accommodate the weight requirements of every format and is susceptible to water and pest damage.

There are also different types of shelving:

All formats, except broken discs, should be shelved standing vertically on their spines.

- ■ **Open shelving**, used for discs, audio tapes, and grouped formats in boxes, should have a back panel to keep items from being pushed off the back of the shelf and lips on the front of the shelf to protect items from rolling or sliding off.
- ■ **Cabinets with drawers** are used for cylinders, cartridges, CDs, and other small formats.

Shelving should also have smooth, finished surfaces without gaps or protruding hardware.

The shelves should be installed on level flooring and evenly loaded on either side of the unit to balance weight, with heavier or more fragile items on the bottom shelves. Make sure the unit is secured to the floor and stabilized above, regardless of whether the unit is compact or stationary shelving. There should also be enough space between shelving units to allow the use of ladders and to provide enough clearance when cabinet drawers are opened. Try to avoid storing collection items on shelves near pipes or electrical conduits, in direct light, or in front of a heating, ventilation, or air conditioning (HVAC) vent.

Open shelving with back panels and dividers

Common Shelving Measurements and Accessories

- Length: 3 feet
- Height and depth: 16, 12, 10, and 7 inches plus 2–3 inches for clearance when moving items
- Floor height clearance: no less than 6 inches
    — For protection against dust or bumps from ladders or stools
    — If worried about flooding, increase the minimum to 1 foot
- Shelf dividers
    — Discs and open reel audio tapes should have additional dividers installed throughout each shelf to prevent items from leaning and to provide extra weight-bearing support

Summarized from Warren 1993, 147.

STRUCTURAL CONSIDERATIONS AND BUILDING LOCATIONS

Audio collections should be stored in locations with

- Reliable climate control (see section 4.7)
- Good ventilation
- Sufficient floor loading capacity
- Fire suppression systems
- Security[11]

Recordings should also be protected against damage from

- Light
- Flooding
- Earthquakes and other vibrations
- Magnetic fields
- Pest infestations

Floor Loading Capacity. Recorded sound formats become extremely heavy when grouped together on shelves, so it is important to know the floor loading capacity. Ground floors are typically the best place to store audio collections; however, they may be a poor choice if the storage location is in a designated flood zone. In any environment, it is important that the lowest shelf be no less than six inches from the floor.

Magnetic Fields. Equipment and machines in neighboring rooms or buildings may emit a magnetic field strong enough to disrupt magnetic audio recordings. Magnetic fields should not harm CDs and other optical media, but they may harm or erase wire recordings, magnetic tape formats, and digital files stored on portable drives (Byers 2003, 18). Magnetometers can be used to test for magnetic fields in and around storage and working areas.

If items are to be shipped to locations with high security, irradiation screening methods should not be used on packages containing audio recordings, as they may melt or warp plastic-based items and discolor optical media. The data on optical discs, however, may remain unaffected as long as the disc is physically still playable (Byers 2003, 18).

---

[11] List adapted from Council on Library and Information Resources and Library of Congress 2012, 21.

Fire Suppression Systems. If a fire suppression system is installed, it should be a clean agent system that does not release water or dry chemicals. Both are damaging to audio collections. It is recommended that you consult with your facilities manager to determine whether your system is appropriate for media collection storage and that it is regularly maintained.

4.6 ARRANGEMENT

There is no universal classification system to dictate the arrangement of recorded sound formats. The following two arrangement styles are most common:

1. Interfiling commercial items by publisher name and number
2. Assigning an acquisition or shelf number to individual items; certain prefixes may also be assigned for each format type and size

Arranging by publisher name and number allows collection items to be accessioned quickly into storage, which can be more time-efficient for larger commercial collections. However, adopting this arrangement method may require constant shifting of collection items as new materials are added.

Arranging items in the collection with assigned shelf numbers is more time-consuming in the beginning, because the items must be cataloged first. This method is preferred, as it limits the number of times an item is shifted and ensures bibliographic control for quick search and retrieval.

To maximize space, large collections of varying audio formats should be arranged, first, by format type (e.g., vinyl, shellac, CDs, DATs), and second, by height (16 inches, 12 inches, 10 inches, and 7 inches or less).

You may want to group a small number of audio formats within a larger collection together in archival boxes and store the collection as one unit. If there is extra space in the box, use a space filler so that the items do not tip inside the box. Loose, unsupported items may warp, crack, or break.

Recorded sound formats can be large, heavy, and awkward to maneuver from shelves. To limit damage to the item (and to the person retrieving the item), it is best to retrieve items on shelves no higher than an arm's length above the person. Richard Warren suggests storing items that "weigh more than one pound each no higher than 6 feet (1.8 m) with heavier items no higher than 4-5 feet (1.2-1.5 m)" off the ground (Warren 1993, 146).

Ideally, multiple exact copies of a recording should be shelved separately from each other to protect the collection from complete loss if one part is stolen or partially damaged by fire or flooding. If you have both preservation and access copies, consider placing access copies closer to the processing or listening areas to limit traffic near the long-term preservation copies.

Multiple exact copies of a recording should be shelved separately from each other to protect the collection from complete loss if one part is stolen or partially damaged by fire or flooding.

4.7 CLIMATE CONTROL

Audio recordings should be kept at a consistently low temperature and humidity. Although exact guidelines for the best temperature and humidity levels have yet to be agreed upon through conclusive scientific research of individual audio formats, common best practices have emerged (Audio Engineering Society 2006, Byers 2003, and Van Bogart 1995).

Short-Term Storage (less than 10 years)
- Cooler than room temperature, <68°F (20°C)
- 30–50 percent relative humidity

Long-Term Storage
- 46–53°F (8–12°C)
- 25–35 percent relative humidity

Magnetic tape should not be stored below 46°F (8°C), and no audio format should be stored at or below freezing temperatures (Library of Congress, *Care, Handling, and Storage of Audio Visual Materials*; IASA 2014, 33–34). Isolated damaged items should be stored in a separate climate controlled unit or space while awaiting stabilization and cleaning.

VARIABILITY

Keeping fluctuations in temperature and humidity from hour to hour and season to season to a minimum (+5 percent relative humidity, +3°F [1°C]) slows deterioration, which is why investment in a reliable HVAC system should be a high priority. For example, temperature fluctuations affect cylinders and tapes, increasing the chance of print-through on tapes. Humidity fluctuations affect shellac and laminate formats, increasing the chance of brittleness and flaking (Warren 1993, 140).

NO AVAILABLE CLIMATE CONTROL

The goal of basic storage is to maintain a consistent environment with as few fluctuations as possible year-round.

If there is no option for cold storage, audio materials should be stored in a relatively cool and dry place with portable dehumidifiers, air conditioners, and heaters to be switched out as seasons change. The goal of basic storage is to maintain a consistent environment with as few fluctuations as possible year-round. Avoid high-risk places, such as attics and basements.

ACCLIMATIZATION

If there is more than a 10-degree difference between cold storage and working spaces, recordings should be gradually acclimatized in a separate room before they are taken into a working area. Acclimatization provides an intermediate temperature and humidity so that items will slowly transition to the temperature and humidity of the processing and listening areas. Ideally, items should be acclimatized over a 24-hour period before they are moved to working areas. If a quicker turnaround is needed, items should be acclimatized for at least two hours. Without sufficient acclimatization you may be subjecting your collections to damaging moisture and condensation (Van Bogart 1995, 26).

4.8 TRANSPORTATION

Certain guidelines should be followed when audio formats are being moved, both onsite and offsite. They should be transported

■ Vertically, on the spine or edge (unless broken)
■ With like formats or with extra padding to fill sizing gaps
■ In trays, boxes, or on carts (padded for cylinders and discs)
■ In mild weather conditions or an environment similar to that of their storage areas

Audio formats should preferably be moved at the times of day when conditions are most similar to their storage conditions (Warren 1994, 147).[12] If transporting multiple boxes of audio formats on pallets, place fragile items on top and heavier items on the bottom.

When transporting items, be aware of obstacles, such as seams in the flooring or changes from concrete to carpet, that can cause bumps for carts or become tripping hazards. Glass discs are particularly susceptible to jolts and can easily crack or break if they are moved quickly or bumped the wrong way. Always start or stop slowly when transporting fragile formats in a cart.

Carts with flat shelves are best for audio tapes and formats that are housed in boxes. Discs should be transported in carts with padding and sides high enough to support all or most of the height of the disc.

Metal cart with Library of Congress designed "topper." A Velcro strap provides added protection in case items roll or slip.

Wood cart with tapes and foam spacers

Metal cart with foam padding

---

[12] To follow this recommendation, be aware of your local area's temperature and humidity trends. In most areas, humidity levels are lowest during the night or early morning, so these are the best times to transport audiovisual media. However, in some areas, such as Southern California, humidity is higher in the mornings and evenings.

4.9 PLAYBACK

When deciding to play back audio recordings it is important to first identify the purpose of playback. The rarity of the content on the recording will dictate how often it should be played and to what purpose.

There are three main categories for playback:

1. Access
2. Preservation/restoration
3. Educational demonstrations

> **Limit Wear. Go Digital.**
>
> Creating digital access copies of recordings will limit wear caused by repeated plays.

Additionally, IASA (2014) suggests that mechanical media (e.g., cylinders, discs) should have limited playback, because each transfer causes some deterioration of the playing surface. Magnetic media in good condition can be played back many times without any measurable loss of quality, as long as the playback equipment is of a newer generation, well maintained, and operated by an experienced engineer (IASA 2014). Creating digital access copies of recordings will limit wear caused by repeated plays of the original recordings.

Playback equipment needed for access can be minimal compared with the equipment needed for preservation transfers and restoration. Listening equipment can be as simple as a reel-to-reel deck for ¼-inch audio tape and amplifier speakers (if the deck does not already have them), or a CD player and amplifier speakers.

Preservation transfers should provide quality control through the use of analog-to-digital converters, digital audio workstations with tone generation, mixing boards, professional speakers, transfer software, and the like.

Regardless of format, when reformatting for preservation, it is best to use a trained audio preservation engineer to ensure quality transfers and the safeguarding of the original recording.[13] Preservation engineers are specially trained to understand recording equipment, correct handling, the recording history of each format, the creation of audiovisual metadata and preservation files, and individual playback challenges. Some engineers offer additional services, such as the provision of professional restoration software that can remove hiss, crackle, or other problems. If the services of professional preservation engineers are not available to your institution, be sure that, at a minimum, your playback equipment is maintained by a professional and that training and product quality control are done by experienced engineers. See chapters 6 and 7 for details on preservation and digitization.

If playing back recordings for educational demonstrations, legacy equipment provides an effective listening and visual experience. However, legacy equipment can be harmful to recordings; for example, the weight of the tonearm and the steel needles used to play acoustic shellac discs can harm them. Only duplicate recordings should be used for demonstrations of historical playback machines.

---

[13] ARSC maintains a directory of audio preservation and restoration engineers and companies on its website, http://www.arsc-audio.org/audiopreservation.html.

EQUIPMENT

Some formats can be played back only on legacy equipment. Other formats can and should be played back on newer equipment, such as shellac discs on contemporary turntables. It is recommended that only preservation specialists play back wax cylinders and all instantaneous discs because of their extreme fragility. Trained staff can safely play back recordings on shellac discs and microgroove discs (IASA 2014). A damaged recording should never be played back without first consulting a specialist, as playing it back may further damage the recording and may damage the equipment.

FORMAT-SPECIFIC PLAYBACK EQUIPMENT

1. Cylinders

There are some archival-quality cylinder players available on the new- and used-equipment market. One such machine is the Archéophone. Some archives have had cylinder recordings reproduced through the IRENE 3D transfer system. The cylinder phonograph player should be used only for educational demonstrations.

Right: The Archéophone player was designed by Henri Chamoux and is used by various institutions for transfer of their cylinder collections. It is no longer produced.

Right: An early Edison "yellow wax" cylinder being mounted on IRENE 3D

2. Grooved discs

Modern professional turntables with speed options for 33⅓, 78, and 45 rpm, as well as an option for incremental changes to speed, should be used to play back grooved discs. Many of the discs known as 78-rpm discs should actually be played back at a slightly lower or higher speed (e.g., 76 rpm, 79 rpm).

Choosing the appropriate stylus (needle) depends on several factors:

- Disc type
- Recording label
- Recording era
- Wear/condition of the grooves

Before operating a turntable, be sure that the tonearm is balanced (tracking force), can track out wide enough if playing a 16-inch disc, and is set to the right height. Preservation engineers tend to keep a range of styli on hand to test on earlier disc formats before transferring the recordings from them. Because of wear, some grooves may sound better with a larger or smaller needle than would have been used originally.[14]

When playing back a disc, make sure that it is already spinning before the stylus is set down. Never leave a disc unattended during transfer in case it begins to skip. Remove the tonearm quickly after the recording has finished, as leaving the stylus playing in the runoff groove will wear out the stylus more quickly.

3. Magnetic wire recordings

Working wire recording machines are no longer manufactured and are hard to find. It is best to contact a specialist for access and preservation transfers of recordings from magnetic wire recordings.

4. Dictabelts

Like magnetic wire machines, dictabelt machines are no longer manufactured and hard to find.[15] It is best to contact a specialist for access and preservation transfers of recordings.

5. Open reel audio tape

New open reel playback decks are no longer manufactured but many are available used or refurbished.

Ideally, an audio preservation engineer should be used for preservation transfers of all audio tape. All playback engineers should have a basic knowledge of how to realign the azimuth and playback head to maintain the integrity of the recording. The tape should move freely through the guides and across the playback head without being scraped or stretched. Machine surfaces and metal guides should be cleaned after every reel with isopropyl alcohol (preferably 99 percent). Pinch rollers should be

---

Typical Styli Sizes and Styles

- Elliptical or conical
- Size ranges from .075 to 5.0
- Truncated or not; truncated styli have the tip of the diamond shaved off so that the needle does not grind up against the bottom of the groove and against dust and dirt, creating extra noise

---

[14] There are many styli vendors that can provide greater detail on correct styli selection; they include Needle Doctor, KAB, Esoteric Sound, TurntableNeedles.com, Expert Stylus, and LP Gear.

[15] The Archéophone produced a dictabelt mandrel for preservation transfers.

cleaned with polyurethane cleaner. Additionally, playback heads should be demagnetized periodically. Larger open reel formats, such as those using ½-inch or 2-inch tape, require preservation engineers, as their playback equipment is more complex than consumer machines and servicing can be both expensive and difficult to find.

6. Cartridge audio tape

Quality audiocassette and mini-cassette decks are becoming harder to find. If possible, use a higher-end professional deck for playback. Cheap decks will break more quickly and risk damaging the tape.

Other rare cartridge tape media, such as 8-track or 1/8-inch dictation cartridges, should be transferred by preservation engineers with specialized equipment.

DAT decks, which are also becoming increasingly difficult to find, may not play all DATs because of coding errors and the failure rate of the media. Even if a deck is acquired, you may have to send certain DATs to a specialist for content recovery.

7. Optical discs

CD players are relatively easy to find, and their operation remains widely known. It may be harder to find equipment for other optical discs, such as MiniDiscs.

MAINTENANCE OF EQUIPMENT

Regularly scheduled maintenance of all playback equipment is important for continued reliable damage-free playback of recordings. Do not use equipment if it is twisting, stretching, scratching, or knocking a recording in a way that could damage the playing area or overall integrity of the format.

Equipment should be cleaned after each pass or playing. For discs, the styli should be cleaned with styli-cleaning solution and a styli-cleaning brush, wiping from back to front over the diamond. Make sure the solution does not leave residue on the disc when played back. For open reel tape decks, properly clean the playback path to remove dirt, dust, and buildup of binder (from sticky tapes). If you have to stop a tape in the middle of a recording, check the playback head before starting again in case any binder has built up.

4.10 CONCLUSION

The commonly quoted window of 10–15 years for optimal transfer conditions is unattainable for many collections. However, regardless of your capabilities, any action you take today to provide better quality care and maintenance of an audio recording, such as better climate control and more stable housing, will help prolong its life until a time when you can carry out further preservation efforts.

Keep in mind, too, that even after an item is digitized for preservation, if it is historically or culturally significant, it should be retained in a climate-controlled storage environment. This safeguards against loss of the preservation master and allows you to take advantage of any future improvements in reformatting technology, as was the case with the recent reformatting of the Passamaquoddy Indian cylinders mentioned in chapter 1.

REFERENCES

All URLs are current as of May 1, 2015

3M. 1994. *Analog Audio Mastering Tape Print-Through*. Technical Bulletin A011194. Available at http://www.aes.org/aeshc/docs/3mtape/print-through.pdf.

Association of Recorded Sound Collections. 2014. *Audio Preservation & Restoration Directory*. ARSC Technical Committee. Available at http://www.arsc-audio.org/audiopreservation.html.

Audio Engineering Society. 2006 (r2012). *AES Information Document for Preservation of Audio Recordings–Extended Term Storage Environment for Multiple Media Archives* AES-11id-2006 (r2012). Available at http://www.aes.org/publications/standards/search.cfm?docID=56.

Byers, Fred. 2003. *Care and Handling of CDs and DVDs: A Guide for Librarians and Archivists*. Washington, D.C.: Council on Library and Information Resources and Gaithersburg, MD: National Institute of Standards and Technology. Available at http://www.clir.org/pubs/reports/reports/pub121/pub121.pdf.

California Audiovisual Preservation Project. 2013. *Audiovisual Formats: A Guide to Identification*. Available at http://calpreservation.org/wp-content/uploads/2013/10/2013-Audiovisual-Formats_draft_webversion-2013oct15.pdf.

Council on Library and Information Resources and Library of Congress. 2012. *The Library of Congress National Recording Preservation Plan*. Washington, D.C.: Council on Library and Information Resources and Library of Congress. Available at http://www.clir.org/pubs/reports/pub156/pub156.pdf.

Hess, Richard L. 2008. "Tape Degradation Factors and Challenges in Predicting Tape Life." *ARSC Journal* 34: 241–274.

IASA (International Association of Sound and Audiovisual Archives). 2014. *Handling and Storing of Audio and Video Carriers*, IASA-TC 05.

Keller, Michael. 2013. Shelving and Storage for Archival Sound Recordings. Final Report, Grant PF-50169-11, to Stanford University: Planning: Upgrading Climate Control to Preserve Audiovisual Collections. Environmental Conditions for Archival Sound Recordings. Stanford University Libraries. Available via https://securegrants.neh.gov/publicquery/main.aspx?f=1&gn=PF-50169-11.

Library of Congress. n.d. *Care, Handling, and Storage of Audio Visual Materials.* Available at http://www.loc.gov/preservation/care/record.html.

Van Bogart, John W. C. 1995. *Magnetic Tape Storage and Handling Guide.* Washington, D.C.: Commission on Preservation and Access. Available at www.clir.org/pubs/abstract//reports/pub54.

Vinylville. n.d. Cleaning and Caring for 78s and Cylinders. Available at http://vinylville.tripod.com/clean-6.html.

Warren Jr., Richard. 1993. "Storage of Sound Recordings." *ARSC Journal* 24(2):130–175.

Warren Jr., Richard. 1994. "Handling of Sound Recordings." *ARSC Journal* 25(2):139–162.

ADDITIONAL RESOURCES

Casey, Mike. 2007. *The Field Audio Collection Evaluation Tool: Format Characteristics and Preservation Problems Version 1.0.* Bloomington, IN: Indiana University. Available at http://www.dlib.indiana.edu/projects/sounddirections/facet/facet_formats.pdf.

Casey, Mike, and Bruce Gordon. 2007. *Sound Directions: Best Practices for Audio Preservation* Bloomington: Indiana University.

Hortz Stanton, Laura. 2013. Preservation Best Practices: Fundamentals and Facilities Infopeople webinar series. Available at https://infopeople.org/civicrm/event/info?reset=1&id=196.

Library of Congress. n.d. *CD-R and DVD-R RW Longevity Research.* Available at http://www.loc.gov/preservation/scientists/projects/cd-r_dvd-r_rw_longevity.html.

CHAPTER 5

Description of Audio Recordings

By Marsha Maguire

Preserving the richness and variety of sound recordings is a worthwhile undertaking in itself, but it is the interaction between listener and sound, an interaction that can take place only if preceded by discovery of recorded sound content, that makes recordings come alive. Preservation is a crucial part of the picture, but the ultimate goals of preservation are sustained discovery and use.

Technology is playing an ever greater role in the discovery—and analysis—of audio content. The music information retrieval community, for example, is developing music retrieval systems that query the music itself; these systems include techniques such as query-by-singing and audio melody extraction (MIREX 2014). Legal, government, and corporate clients can use patented technologies such as Nexidia that locate, analyze, and organize large volumes of spoken word recordings for purposes such as presenting information at trials and determining compliance with regulations. For the foreseeable future, though, metadata will continue to play the central role in audio discovery.

Metadata also inform internal collection management decisions and workflows. Information about content and carriers, creators, and donors is required for

- Acquiring audio resources that fulfill an institution's mission and effectively serve its users
- Making prudent decisions about costly storage space, housing supplies, and staff time
- Understanding the long-term implications of donor-imposed, copyright, and other restrictions on access and use
- Making the best use of available preservation resources

Over the past several decades, especially with the explosive growth of digital resources on the web, diverse organizations and communities have developed *metadata schemas*, structured sets of elements intended to describe information resources of specific areas of endeavor (science, business, arts, and humanities); specified formats of material (e.g., books, graphic materials, media resources); or certain information environments (e.g., the online library catalog, the World Wide Web). Metadata schemas may be simple or extremely complex in structure, and they may or may not require that the content of one or more elements be taken from controlled vocabulary lists or authority files, or adhere to external rules governing how data are formulated or represented.

A metadata schema is usually accompanied by some kind of documentation or data dictionary that describes the schema's purpose and structure, the number and names of elements, the relationships among those elements, whether a given element is required or may be repeated, and, sometimes, rules governing the nature of the information (or value) each element may contain. Regarding the level of detail provided in a description, most metadata standards are flexible, allowing institutions to prepare descriptions as local resources and policies permit.

Perhaps the most crucial feature for assessing the usefulness of a metadata schema is its degree of interoperability for purposes of data sharing, cross-repository searching, harvesting, and transformation or migration to other schemas or systems. Within an organization, consistent use of standard and interoperable schemas (containing elements that can be mapped to one another with relative ease) reduces duplication of effort while effectively serving multiple purposes over time. Interoperability ensures, for example, that a detailed collection inventory originally prepared to inform preservation work carried out by an external audio lab may be reused, at least in part, to generate Dublin Core or other metadata records intended for public discovery.

Perfect Is the Enemy of the Useful

The two most challenging responsibilities related to the care of an audio collection are processing and preservation. Each set of actions requires significant resources to plan, prioritize, and perform. The discussion of preservation programs in chapter 7 cites a study noting that a "misleading perception about digital preservation investments is that…choices are binary: either we implement intensive preservation…immediately and forever; or we do nothing" (Blue Ribbon Task Force 2010, 99).

The same may be said of providing bibliographic control over a collection. The creation of detailed item-level cataloging of a collection of nearly any size is a formidable task. But managers responsible for sound recording collections should never allow such challenges to intimidate them to the extent that no inventorying or cataloging is done because the ideal cannot be achieved.

Most researchers are grateful for access to any type of inventory or catalog records that describe a collection. A minimal list of items in a collection is infinitely superior to no list at all. If potential users of your collection have no concept of your holdings, your collections may be of little value to anyone. A very basic inventory will serve many internal needs as well, including collection development activities, preservation planning, and space allocation.

There are several tools available at no cost through the web that make it easier than ever before to prepare collection inventories. View thorough, but simple, inventories of your collection as the foundation for professional management of your audio collections, as well as a service to your users.

5.1 METADATA AND TOOLS FOR COLLECTION MANAGEMENT

Descriptive metadata play an important role in most of the major functions performed in a cultural heritage repository:

- Documenting what the repository has in its possession
- Preparing for preservation reformatting
- Planning to meet space, supply, and budget needs
- Clarifying rights information for potential users
- Tracking location, use, and preservation activity over time
- Preparing local and online exhibitions, collection guides, etc.
- Complying with internal reporting requirements (e.g., annual reports)
- Finding the resources needed by researchers

The first step in undertaking these tasks is the preparation of an inventory that identifies every item in a collection.

ITEM-LEVEL COLLECTION INVENTORY

Item-level metadata inform crucial collection management functions, especially those relating to preservation planning. For this reason, an inventory should be provided for each collection if possible and as soon as possible. To help the repository gain basic intellectual and physical control of a collection, the initial inventory should include for each recording, at a minimum, the title (or titles if there are more than one on the recording) and location of the recording in the repository.

What Are Metadata?

Given their critical role in all areas of audio discovery, management, and use, what exactly are metadata, and how can they be put to effective and efficient use in your institution?

The National Information Standards Organization (NISO) booklet, *Understanding Metadata,* offers a useful definition of metadata as "structured information that describes, explains, locates, or otherwise makes it easier to retrieve, use, or manage an information resource" (NISO 2004, 1). There are three main types of metadata, although most descriptive records include elements of all three:

1. *Administrative:* Information about provenance, technical characteristics, intellectual property rights, preservation issues and actions, and location
2. *Structural:* Information that clarifies the structure of a compound object (such as an album and its individual tracks or the components of an oral history collection)
3. *Descriptive:* Basic identification and discovery elements (such as creator, title, dates, contents, subjects, and genres)

If there is no formal title on a published recording or its accompanying documentation, transcribe any potentially identifying information from the recording's container or label. If more complete information becomes available later (as supplied by the donor or creator, or provided by a staff member or audio engineer working with the recording), it can replace a provisional title.

For an unpublished recording, a title may be devised from information taken from accompanying documentation (such as donor-supplied lists, inventories, letters, notes, etc.), from labels or notes on the recording or its container, or from other reliable sources. A devised title should include the following, as known and needed for identification:

- Name element (name(s) of performers, speakers, interviewees)
- Activity/event element (generic word or words that describe the nature of the recorded content or the type of recorded activity or event, if needed for clarity, e.g., "radio news programs," "performance," "lectures," "jam session")
- Topic or focus of event/activity (usually for spoken-word recordings, e.g., subject of a lecture)
- Venue or place of event

The location of a recording can be a room or shelf number or, for a digital audio file, the domain, path, and file name.

Other elements of information can be added to the collection inventory either right from the start or as needed for specific collection management tasks or preservation actions. An audio engineer digitizing a recorded sound collection for preservation purposes, for example, needs a detailed inventory of the collection, one that provides not only the title (or provisional title) of each recording, but also physical details, such as format, size, and speed, to the extent that information is known. It is also helpful to provide condition information and comments regarding potential duplication problems (e.g., speed changes or gaps in recorded content on a reel of tape). Some collection management tools, such as AVCC (described on pp. 82–84), offer suggestions about useful information elements to include in a collection inventory list, spreadsheet, or database. Such suggestions are especially helpful for institutions unfamiliar with inventorying or cataloging recorded sound collections.

Because metadata are critical in managing a collection from the moment it comes in the door, the collection's creator or donor should be asked to provide as much documentation as possible.

SOURCE OF THE METADATA

Because metadata are critical in managing a collection from the moment it comes in the door, the collection's creator or donor should be asked to provide as much documentation as possible: databases, spreadsheets, word processing lists and tables, appraisals, correspondence, even handwritten notes and card files. Donors sometimes forget to include documentation with collection items, but a gentle reminder in the form of a letter, phone call, or even a "donor guidelines" statement or inventory form can prompt a donor to submit vital collection descriptions. If donor-provided documentation is unavailable, a staff member or volunteer should arrange to review the collection and prepare a preliminary inventory, if possible before the items are transferred to the repository. It is easier to contend with unpleasant surprises, such as multiple exact item duplicates, missing materials, or quantities of completely unidentified or blank recordings before the collection is on your doorstep. Electronic documentation is preferable, but any documentation is better than none, especially for unpublished recordings.

METADATA TOOLS FOR COLLECTION MANAGEMENT (AND BEYOND)

When it is time to edit documentation acquired from a donor or, if necessary, to create metadata from scratch, quite a few tools are available to the archivist.[1]

Desktop Office Tools. Commercial desktop applications that may already be in use in the repository—MS Word, Excel, Access, and Filemaker Pro, for example—are generally familiar, easy to use, and highly functional for data entry and manipulation. Open source applications, such as Open Office and Google Drive tools, offer the same advantages to individual collectors and institutions with small budgets. Learning how to perform basic data manipulations in a spreadsheet through online tutorials, support sites, and forums is well worth the effort. Common spreadsheet features such as auto-filling a column of text, splitting and merging text strings, understanding and changing data formats, using find/replace operations, and concatenating new data to existing information save time and result in more consistent and well structured metadata.

Keeping standards in mind when designing a metadata spreadsheet or database will generate metadata that are more effectively searched, shared, and reused. For example, staff who wish to use a collection spreadsheet to create simple Dublin Core metadata records for eventual harvesting and migration into a publicly accessible digital repository (see section 5.6) might match each column header in the spreadsheet to a Dublin Core element (in other words, establish one column each for the Dublin Core elements Title, Creator, Date, Description, etc.). The Dublin Core–compliant spreadsheet data could then be exported as XML-formatted metadata,[2] requiring only minor editing to each record prior to publication in a web-based digital repository.

Because of improvements in office software design and interoperability in recent years, a nontechnical user can import and export data in a variety of formats, making it easy to use different applications for different metadata editing and reformatting purposes. There is one caveat, however: A spreadsheet is an inherently flat structure; some level of programming is usually required to make a spreadsheet accommodate hierarchical relationships, for example, among instances of the same sound recording or descriptions of individual movements in a musical work. A relational

---

[1] Discussion of a software application in this chapter does not necessarily constitute its endorsement.

[2] XML (EXtensible Markup Language) is a commonly used language for marking up the structure and other features of electronic documents. Basic XML tutorials are available at the w3schools.com website.

database, such as MS Access or Filemaker, may be a better choice for hierarchically structured metadata.

An extremely useful desktop office tool for reviewing, cleaning, and restructuring existing metadata, especially messy and inconsistent legacy or donor-provided metadata, is OpenRefine (formerly GoogleRefine). This free and open source tool is available at the OpenRefine website, which also supplies videos, links to tutorials, and a user manual.

Dedicated Metadata Database Tools. In addition to desktop office applications, archivists have a number of open source collection management and description databases to choose from that were not available just a few years ago.

- ■ **CollectiveAccess:** Free, open source software for creating and publishing collection metadata, CollectiveAccess is preconfigured for several descriptive standards (including Dublin Core, PBCore, Encoded Archival Description [EAD], and more), but may be customized for additional uses. It is "integrated" with several widely used controlled vocabularies (e.g., the Library of Congress Subject Headings, the Getty Vocabularies) and can accommodate hierarchical relationships for complex collections. Viewing and annotation tools are provided for digital images, audio and video files, and multipage documents; an optional web publication and a discovery platform are also available. Although users need not have programming expertise, the database application runs on a designated server and requires the installation of three open source software packages. Users include Northeast Historic Film and the National Folklore Archives Initiative.

- ■ **Audio-Visual and Image Database (AVID):** An MS Access–based desktop application, AVID is a tool for managing and tracking audio, moving image, and still image materials. Developed by the audiovisual and image archivist at the University of Florida's George A. Smathers Libraries, AVID specifically addresses some of the more challenging issues in providing metadata for media materials. It enables description at both the collection and item levels, and it makes the relationship between a physical object and its parent library or archival collection clear. A physical original and all of its analog and digital copies can be associated, and fields are included for specific physical characteristics, condition, preservation reformatting priority, and rights information. AVID is intended to support complex workflows and can import and export metadata from other applications. A brief article about the application by its developer is available (Martyniak 2013).

- ■ **AudioVisual Collaborative Cataloging (AVCC)**: A promising tool for item-level description of audio, video, and film collections, AVCC is a free, open source web application developed by AVPreserve and funded by the Library of Congress National

Required Fields

Unique ID assigned to the item

Format Specific format, e.g., DAT, ¼ Inch Open Reel Audio. *Drop-down list*

Title Title of the object. Generally transcribed from a published item or devised by the cataloger for an unpublished item

Storage Location Code Local code indicating location (e.g., shelf number, container number)

Media Diameter Percentage of tape filling a reel. *Drop-down list*

Fields Needed for Report Generation

Media Type Audio, video, or film. *Drop-down list*

Creation Date Date of object creation. Formatted yyyy/mm/dd; date ranges and time periods acceptable

Media Duration Full capacity of object. *Drop-down list*

Content Duration Run time of recorded content in minutes

Base Physical material object is made from. *Drop-down list*

Reel/Disc Diameter Two fields; both have *Drop-down lists* (e.g., 7", 10", 12")

Media Diameter Percentage of tape filling a reel. *Drop-down list*

Optional Suggested Fields

Collection Name of parent collection, if applicable

Description Used for contents, contextual information (e.g., place and type of event where contents were recorded), alternate title(s), provenance of physical item

Content Date Date of content creation. Formatted yyyy/mm/dd; date ranges and time periods acceptable

Genre/Subject One or more terms taken from an authorized or local list; indicates what genre/style the object is an example of (genre terms) and what item is about (subject terms)

Contributor Name(s) of person(s) or corporate bodies involved with the creation of item's content; optionally include role term(s). Take names from authorized or local list, or, minimally, format names consistently

Generation Relationship between original material and copies (e.g., Original, Production Master, Access Copy)

Part Indicates if object is one of a number of objects (e.g., "Reel 1 of 4")

Commercial or Unique Indicates whether item is published or unpublished. *Drop-down list*

Copyright/Restrictions Legal or donor-imposed rights on access and use

Duplicates/Derivatives States if the institution has multiple original copies of an object or if there are derivatives; location information optional

Related Material Notes on associated objects

Condition Chemical or physical damage or degradation that may impact playback (e.g., mold, shrinkage, brittleness)

Tape Thickness 0.5 to 2 mil. *Drop-down list*

Sides Item recorded on one or both sides. *Drop-down list*

Track Type Indicates number of tracks on tape (e.g., full track, 8-track). *Drop-down list*

Mono or Stereo *Drop-down list*

Noise Reduction States any noise filtering devices used during the object's recording (e.g., Dolby A, Dolby S). *Drop-down list*

Recording Speed e.g., SP, LP, 7.5 ips, 15 ips, etc.

Table 5.1: AVCC Beta version, audio cataloging fields. The extensive use of drop-down lists in AVCC helps maintain a controlled vocabulary for the description of audiovisual items.

Recording Preservation Board, METRO, and AVPreserve. A "sandbox" version of AVCC, and link to the source code, is available at http://www.avpreserve.com/tools/avcc. Sample layouts used by AVCC may be viewed at the website of an earlier version of the tool, at http://keepingcollections.org/avcc-cataloging-toolkit/.

AVCC enables collaborative, efficient item-level cataloging of audiovisual collections in order to gain the intellectual control necessary to make decisions about collection management and aid in obtaining preservation funding. There are several built-in reports and graphs that make it easy get key metrics and documentation. These include collection statistics, digital storage calculations, shipping manifests, and other data critical to setting priorities and planning preservation work for audiovisual materials.

Other features include a browser-based web application that works on any Windows or Mac operating system using all popular browsers; support for video and film, as well as audio; and controlled vocabularies and field validation to help ensure consistent data entry. The tool allows teams to enter and edit data simultaneously; provides mechanisms for bulk editing and efficient record creation; and incorporates MediaSCORE base scores for assigning preservation priority.

Although AVCC was originally envisioned as supporting volunteer-based teams, it offers an effective platform for working with a team of any kind. Catalogers and archivists who have limited experience with media, especially legacy tape, disc, and wire audio formats, will find the forms and guides highly useful. AVCC software needs to be installed and configured on a server, requiring the proper expertise. AVPreserve is planning to offer AVCC as a hosted application on a monthly subscription basis.

PBCORE FOR COLLECTION MANAGEMENT AND PRESERVATION

The metadata schema PBCore is described in this section (as well as under Dublin Core Initiative Metadata Standards and Tools) because it is designed to handle the descriptive details and hierarchical relationships needed for preservation and management of time-based media such as sound recordings and other audiovisual materials. Collection management software that can receive, manipulate, create, and export PBCore metadata can be useful for sound recordings.

Developed by the public broadcasting archival community, PBCore is an XML-based metadata schema for describing digital and analog audiovisual media. It has been in use since 2004; the most recent version is PBCore 2.0, released in January 2011. PBCore development was in decline for a number of years, but with the release of version 2.0 and the selection of PBCore in 2013 as the metadata standard for the American Archive of Public Broadcasting (see Archival Management System in section 5.6), it is being revitalized by a growing community of users.

Most metadata standards used in cultural heritage institutions include general descriptive fields or elements, such as title, creator, subject, description, and identifier. As one of the few metadata standards intended specifically for audiovisual materials, PBCore accommodates not only those basic identifying elements, but also more granular (i.e., more finely detailed) elements regarding technical and time-related characteristics of analog and digital sound, film, and video materials. It directly addresses the complex relationships that so often bedevil audiovisual archivists who must decide, for example, how to describe specific content, such as an episode in a series or an oral history interview that extends across multiple, sometimes out-of-sequence, tape reels.

PBCore also offers the option of tracking preservation-related needs and actions. Elements are available that can help staff monitor digital file integrity over time, for example, or that relate digital master and access copies to the original analog recording from which they were derived. If the staff prefer to track preservation actions using elements from a different metadata standard (such as PREMIS preservation metadata), they can wrap PREMIS elements within a PBCore Extension "container" element.

A PBCore description may be as simple or as detailed as the institution prefers; it may consist of a single document, or it may contain multiple component documents. A document may describe an "asset" (which refers to the content of an audiovisual resource), an "instantiation" (which is a physical or digital occurrence of an asset), or both. A PBCore document can also describe a collection or grouping of resources along with all of the collection's component assets and instantiations. Only a few elements are required to create a "valid" PBCore record (i.e., a record that complies with rules regarding required and optional elements, the order of elements, allowed data types, etc., when checked against the PBCore XML schema). The example in Figure 5.1, taken from the PBCore website, is a valid PBCore instantiation record containing only an item's identifier and location information.

```
<pbcoreInstantiationDocument xmlns="http://www.pbcore.org/PBCore/
PBCoreNamespace.html" xmlns:xsi="http://www.w3.org/2001/XMLSchema-
instance" xsi:schemaLocation="http://www.pbcore.org/PBCore/PBCore-
Namespace.html http://pbcore.org/xsd/pbcore-2.0.xsd">

<instantiationIdentifier source="McHale University">MCU_v0123_01</
instantiationIdentifier>

<instantiationLocation>McHale University</instantiationLocation>
</pbcoreInstantiationDocument>
```

Fig. 5.1: PBCore simple instantiation record, PBCore website

PBCORE TOOLS

Although PBCore is expressed in XML, PBCore-compliant metadata may be built, enhanced, and revised in a variety of familiar applications and then exported as XML (or CSV that can be converted to XML). These applications include databases, such as Filemaker Pro, and spreadsheets.

As discussed earlier, spreadsheets are quick and easy to build. Their flat structure, however, does not accommodate PBCore's potentially complex hierarchical structure. Guidance on generating hierarchical PBCore metadata from spreadsheets is available; see the Community section of the PBCore website. The user community has also developed PBCore templates for Filemaker Pro. Plug-ins that generate PBCore XML documents are available for some content management systems, such as Omeka (described below) and CollectiveAccess (described earlier). Keep in mind that PBCore as an XML schema is also intended for search and retrieval, as well as creating or harvesting descriptive audiovisual metadata. See PBCore in section 5.6, and see the PBCore website for more information.

5.2   EXPOSING METADATA FOR PUBLIC DISCOVERY

Discovery generally refers to the ability to find described resources (e.g., books, sound and video recordings, maps) through search and retrieval. In a library environment, a discovery tool is a commercial or locally developed solution for finding resources described in the local catalog and other local and remote databases.

The cultural heritage community (libraries, archives, museums) has developed a broad range of descriptive metadata standards, many of which are interoperable, at least in part.

As a medium for making metadata available to the widest possible audience, the World Wide Web is, of course, the obvious choice. A local database or catalog can be published to a locally produced website, an option that may be chosen by large repositories, such as college libraries and government archives. Institutional websites usually require sizable and ongoing investments in equipment and technical expertise. Staff at an institution that lacks those resources may elect to use one of the many and varied web hosting services on the Internet. Such services span a wide range and include free or ad-supported hosting (that may offer limited server and software components); web hosting in which clients share server space, software, and other features; web services controlled by a service provider; and cloud hosting, which, although incurring charges only for resources used, could result in a client's loss of control over data location and even security issues.

An institution with limited resources could publish a simple, static HTML page containing descriptive information about one or more collections. This kind of web page, although inexpensive to produce, is usually difficult to update and offers minimal functionality. Users cannot browse by controlled access points (names, subject headings, titles, etc.) on a static HTML page, for example.

One intriguing option is Omeka, a free and open source web publishing tool for cultural heritage collections. Omeka provides publishing "themes" and add-ons that allow online access to digital collection items (including audio and video formats) and their metadata. One of these add-ons generates PBCore metadata (see the PBCore discussions in this chapter). The Omeka website features a wiki and user forums.

For repositories whose staff are unable or disinclined to manage a website, other choices are available for providing widespread access to recorded sound collections. Descriptive metadata about audio resources may be harvested by metadata aggregators (see section 5.6) or contributed to union databases, shared online catalogs, and, increasingly in the cultural heritage community, linked data portals.

All of these methods either require or are optimized by metadata that are well structured and consistent, a goal that is most effectively attained through the implementation of appropriate standards.

5.3   CHOOSING AMONG METADATA STANDARDS

Different metadata standards have different uses. In determining which descriptive metadata standards would best serve your institution and its users, consider how you will use metadata.

The cultural heritage community (libraries, archives, museums) has developed a broad range of descriptive metadata standards, many of which are interoperable, at least in part. Readers are encouraged to visit the official website of each structural and content standard of interest, as well as related websites, blogs, tutorials, and print publications, for more detailed information. Use of a metadata standard, especially consistent use, increases the discoverability of your resources, interoperability of your data with others, and efficiency in metadata creation over time.

Just as there is no single audio format ensuring the permanent preservation of recorded content, there is no single, universally accepted descriptive metadata standard leading to maximally effective identification, discovery, and control of audio resources. At each public or private repository, it is necessary to evaluate the available standards and tools, and adopt what best serves the repository's particular users, mission, collections, day-to-day management requirements, and available resources (such as technical and cataloging expertise and funding).

Different metadata standards have different uses. In determining which descriptive metadata standards would best serve your institution and its users, consider how you will use metadata. Do you need to report on audio quantities and formats in order to assess future shelving needs? Would more detailed technical information about specific audio formats, as well as descriptions of their condition, help with conservation planning and budget requests? Does the repository hold many sound recordings in a variety of formats, or are your holdings relatively small and limited to one or two fairly current formats? Does your institution chiefly acquire published or unpublished materials?

For uses requiring detailed technical and physical condition information on a regular basis, a standard developed specifically for audiovisual materials, such as PBCore, may be most appropriate, whereas a simple spreadsheet can generate a basic inventory for tracking and managing a few hundred sound recordings. An open source library application through which a staff member could search and download machine-readable cataloging (MARC) records from other libraries may answer all of the descriptive audio metadata needs of a small, financially strapped library holding a collection of published compact discs (CDs). A local history society that acquires unpublished archival collections may find that Describing Archives: A Content Standard (DACS), in combination with Encoded Archive Description (EAD), successfully addresses the characteristics and concerns of archival materials overall. Resource Description and Access (RDA) and PBCore, both of which offer controlled vocabularies for audio-related items, are useful guides to describing the content of sound recordings included in an archival finding aid.

Another factor in the adoption of one or more descriptive metadata standards is your institution's familiarity with creating and using metadata. Larger libraries and archives with professionally trained staff obviously will find it easier to use the standards, as complex as they might be, developed specifically for libraries and archives (e.g., RDA and MARC for libraries, DACS and EAD for archives). XML or even HTML familiarity will reduce the EAD or PBCore learning curve because those standards are expressed in the XML markup language.

Institutions with little metadata experience may wish to begin by creating simple inventory spreadsheets (see Item-level Collection Inventory in section 5.1) or by selecting a simple but effective metadata standard such as Dublin Core (see section 5.6). Metadata created according to simpler standards could be migrated to more detailed and complex standards at a later time if considered useful to the institution and its users.

Of primary importance to any institution is its user base. Does your institution serve primarily casual or relatively inexperienced users, or do significant numbers of them conduct serious academic or professional research? Do patrons typically search the library catalog when seeking materials, or do most of them rely on web search tools like Google or Yahoo? Are your audio holdings an important consideration in a potential researcher's decision to use your institution? Keeping user research needs and preferences in mind as you evaluate standards is essential to making informed and appropriate metadata decisions.

METADATA STANDARDS IN TRANSITION

Descriptive metadata standards are in a period of immense transition. Widely used content rules and data structures in both the library and archival communities in the United States have recently been revised (DACS, EAD), completely replaced (*Anglo-American Cataloguing Rules*, 2nd edition [AACR2]), or newly implemented (RDA), while others are just being introduced (Encoded Archival Context–Corporate Bodies, Persons, and Families [EAC-CPF]). An even more dramatic change for libraries and archives is the new discovery environment of the Semantic Web of linked data (World Wide Web Consortium 2014). Readers should keep a watchful eye on linked data and conceptual modeling efforts such as the Library of Congress's emerging Bibliographic Framework Initiative (BIBFRAME) and the international archival community's Experts Group on Archival Description (EGAD) conceptual modeling endeavor.

5.4 LIBRARY METADATA: STANDARDS AND TOOLS

Library standards include rules governing the content of metadata (e.g., AACR2, RDA) and standards for the technical data structure that holds the metadata (e.g., MARC21, MODS, BIBFRAME). Based on the types of material most commonly held in libraries, as well as the nature of access tools traditionally used in libraries (namely, item-level catalogs), library standards have generally been shaped by the following assumptions.

Published materials: Libraries traditionally acquire and catalog published materials in many forms—books, sound recordings, serials, videos, maps, reports, and so forth. Published items are intended for distribution, often mass distribution. They are not unique, which means that a catalog record for a specific edition of a commercially released sound recording can be used in many library catalogs. Libraries contribute original catalog records to large union databases such as the OCLC global cooperative and, in turn, use (and sometimes locally edit) records prepared by other libraries in their own catalogs.

The fact that published materials are self-describing also influences the library approach to descriptive cataloging. Published books, digital video discs (DVDs), CDs, and other items usually feature recognizable, often formal title pages, disc and tape labels, printed container information, and so forth. Library cataloging rules require, therefore, the transcription of basic, identifying elements of information directly from the items.

Item-level cataloging: Cataloging is done at the item rather than the collection level in libraries; one catalog record is prepared for one book, CD, DVD, and so forth. A MARC catalog record, the cataloging structure used in most libraries, is flat because of this simple, one-to-one relationship (although MARC has never been adequate for audio items such as albums and other carriers that contain multiple individual musical works, composers, and performers). Today, new metadata models and content standards in libraries are leading to MARC's demise, but item-level cataloging is still the norm.

Online catalogs: A library user searches an indexed, online public access catalog to find and identify published library materials. In many institutions, digital assets, unpublished materials, and individual journal articles must be searched in databases other than the online catalog. Increasingly, though, separate metadata "silos" are being merged or presented as a single, unified system for resource discovery.

SPECIFIC LIBRARY STANDARDS: DATA CONTENT

AACR2 (Anglo-American Cataloguing Rules 2002, 2005). For bibliographic description in AACR2, general rules govern metadata syntax, information transcription, capitalization, abbreviation, punctuation, and the like. Chapter 6 of AACR2 covers sound recordings; chapter 5 covers music.

For authority control (in AACR2 and RDA), the second half of AACR2 governs controlled access points (headings) for names of people, geographic names, corporate bodies, and titles. Librarians now follow RDA to create name and title authority records containing the preferred access point, alternate access points (e.g., alternate spellings and forms of a name or title), certain biographical and historical characteristics, usage notes, and sources of information consulted. In both AACR2 and RDA, rules for establishing uniform titles (basically, distinct composer-title access points, called preferred titles in RDA), especially for Western art music, are complex. Institutions should use preferred names and titles established in the Library of Congress Authority Files (see Authorized Access Points, next page). Additionally, the Music Cataloging at Yale web pages provide extremely helpful resources on these and other music and recorded sound cataloging rules and practices. Officially obsolete since 2013 because of its replacement by RDA, AACR2 is still in use at many institutions.

RDA (Resource Description and Access). RDA was developed by the American Library Association (ALA), the Australian Committee on Cataloguing, the British Library, the Canadian Committee on Cataloguing, the Chartered Institute of Library and Information Professionals (CILIP), and the Library of Congress. It is available in electronic form through paid subscription to the RDA Toolkit or the Library of Congress's Cataloger's Desktop. A printed version of the rules is also available for purchase.

RDA is the replacement content standard for AACR2; it was implemented in libraries in many (but not all) countries starting in 2013. Although it is the current Library of Congress–wide standard for name and title access points and authority records, RDA has not been implemented for bibliographic description in either the Motion Picture, Broadcasting, and Recorded Sound Division or the American Folklife Center, the two Library of Congress divisions that are chiefly responsible for recorded sound cataloging. Those divisions are participating in the development of BIBFRAME as an alternative to RDA for describing audiovisual materials (Van Malssen 2014).

RDA is based on the Functional Requirements for Bibliographic Records (FRBR) conceptual model, which emphasizes four major "Group 1" entities and the relationships among them:

1. *Work:* intentionally created intellectual work
2. *Expression:* realization of the work in text (original language or translation), e.g., spoken word, musical performance, motion picture
3. *Manifestation:* an embodiment (basically, an edition) of a particular expression of a work
4. *Item:* an example of a manifestation; a specific, physical item

Rules for describing sound recordings are scattered throughout RDA, making it difficult to learn the rules by wading into the text. Exploring training sites, best practice guidelines, and webinars like the ones listed on the next page is probably a clearer and more efficient way to get started with RDA. The Library of Congress and the Program for Cooperative Cataloging (PCC) have developed policy statements (each known as an

LC-PCC PS) on many RDA rules; these are included in the RDA Toolkit. The following sources provide additional information on RDA:

- Library of Congress RDA Training Materials.
- *Best Practices for Music Cataloging Using RDA and MARC21* (Music Library Association 2014). The appendix to chapter 3 is especially useful for media and carrier terms as well as technical characteristics for analog and digital sound captured on a large variety of physical carriers.
- Bibliographic Control Committee website (Music Library Association). The site includes an overview of RDA descriptive elements.
- RDA: Resource Description & Access Toolkit (American Library Association, Canadian Library Association, and CILIP: Chartered Institute of Library and Information Professionals). The site includes RDA record examples in MARC format.
- RDA webinars on cataloging popular/jazz/ethnographic recordings, classical music recordings, and musical scores (Cornell University 2014).

Authorized Access Points. For consistent access points for names, titles, places, subjects, and genres and forms of material, catalogers acquire name and term forms from the Library of Congress Authorities or the Virtual International Authority File (VIAF) (names only). Additional name and subject headings, genre terms, and medium of performance terms for musical works are available at the Library of Congress Linked Data Service website.

SPECIFIC LIBRARY STANDARDS: DATA STRUCTURE

MARC21 (Machine-Readable Cataloging). MARC is a data structure devised for exchange of metadata (e.g., catalog card data) among libraries and other similar institutions. The MARC standard has accommodated both bibliographic and authority metadata since the 1960s; the current version is known as MARC21. Still in use internationally, MARC will be replaced by BIBFRAME (based on linked data principles) in coming years.

Originally conceived as a machine-readable way to communicate the data on a traditional catalog card, MARC is structured to hold descriptive information about the resource described (e.g., title, edition, publication information, physical characteristics, standard numbers, and notes), "main entry" and "added entries" (headings for persons and corporate bodies responsible for creating the resource), subject headings, classification or shelf number, and more. Each major area of description is represented in MARC by a specific numeric tag or label:

1XX fields accommodate the controlled access point for the creator/ author primarily responsible for the resource.
24X fields accommodate the title and statement of responsibility.
25X fields cover edition information.
26X fields are for publication, distribution, etc., metadata.
3XX is the physical description area.
    …and so forth.

Figure 5.2 shows an example of a MARC record for a compact disc. For a basic introduction to the MARC data structure, see *Understanding MARC Bibliographic: Machine-Readable Cataloging* (Library of Congress 2009).

BIBFRAME (Bibliographic Framework Initiative). An emerging structural standard based on linked data principles and expressed through the Resource Description Framework (RDF) data model, BIBFRAME is intended not only to replace MARC, but also to expand the environment of descriptive metadata for all types of materials of interest to libraries, archives, and museums. The initiative is based at the Library of Congress, but input is requested from anyone interested in cultural heritage information.

000	01482njm a2200373 a 4500	
001	5656840	
005	19930423063704.0	
007	sduzunznnmlne ***Coded physical details about the CD***	
008	920824r1992 nyujzn f eng d ***Coded data about the publication, language, music genre***	
035	__	‡9 (DLC) 92767955 ***OCLC record ID number***
906	__	‡a 7 ‡b cbc ‡c copycat ‡d 4 ‡e ncip ‡f 19 ‡g y-soundrec ***Local field***
010	__	‡a 92767955 ***Library of Congress Control Number***
028	02	‡a 07863 61071-2 ‡b Bluebird ***Publisher number***
033	2_	‡a 1941---- ‡a 1946---- ***Coded data about recording dates***
035	__	‡a (OCoLC)25778789 ***OCLC record ID number***
040	__	‡a MoS ‡c DLC ‡d DLC ***IDs of libraries that created, edited the catalog record***
042	__	‡a lccopycat
050	00	‡a Bluebird 07863 61071-2 ***Library of Congress shelf number***
100	1_	‡a Ellington, Duke, ‡d 1899-1974. ***Main entry (Performer)***
245	10	‡a Sophisticated lady ‡h [sound recording] / ‡c Duke Ellington. ***Album title, statement of responsibility***
260	__	‡a New York, N.Y. : ‡b Bluebird : ‡b Distributed by BMG Music, ‡c p1992. ***Publication information***
300	__	‡a 1 sound disc : ‡b digital ; ‡c 4 3/4 in. ***Physical description of CD***
306	__	‡a 003200 ***Duration***
440	_0	‡a Masters of the big bands ***Series title***
511	0_	‡a Duke Ellington, piano ; with orchestra and vocals. ***Performers and their roles***
518	__	‡a Songs originally recorded between 1941 and 1946. ***Place/date of publication note***
500	__	‡a Compact disc. ***Carrier format note***
500	__	‡a Program notes by Ira Gitler on container insert. ***Accompanying information note***
505	0_	‡a Take the «A» train -- I got it bad (and that ain't good) -- Chelsea Bridge -- Perdido -- The "C" jam blues -- Caravan -- Mood indigo -- It don't mean a thing (if it ain't got that swing) -- Sophisticated lady -- Things ain't what they used to be (Time's a wastin') -- Just squeeze me. ***Contents note***
650	_0	‡a Big band music. ***Subject access point for type of music***
650	_0	‡a Jazz ‡y 1941-1950. ***Additional subject access point for type of music and its time period***
952	__	‡a New ***Local note***
953	__	‡a TA28 ***Local note: Library of Congress cataloger ID code***

Fig. 5.2: MARC record based on AACR2 rules for a CD. This record was downloaded from the OCLC union database into the Library of Congress online catalog, where it received further editing.

For information, see the BIBFRAME official website and the Linked Open Data in Libraries, Archives, and Museums (LODLAM) website.

MODS (Metadata Object Description Schema). For those who wish to work within a library-oriented metadata environment but avoid the complexities of MARC, there is MODS, a simplified XML version of MARC that may be used to describe all types of material. Any content standard may be used with MODS. As is the case for all XML schema–based standards, an XSLT stylesheet is needed to convert an XML MODS record to HTML for web display. (For more detail about working with XML-based structural standards, see EAD/EAD3 [Encoded Archival Description] on p. 97.)

The official MODS website at the Library of Congress is the best source for obtaining the MODS XML schema, user guidelines, record examples, element and attribute lists, and tools for creating and editing MODS metadata.

LIBRARY CATALOGING TOOLS

Most large and even medium-sized libraries use expensive vendor-provided software for cataloging, public search and retrieval, and other library tasks. Acquiring and maintaining these applications requires substantial investments in technical staff, hardware, and software. Many libraries and consortia across the globe also participate in OCLC, a cooperative that allows a subscribing institution to use existing records in its

Discovery Tools in Libraries

In recent years, vendors that provide libraries with catalog systems and subscription databases of articles and other content have developed tools (called "discovery tools" or "discovery services") that search large indexes of aggregated catalogs and databases. Examples of discovery tools are Primo, Summon, EBSCO Discovery Service, and OCLC's WorldCat Discovery Services. The idea is to offer users simple, one-stop searching that covers all or most of the resources available from a library (or similar institution), rather than requiring researchers to conduct separate queries in the library's catalog, newspaper database, digital repository, general article database, and specialized topical databases. This effort to do away with separate silos of data is rooted in the success of Internet search tools such as Google and Yahoo. One-stop searching has, rightly or wrongly, accustomed users to the idea of finding everything they need though a single search.

Many users may end their search efforts after querying a single system, usually the online library catalog because of its central position on most library home pages. Therefore, some repositories have elected to describe as many of their local holdings as possible in the catalog, which typically handles only library-standard MARC records. For curators of audio content, especially unique recordings that have been digitized and included in an institution's digital repository or other database, discovery tools mean that it may be increasingly possible for users to retrieve in one search metadata descriptions of a repository's books, serials, archival collections, general and specialized articles, and digital collections. As a result, a small library or historical society may no longer need to provide access to its specialized audio holdings principally via MARC records in the library catalog. If PBCore (with its audiovisual-specific structure and accommodation of format-specific technical details) or DACS/EAD finding aids (with their emphasis on contextual information for unpublished collections) were considered more appropriate to the material and its potential users, the institution could use those standards without worrying that important audio content would be less findable in a database other than the online library catalog.

This is something to consider in determining—or rethinking—the most appropriate descriptive metadata standards and tools for your institution.

local MARC database and contribute new (original) records to the huge OCLC WorldCat database, a worldwide online catalog of records describing library and archival materials in all formats. For smaller institutions, opportunities for no-cost downloading and editing of existing MARC records have increased in recent years.

Commercial, but also open source, applications enable the cataloger to search and download catalog records from various libraries, including major cataloging libraries such as the Library of Congress, into local databases. For information on how to find and evaluate these applications, see *Automating Libraries* (American Library Association 2014).

MarcEdit. A free MARC editing utility from Terry Reese of Ohio State University Libraries, MarcEdit can be used to search, download, edit, and create new MARC records individually or in batches. In MarcEdit, existing MARC21 records (which usually must be created and edited in specialized, often expensive library cataloging applications) are converted to a "mnemonic" file format for record edits or updates; the utility also accepts descriptions in XML, Excel, Access, and any delimited format (such as tab- and comma-delimited files) and converts that data to MARC. Record files may then be imported into a database or integrated library system. MarcEdit is also equipped with a MARC validator, an Open Archives Initiative (OAI) harvester, and functions that convert various metadata and MARC files into other formats and standards (e.g., Dublin Core, EAD, MODS, various delimited text formats). Assistance is widely available and includes Reese's online tutorials. Reese frequently incorporates new features into MarcEdit.

5.5   ARCHIVAL DESCRIPTION: STANDARDS AND TOOLS

The arrangement and description of very large collections is based on archival principles that emphasize provenance and context.

Like librarians, archivists have developed standard rules for metadata content (DACS in the United States), as well as standards for the data structure that holds that metadata (EAD, EAD-CPF). Archival collections have special characteristics that distinguish them from the published materials typically acquired by libraries, and archival description reflects those characteristics.

Archives and manuscript repositories often acquire materials that have been created or accumulated by a person, family, or organization during the course of their daily affairs. The arrangement and description of these sometimes very large collections is based on archival principles that emphasize provenance and context. Archival description is chiefly intended to communicate not only what a collection consists of but how the materials are related to one another and to the collection's creator. When thinking about archival description, it might be helpful to keep the following of its characteristics in mind.

Unpublished collections: Archivists work with unpublished collections of personal, family, and organizational records, and sometimes collector- and repository-created collections (built around a topic or format, for example). They also, as appropriate to the arrangement of the collection, describe component groupings of collection materials: series, subseries, files, items. The size of an archival collection can range from a single item to hundreds or even thousands of cubic feet of material.

Forms of material: Archival collections may consist of one or many formats (including sound recordings); the materials may be in analog or digital form or both. Although audiovisual materials are often transferred from an archives or manuscript division within a larger institution to an audio or audiovisual repository or division for shelving and preservation purposes, those audiovisual materials should, in general, be identified as part of the larger archival collection in which they originated.

Collection-level cataloging: Because archival collections are often quite large, description is generally done at the collection or series level. Item-level description is perfectly acceptable, however, when appropriate to the material. Archival description is suitable for unpublished audio collections, individual recordings, and sound recordings that form part of larger, multiformat collections.

Archivist-supplied information: Because unpublished materials lack designated "title pages" or publisher-supplied labels providing basic identifying information, the archivist usually synthesizes available information (from accompanying documents and other sources) in order to devise titles and provide dates, content information, and the like.

Finding aids, collection-level catalog records: The most common archival descriptive tool is the finding aid, a document that describes a collection's provenance (information about the creator of the collection), overall content and coverage, arrangement, access and use restrictions, and processing. A finding aid also contains name and subject access points and an inventory or container list of the collection's components. The inventory, structured hierarchically according to the manner in which the collection is arranged, may describe series, subseries, files, and sometimes items. Archivists frequently prepare a collection-level MARC catalog record that contains a link to the more detailed finding aid.

Conceptual model: In 2012, the International Council on Archives (ICA) appointed an Experts Group on Archival Description (EGAD) to develop a conceptual model for archival description. The model will provide a foundation for description systems that enhance access to archival resources in a linked data environment (Gueguen et al. 2013).

SPECIFIC ARCHIVAL STANDARDS: DATA CONTENT

DACS (Describing Archives: A Content Standard, 2013). The U.S. content standard for archival description, DACS is based on the international standards for describing archival materials and their creators: *General International Standard of Archival Description* (ISAD[G], International Council on Archives 1999) and *International Standard Archival Authority Record for Corporate Bodies, Persons, and Families* (ISAAR[CPF], International Council on Archives 2004).

The standard is output neutral. DACS-based content can be expressed in MARC records, EAD finding aids, local databases, etc. DACS itself consists of two parts: Describing Archival Materials and Archival Authority Records.

Flexible and easier to use than RDA, DACS allows for just a single level of description (as in a collection-level MARC record) or multiple levels of description (as in a finding aid that describes a collection at successively narrower levels of arrangement—from the collection as a whole to series, subseries, and items). In a finding aid, in fact, some series may be described in general terms, while others are broken into narrower levels of detail (e.g., a series description followed by entries for all or for selected items included in that series).

As appropriate to the material described, access points should be provided for names, places, subjects, documentary forms, occupations, and functions. DACS is not prescriptive about sources of controlled access points, but does offer as one source of authorized names and subject headings the Library of Congress Authority files. Additional sources of standardized names, subjects, and genre/form terms include VIAF and the *Art & Architecture Thesaurus Online* (a good source for genre and form terms). Other vocabularies available at the Getty Research Institute website may be helpful as well. The American Folklore Society's *Ethnographic Thesaurus* is appropriate for folklife and ethnomusicology materials.

DACS for Audio Description. Archival description is appropriate for unpublished audio collections, individual recordings, and sound recordings that form part of larger, multiformat collections. DACS applies to all forms of material, but because it does not cover physical and technical aspects of media materials, other content standards must be used to describe special characteristics of analog and digital sound recordings. At present, there are no DACS-compatible content standards or guidelines for describing unpublished sound recordings. An archivist, therefore, may apply DACS in formulating the title, creation date, and shelf location of an open reel tape, but consult AACR2, RDA, or PBCore for guidance on recording physical and technical details; musical contents notes; and notes indicating place and date of recording, names of performers, and their roles. PBCore, a structural standard for describing and managing audiovisual media, provides a set of XML elements and attributes, as well as a set of controlled vocabularies, that, although not a content standard per se, is another potential source of consistent terminology for physical and technical descriptions within an EAD finding aid. (For more information, see pp. 98-101.)

Sound recordings included in a collection may be described at any level—or combination of levels—of granularity considered appropriate according to institutional policy and archivist's judgment.

Let NUCMC Do the Cataloging. Especially useful for repositories with limited means is the National Union Catalog of Manuscript Collections (NUCMC) at the Library of Congress. NUCMC catalogers prepare MARC21 records for eligible U.S. repositories and include them in OCLC WorldCat. NUCMC services are free of charge. To be eligible for participation, an archival repository must be located in the United States or its territories, be open to researchers on a regular basis, and be unable to contribute national-level catalog records to OCLC WorldCat (because of OCLC participation costs, for example). Oral histories that include tapes or transcripts are eligible, but collections consisting entirely of nontextual materials may or may not be.[3]

SPECIFIC ARCHIVAL STANDARDS: DATA STRUCTURE

EAD/EAD3 (Encoded Archival Description). EAD is an international, nonproprietary, XML-based structural standard for electronic finding aids. It was first published in 1998, version 2 appeared in 2002, and EAD3 was implemented in 2015. The Society of American Archivists and the Library of Congress maintain this standard. Content provided in EAD elements is generally based on DACS in the United States.

As structured data, EAD can provide searchable, sortable, and browsable access to collections and their components. EAD documents are generally accessible to web search engines such as Google and Yahoo, and they can be included in XML databases, such as MarkLogic and eXist, as well as some digital repositories, such as Fedora.

An EAD finding aid consists of XML elements and attributes that represent recognized parts of the standard archival finding aid and reflect the hierarchical nature of archival arrangement. The elements and attributes themselves, as well as machine-readable rules for using them, are stated in the EAD schema document, which is available at the EAD official website at the Library of Congress. Sophisticated XML editing tools, such as Oxygen and XMLSpy, can be pointed to the desired EAD schema file in the opening section of a finding aid; the schema file then controls which elements and attributes are available for use at given locations in the finding aid document.

A typical EAD finding aid consists of the following:

- Essential identifying elements, such as collection title, dates, extent, location of collection materials, and abstract
- Elements containing controlled access points for important names, subjects, places, titles, functions, occupations, and forms and genres of material
- Notes for describing the content and forms of material in the collection; the history of the collection's personal, family, or organizational creator; the arrangement of material; access and use rights; and other optional information
- Description of subordinate components that constitute the collection (also called an inventory or container list). All of the elements available at the collection level of description are also available for describing components in the inventory

Linking elements enable hypertext linking both within and beyond the finding aid document. For example, links can target digitized or

---

[3] The NUCMC team may be reached via http://www.loc.gov/coll/nucmc/index.html.

born-digital items in the collection along with metadata describing those items.

Displaying EAD Finding Aids on the Web. A "raw" EAD finding aid document in XML format must be converted to HTML or PDF in order to be displayed to end users on the web. The Society of American Archivists (SAA) has made a number of XML-to-HTML conversion stylesheets available for download:

- *SAA Standards: Encoded Archival Description (EAD)*
- SAA EAD Roundtable at Github
- *The EAD Cookbook*, originally developed by Michael Fox

EAD finding aids may be published to an institutional website, database, or digital repository. Finding aids may also be contributed to ArchiveGrid, OCLC's extensive archives discovery system, or to one of the many regional or local finding aids consortia, such as Mountain West Digital Library, the Northwest Digital Archives, the Virginia Heritage Project, OhioLINK, and many more. Prior conversion to HTML is usually not required.

Adapting EAD for Audio Description. As noted previously in connection with DACS, there are at present no widely accepted, up-to-date content rules for the description of unpublished sound recordings,[4] and DACS does not specifically address audiovisual materials; therefore, there is great variety in existing EAD finding aids that describe sound recordings. In the absence of specific guidelines, a few suggestions may be helpful.

DACS is useful in formulating and recording information in general, not format-specific, data elements such as collection title, date or date range, creator name(s), biographical or historical note, scope and content or summary note, language and restrictions information, and non-audio, non-music-related access points. In addition to DACS general guidance, consult a standard such as AACR2, RDA, or PBCore regarding the content of audio- or music-related elements such as extent and duration statements, physical and technical characteristics, dimensions, and music-related notes (e.g., contents, performer, alternate form, and place and date of recording notes).

EAD3 contains an element, <unittype>, that may be used along with other elements within a <physdescstructured> element set to describe object type and physical characteristics of sound recordings. For audio materials, use RDA or PBCore controlled vocabularies for stating information in <physdescstructured> child elements consistently. Both vocabularies are available in the Open Metadata Registry. Terms taken from RDA, PBCore, or any other controlled vocabulary should be identified in the pertinent element's SOURCE attribute and used consistently across all metadata records.

---

[4] Some institutions use the IASA Cataloguing Rules (Milano 1999).

If possible (depending on institutional policy and availability of information), identifying elements and audio-related notes should describe the *original* audio format. If a digital version of the recording is available for listening, a link to the audio file can be provided, along with basic technical information, such as file format, bits per sample, sampling rate, and file size or duration in a <dao> element or element set. The original recording (or the closest generation to it that the institution holds) has both factual and evidentiary value as a content carrier and as an artifact in itself. It is equally important to inform users if changes have been made to recorded content during digitization (e.g., noise reduction, editing).

I have used my own EAD (version 2002) encoding in the following examples, although other staff in the Library of Congress's Recorded Sound Section originally provided the content. The examples are not intended to be prescriptive. Decisions concerning the amount and type of item-level information given in each of the two collections were based not on any ideal of an EAD-structured audio description, but rather on the availability of existing metadata, institutional cataloging priorities, perceived user interest in the content, and available technical assistance when conversion problems arose. Figure 5.3 shows a section of the collection-level description of the Emile Berliner Collection at the Library of Congress. Figure 5.4 is an item-level description of one disc from that collection.[5] The description of the disc derives from an AACR2/MARC catalog record. Figure 5.5 is an item-level record from the Joe Smith Collection at the Library of Congress, oral history interviews on audiocassettes.[6] This EAD record derives from an in-house collection management system. As well as describing the cassette, it references a written transcript of the interview and provides a link to online audio of the interview.

One option for providing detailed, item-level information about a collection's sound recordings despite the lack of specific guidance in DACS and EAD is to use PBCore for individual audio descriptions. For example, an EAD finding aid might include a single series-level description of a group of audiocassettes. That series-level description would include a link to digital listening copies of the audiocassettes in the institution's digital repository. Each listening copy of an audiocassette in the digital repository would be accompanied by an its own item-level PBCore record; in turn, each individual PBCore record would link back to the finding aid in order to provide context.

EAD TOOLS

In addition to the EAD stylesheet resources listed on page 98, archivists have discussed and posted online an abundance of tools and ideas for

---

[5] The full finding aid may be found at
http://findingaids.loc.gov/db/search/xq/searchMferDsc04.xq?_id=loc.mbrsrs.eadmbrs.
rs011001&_start=242&_lines=125. To examine the EAD/XML encoding for the collection, click the Print/Download tab and select Full Text, XML format.

[6] The full finding aid may be found at http://findingaids.loc.gov/db/search/xq/searchMfer02.
xq?_id=loc.mbrsrs.eadmbrs.rs012001&_faSection.

```
<archdesc type="register" level="collection" relatedencoding="MARC21">
     <did>
          <unittitle label="Title" encodinganalog="245$a">Emile Berliner collection
          <unitdate label="Inclusive Dates" type="inclusive" encodinganalog="245$f"
          normal="1871/1965" era="ce" calendar="gregorian">1871-1965</unitdate>
          <origination label="Creator">
               <persname source="lcnaf" encodinganalog="100" role="creator">Berliner, Emile,
               1851-1929</persname>
          </origination>
     <physdesc label="Extent (Sound Recordings)"><extent encodinganalog="300">over 400 sound discs, including
     zinc, copper, celluloid, rubber, shellac, and vinyl pressings and masters, in various speeds, and in sizes ranging from
     5 to 12 inches in diameter</extent>
     </physdesc> …
```

Basic identifying elements at collection level: title, creation date range, creator name, collective physical description.

WEB DISPLAY: ⎯⎯⎯⎯⎯⎯⎯⎯⎯⎯⎯⎯⎯⎯⎯⎯⎯⎯⎯⎯⎯⎯⎯⎯⎯

Title Emile Berliner collection, 1871-1965
Inclusive Dates 1871-1965
Creator Berliner, Emile, 1851-1929
Extent (Sound Recordings) over 400 sound discs, including zinc, copper, celluloid, rubber, shellac, and vinyl pressings and masters, in various speeds, and in sizes ranging from 5 to 12 inches in diameter

Fig. 5.3: Segment of collection-level EAD tagging, with broad physical description of early sound discs, followed by web display of the same content.

```
<c02 level="item"
     <did>
          <container type="disc">Berliner 0504</container>
          <unittitle type="transcribed">Admiral Dewey march, </unittitle> <unitdate>1899 </unitdate>
          <origination label="Composer">
               <persname role="creator" source="lcnaf">Santelmann, William H. (William Henry), 1863-1932</
               persname>
          </origination>
          <physdesc>
               <extent>1 sound disc : </extent><physfacet>analog, 66.4 rpm, mono. ;</physfacet><dimensions>7
               in.</dimensions>
          </physdesc>
          <unitid label="Original issue number">E. Berliner's Gramophone 0504</unitid>
     </did>
     <note><p>Performed by the United States Marine Band; William H. Santelmann, conductor.</p></note>
     <note><p>Recorded at an unknown location, Sept. 20, 1899.</p></note>
     <note><p>Autograph of Santelmann (conductor) inscribed in zinc master.</p></note>
     <daogrp xmlns:xlink="http://www.w3.org/1999/xlink">
          <daoloc xlink:type="locator"
               xlink:href="http://hdl.loc.gov/loc.mbrsrs/berl.130504">
               <daodesc><p>Online digital audio.</p></daodesc>
          </daoloc>
     </daogrp>
</c02>
```

Physical description elements

EAD linking element group. <daoloc> contains URI to linked object; <daodesc> contains display text

WEB DISPLAY: ⎯⎯⎯⎯⎯⎯⎯⎯⎯⎯⎯⎯⎯⎯⎯⎯⎯⎯⎯⎯⎯⎯⎯⎯⎯⎯⎯⎯⎯⎯⎯⎯⎯

DISC Berliner 0504   Admiral Dewey march, 1899
Composer: Santelmann, William H. (William Henry), 1863-1932
1 sound disc : analog, 66.4 rpm, mono. ; 7 in.
Original issue number: E. Berliner's Gramophone 0504
Performed by the United States Marine Band; William H. Santelmann, conductor.
Recorded at an unknown location, Sept. 20, 1899.
Autograph of Santelmann (conductor) inscribed in zinc master.
Online digital audio.

Fig. 5.4: Item-level EAD tagging, with detailed physical description of an early sound disc, followed by web display of the same content.

```
<c01 level="item"
    <did>
            <container type="CASS ">RYN 0159</container>
            <unittitle>Off the record interview with Tony Bennett,<unitdate>1987-09-27</unitdate></unittitle>
            <physdesc><extent>1 analog audiocassette</extent></physdesc>
            <unitid type="MAVISno" label="Local ID number">1836250</unitid>
    </did>
    <note><p>Transcript available in box RPA 00461.</p></note>
    <daogrp xmlns:xlink="http://www.w3.org/1999/xlink">id="magby240XD.rs012001.rs012001.mavis1836250-1-1"
    xlink:type="extended">
            <daoloc xlink:type="locator"
                xlink:href="http://hdl.loc.gov/loc.mbrsrs/rs012001.mavis1836250-1-1">
                <daodesc>
                    <p>Digital content available.</p>
                </daodesc>
            </daoloc>
    </daogrp>
</c01>
```

WEB DISPLAY: ————————————————————————————

cass RYN 0159   Off the record interview with Tony Bennett, 1987-09-27
1 analog audiocassette
Local ID number: 1836250
Transcript available in box RPA 00461.
Digital content available.

Fig. 5.5: Brief item-level EAD description of an audiocassette and accompanying transcript in the Joe Smith Collection, followed by web display of the same content

simplifying the preparation and publication of EAD finding aids. The following are just a few:

- **EADiva** is a helpful EAD website, especially for beginners, that includes a blog, an EAD element list, record examples, and many links to additional resources.
- On the **EAD Listserv,** available at the EAD official website at the Library of Congress, archivists often offer their own stylesheets, snippets of XSLT conversion code, and suggestions for tackling all kinds of encoding and conversion problems.
- It is often easier and far more efficient to use office tools such as spreadsheets and databases rather than XML editing applications to prepare the container list portion of a finding aid. Converting flat spreadsheets to hierarchical component-level EAD descriptions, however, can be a complex undertaking. The tools and writings below simplify the process:
  - Indiana University Libraries, Digital Projects and Services, EAD page. Scroll down to "Using Excel to Assist with Encoding" for instructions and a template.
  - Steady, an open source Ruby on Rails utility "developed by Jason Ronallo as part of his work at North Carolina State University Libraries." A container list prepared in Excel or other spreadsheet application can be exported as a CSV file and converted to EAD XML using this tool.

— "Tutorial—How to Turn a Spreadsheet into the Contents List of an EAD-Encoded Finding Aid" (Callahan 2014).

■ **ArchivesSpace** is an open source, archival collection management and description system for providing access to archives, manuscripts, and digital objects. The result of a 2013 merger of two earlier open source tools, Archivist's Toolkit and Archon, ArchivesSpace includes a variety of management, description, and authority control tools. The tool permits the import of EAD, MARCXML, and CSV data. Output formats include EAD, MARCXML, MODS, Dublin Core, and more. Membership in the ArchivesSpace community is strongly encouraged, but not required. Benefits include documentation, training, community forums, and more. The annual fee is based on repository size and ranges (as of late 2014) from $300 to $7,500.

For more assistance with implementing and publishing EAD finding aids, see Combs et al. 2010.

EAC-CPF (ENCODED ARCHIVAL CONTEXT–CORPORATE BODIES, PERSONS, AND FAMILIES)

Based on the *International Standard Archival Authority Record for Corporate Bodies, Persons, and Families* (ISAAR [CPF]) content standard and maintained by the Society of American Archivists in partnership with the Berlin State Library, EAC-CPF is a structural standard for XML encoding of authority records about persons, corporate bodies, and families relating to archival materials. Although related to EAD, EAC-CPF is an independent system for encoding not only controlled names of people and organizations but also contextual information about them. EAC-CPF descriptions may be linked to other EAC-CPF records for people and organizations or to EAD descriptions of collections created and used by those entities. The standard is not described in detail here because implementation of EAC-CPF is relatively new in the United States. At present, some U.S. archivists encode authority data in EAC-CPF XML descriptions, while others prepare DACS or RDA-compliant authority records in the MARC format.

A multiphase, grant-funded project is under way to establish a centralized body of EAC-CPF authority records, including those from the Library of Congress NAR and VIAF databases (see p. 91). The project will include a national cooperative, hosted by the U.S. National Archives and Records Administration (NARA), for maintaining archival authority data and expanding its research potential (Pitti et al. 2014). When fully realized, the cooperative will provide a matchless source of information about the creators of archival resources.

5.6 DUBLIN CORE INITIATIVE METADATA: STANDARDS AND TOOLS

Originally developed in the mid-1990s, the 15-element Dublin Core metadata set was intended to encourage the description of core properties of online resources. It soon came to be used for any type of physical or electronic resource, and it led to the development of schemas representing more specific communities or resource types. PBCore, for example, was initially developed to describe public broadcasting media assets.

The use of the Dublin Core widened when it became the baseline Open Archives Initiative metadata standard: the Open Archives Initiative Protocol for Metadata Harvesting (OAI-PMH). Beginning in 2000, Dublin Core "application profiles" were developed that extended the core element set with elements and terms considered useful in more specialized standards and communities (such as libraries).

There have been major changes in the Dublin Core since the early 2000s. The Dublin Core Abstract Model (2005, current version 2007) was informed by the World Wide Web Consortium's development of the Resource Description Framework (RDF), a data interchange model that constitutes a key standard in the Semantic Web (or "Web of data"). An extended set of Dublin Core metadata terms has become one of the most widely used RDF vocabularies.

The Dublin Core is used in some collection management and web publication systems (e.g., CONTENTdm, Omeka). One OAI-PMH project to investigate Dublin Core use to increase access to electronic collection materials is OAIster, an OCLC union database of more than 30 million records for digital resources. Organizations may upload Dublin Core metadata records to OAIster.

DUBLIN CORE TOOLS

A suite of Dublin Core tools is available at http://dublincore.org/tools/.

PBCore is a Dublin Core-Based Metadata Standard. Because PBCore specifically addresses the time-based and technical aspects of audiovisual materials, it is especially useful as a discovery and exchange format for such materials. In addition, PBCore can accommodate complex relationships, such as multiple instances of audiovisual content in various analog and digital formats and generations, segments or clips that form parts of broader items, and programs or episodes that are parts of broader series. For institutions that hold audio, video, and film content and that wish to make it accessible through consistent, sharable, and technically detailed metadata descriptions, PBCore implementation may be appropriate.

The "About" page on the PBCore website contains useful suggestions on adopting PBCore, either by leveraging existing metadata software tools or by building a new PBCore-based catalog system. The site also offers guidance on using common desktop tools to begin building a media catalog. Metadata reuse and exchange are emphasized.

Dublin Core Elements
Title
Creator
Date
Publisher
Type
Format
Description
Identifier
Contributor
Language
Rights
Subject
Coverage
Source
Relation

Table 5.2: Original Dublin Core element set

Version 2.0 anticipates Semantic Web applications through optional inclusion of unique URLs for media resources and characteristics.

PBCore users include Smithsonian Channel, the Pop Up Archive, Northeast Historic Film, the American Archive of Public Broadcasting, and others.

PBCORE TOOLS

Tools used to create and edit PBCore metadata have varied since the standard's first release in 2004. Some institutions use database software, such as Filemaker Pro; others prefer spreadsheets. XML authoring tools may be used as well. Dedicated collection management applications that accommodate PBCore metadata include the following:

- **Archival Management System (AMS)** is an open source, web-based tool that, as explained by Josh Ranger in a contribution to the American Archive of Public Broadcasting blog on September 18, 2014, was initially developed by AVPreserve to manage more than 2.4 million inventory records provided by stations contributing to the American Archive of Public Broadcasting. The American Archive is a collaboration between the Library of Congress and WGBH Boston to digitally preserve some 40,000 hours of American public radio and television content from the 1950s through the first decade of the twenty-first century. PBCore is the metadata standard for the project.

  A version of the AMS was developed for the Finnish Institute for Archiving for managing digital preservation of audiovisual materials and newspapers in Finnish cultural heritage institutions, and now AVPreserve has made the source code for AMS available on Github. AMS is for institutions that possess the specified equipment, expertise, and software (including the Linux operating system) required to install and run the tool.

- **CollectiveAccess** is a web-based tool preconfigured for creating and publishing metadata in PBCore and other metadata standards. For a more detailed discussion, see p. 82.

5.7 CONCLUSION

No repository can boast unlimited resources. Even the largest institutions must make difficult decisions and accept compromises when weighing metadata quantity against quality, and in-house collection control against user discovery and access.

Such decisions require an eye toward the future. Discovery tools and portals increasingly provide retrieval across standard metadata systems that can, for a single search, locate EAD finding aids, MARC catalog records, and metadata for digital objects. Many cultural heritage institutions already make use of such tools. Emerging web discovery approaches aim to uncover hidden collections and bring scattered resources together in new ways. Linked data technologies, in particular, will change how metadata are provided and used across the Internet. Libraries, archives, and museums are especially interested in linked *open* data. See Voss 2012 for more information on open, web-based cultural heritage metadata.

Although there is no easy descriptive standard that answers all needs, knowledge sharing and collaboration, mapping and conversion options, aggregation portals and services, and the promise of even a partially realized Semantic Web are coming together to make metadata go further. The key is informed selection of tools, detail of description, and standards that not only serve current user and repository needs, but also, because of their consistency and interoperability, may be adapted to future needs and technologies.[7]

REFERENCES

All URLs are current as of May 1, 2015

American Archive of Public Broadcasting website. Available at http://americanarchive.org/.

American Folklore Society Ethnographic Thesaurus. Open Folklore website. Available at http://openfolklore.org/et/.

American Library Association. 2014. *Automating Libraries: A Selected Annotated Bibliography.* ALA Library Fact Sheet 21. Chicago: American Library Association. Last updated October 2014. Available at http://www.ala.org/tools/libfactsheets/alalibraryfactsheet21.

American Library Association, Canadian Library Association, and CILIP. 2010 (with ongoing releases). RDA: Resource Description & Access Toolkit. Developed by the Joint Steering Committee for Development of RDA (JSC). Online toolkit and print version subscription and purchase information available at http://www.rdatoolkit.org/. RDA record examples in MARC format may be viewed at no charge at http://www.rdatoolkit.org/examples/MARC.

Anglo-American Cataloguing Rules, 2nd ed. 2002, 2005r. Prepared under the direction of the Joint Steering Committee for Revision of AACR, a committee of the American Library Association, Canadian Library Association, and Chartered Institute of Library and Information Professionals. Ottawa: Canadian Library Association. Chicago: American Library Association.

ArchiveGrid. OCLC (Online Computer Library Center). Available at http://beta.worldcat.org/archivegrid/.

ArchivesSpace website. Available at http://www.archivesspace.org/.

AudioVisual Collaborative Cataloging. "Sandbox" version available at http://www.avpreserve.com/tools/avcc. Sample layouts used by AVCC may be viewed at the website of an earlier version of the tool at http://keepingcollections.org/avcc-cataloging-toolkit/.

---

[7] The author would like to thank Casey Davis, Alan Gevinson, and Mike Rush for their expertise and assistance.

AVID (Audio-Visual and Image Database) website. Available at http://library.ufl.edu/spec/AVID/.

BIBFRAME (Bibliographic Framework Initiative) official website. Available at: http://www.loc.gov/bibframe/.

Blue Ribbon Task Force on Sustainable Digital Preservation and Access. 2010. *Sustainable Economics for a Digital Planet: Ensuring Long-Term Access to Digital Information*. Available at http://brtf.sdsc.edu/biblio/BRTF_Final_Report.pdf.

Callahan, Maureen. 2014. "Tutorial—How to Turn a Spreadsheet into the Contents List of an EAD-Encoded Finding Aid." Available at http://icantiemyownshoes.wordpress.com/2014/03/04/tutorial-how-to-turn-a-spreadsheet-into-the-contents-list-of-an-ead-encoded-finding-aid/.

CollectiveAccess website. Available at: http://collectiveaccess.org/.

Combs, Michele, Mark A. Matienzo, Merrilee Proffitt, and Lisa Spiro. 2010. *Over, Under, Around, and Through: Getting Around Barriers to EAD Implementation*. Report produced by OCLC Research in support of the RLG Partnership. Available at www.oclc.org/research/publications/library/2010/2010-04.pdf.

Cornell University. 2014. "Hit the Ground Running! RDA Training for Music Catalogers: Training in 2014. A guide to the RDA Preconference at the Music Library Association 2013 meeting." Available at http://guides.library.cornell.edu/c.php?g=32270&p=203375.

Dublin Core Metadata Initiative. A project of the Association for Information Science and Technology (ASIS&T). Available at http://dublincore.org/.

EAC-CPF (Encoded Archival Context–Corporate Bodies, Persons, and Families) website. Available at http://eac.staatsbibliothek-berlin.de/.

EAD (Encoded Archival Description) official website (last modified August 9, 2013). Available at http://www.loc.gov/ead/.

EADiva: A Plain Talking EAD Tag Library. Developed by Ruth Kitchin Tillman. Available at http://eadiva.com/.

Fox, Michael J. 2002. *EAD Cookbook*. Available via http://saa-ead-roundtable.github.io/.

Getty Research Institute. *Art & Architecture Thesaurus Online*. Available at http://www.getty.edu/research/tools/vocabularies/aat/index.html.

Getty Research Institute. Getty Vocabularies. Available at http://www.getty.edu/research/tools/vocabularies/.

Gueguen, Gretchen, Vitor Manoel Marques da Fonseca, Daniel V. Pitti, and Claire Sibille-de Grimoüard. 2013. "Toward an International Conceptual Model for Archival Description: A Preliminary Report from the International Council on Archives' Experts Group on Archival Description." *American Archivist* 76 (Fall/Winter): 566–582.

Indiana University Libraries, Digital Projects and Services. 2012. "Using Excel to Assist with Encoding" (last updated December 13). Available at http://dlib.indiana.edu/services/metadata/activities/eadDocumentation.shtml.

International Council on Archives. 2004. *International Standard Archival Authority Record for Corporate Bodies, Persons and Families (ISAAR[CPF])*, 2nd ed. PDF version available at http://www.icacds.org.uk/eng/isaar2nd edn-e_3_1.pdf.

International Council on Archives. 1999. *General International Standard of Archival Description (ISAD[G])*, 2nd ed. PDF version available at http://www.icacds.org.uk/eng/ISAD%28G%29.pdf.

Koth, Mickey. 2015. "Music Cataloging at Yale." Last updated February 27, 2015. Available at http://www.library.yale.edu/cataloging/music/musicat.htm.

Library of Congress. 2009. *Understanding MARC Bibliographic: Machine-Readable Cataloging*. Washington, D.C.: Library of Congress. Available at http://www.loc.gov/marc/umb/.

Library of Congress Authorities. 2014. Available at http://authorities.loc.gov/.

Library of Congress Cataloger's Desktop website. Available at http://www.loc.gov/cds/desktop/.

Library of Congress Linked Data Service. Available at http://id.loc.gov.

Library of Congress (LC) RDA Training Materials. Available at http://www.loc.gov/catworkshop/RDA%20training%20materials/LC%20RDA%20Training/LC%20RDA%20course%20table.html.

Linked Open Data in Libraries, Archives, and Museums (LODLAM) website. Available at http://lodlam.net/.

MARC21. 1999–2014. Washington, D.C.: Library of Congress, Cataloging Distribution Service; Ottawa: Library and Archives Canada. Available at http://www.loc.gov/marc/bibliographic/ecbdhome.html.

MarcEdit, version 5.9. Developed by Terry Reese. Available at http://marcedit.reeset.net/.

Martyniak, Cathy. 2013. "AVID: A Tool for Audiovisual and Image Collections." *Recorded Sound, the Newsletter of the Recorded Sound Roundtable of the Society of American Archivists* (Spring): 8. Available at http://www2.archivists.org/sites/all/files/2013_Spring_RecordedSoundNewsletter.pdf.

Milano, Mary, ed. 1999. *IASA Cataloguing Rules*. Amsterdam: International Association of Sound and Audiovisual Archives. Print version no longer available; online version available at http://www.iasa-web.org/cataloguing-rules.

MIREX 2014 website (last modified September 24, 2014). Available at http://www.music-ir.org/mirex/wiki/MIREX_HOME.

MODS (Metadata Object Description) official website (last modified July 9, 2013). Available at http://www.loc.gov/standards/mods/.

Music Library Association. 2015. "Metadata for Music Resources. "Developed and maintained by the Metadata Subcommittee of the Music Library Association's Bibliographic Control Committee. Clearinghouse on metadata standards and tools relating to musical resources. Available at http://www.musiclibraryassoc.org/page/bcc_meta_resources.

Music Library Association. 2014. *Best Practices for Music Cataloging Using RDA and MARC21*, version 1.0.1. Prepared by the RDA Music Implementation Task Force, Bibliographic Control Committee, Music Library Association. February 21. Incorporated into the RDA Toolkit in 2014. Available at http://www.rdatoolkit.org/sites/default/files/rda_best_practices_for_music_cataloging-v1_0_1-140401.pdf.

Music Library Association. Bibliographic Control Committee website. Available at http://bcc.musiclibraryassoc.org/bcc.html.

National Union Catalog of Manuscript Collections (NUCMC). Library of Congress. Available at http://www.loc.gov/coll/nucmc/index.html.

NISO (National Information Standards Organization). 2004. *Understanding Metadata*. Available at http://www.niso.org/publications/press/UnderstandingMetadata.pdf.

OAIster database. Available at http://www.oclc.org/oaister.en.html?urlm=168646 or search the database at http://oaister.worldcat.org/ (OAIster records only) or http://www.worldcat.org/ (the complete WorldCat union database).

OCLC (Online Computer Library Center) website. Available at https://oclc.org/.

OCLC (Online Computer Library Center) WorldCat database. Available at http://www.oclc.org/worldcat.en.html.

Omeka website. Available at http://omeka.org/.

Open Archives Initiative (OAI) website. Available at http://www.openarchives.org/.

Open Metadata Registry website. Available at http://metadataregistry.org/.

OpenRefine website. Available at http://openrefine.org/.

PBCore. Public Broadcasting Metadata Dictionary Project. Available at http://pbcore.org/ and at Github, https://github.com/WGBH/PBCore2.0.

Pitti, Daniel, Rachael Hu, Ray Larson, Brian Tingle, and Adrian Turner. 2014. "Social Networks and Archival Context: From Project to Cooperative Archival Program." *Journal of Archival Organization* 12 (1-2). Available at http://www.tandfonline.com/doi/full/10.1080/15332748.2015.999544#.VSr6jJM8qDk.

PREMIS (preservation metadata) official website (last updated September 14, 2014). Available at http://www.loc.gov/standards/premis/index.html.

Society of American Archivists. 2013. *Describing Archives: A Content Standard (DACS)*, 2nd ed. Chicago: Society of American Archivists. Available at http://files.archivists.org/pubs/DACS2E-2013.pdf.

Society of American Archivists. SAA EAD Roundtable. Available at Github. http://saa-ead-roundtable.github.io/.

Society of American Archivists. Standards: Encoded Archival Description (EAD). Available at http://www2.archivists.org/groups/technical-subcommittee-on-encoded-archival-description-ead/encoded-archival-description-ead.

Steady. Developed by Jason Ronallo. Accessed October 9, 2014. Available at http://steady2.herokuapp.com.

Van Malssen, Kara. 2014. BIBFRAME AV Modeling Study: Defining a Flexible Model for Description of Audiovisual Resources. Available at http://www.loc.gov/bibframe/pdf/bibframe-avmodelingstudy-may15-2014.pdf.

VIAF (Virtual International Authority File) website. Available at http://viaf.org/.

Voss, John. 2012. "Radically Open Cultural Heritage Data on the Web. Museums and the Web 2012." Available at http://www.museumsandtheweb.com/mw2012/papers/radically_open_cultural_heritage_data_on_the_w.

World Wide Web Consortium (W3C). 2014. *Standards: Semantic Web*. Available at http://www.w3.org/standards/semanticweb/.

W3Schools XML Tutorial. Available at http://www.w3schools.com/xml/.

ADDITIONAL RESOURCES

Mazé, Elinor A. 2012. "Metadata: Best Practices for Oral History Access and Preservation." In *Oral History in the Digital Age*, edited by D. Boyd, S. Cohen, B. Rakerd, and D. Rehberger. Institute of Library and Museum Services. Available at http://ohda.matrix.msu.edu/2012/06/metadata/.

Riley, Jenn. 2009. "Seeing Standards: A Visualization of the Metadata Universe." Available at http://www.dlib.indiana.edu/~jenlrile/metadatamap/.

CHAPTER 6

Preservation Reformatting

By William Chase

Carrier deterioration and technical obsolescence make reformatting to digital files the only way to ensure future access to legacy format sound recordings. This chapter covers best practices for target preservation formats and provides guidance on making the decision to reformat in-house or outsource, working with vendors, and obtaining funds for reformatting projects.

Preservation reformatting is the process of transferring the essence or intellectual content of an object to another medium. With audio collections, recorded sound content is transferred from one carrier to another without degradation or alteration of the original content. Done correctly, the transfer of analog or carrier-dependent digital audio formats to digital files should not introduce any signal degradation. Given the instability of all digital audio carriers, such as optical discs or Digital Audio Tape (DAT), uncompressed digital audio files are the preferred format for preservation.

A successful preservation transfer captures the essence of the audio as it is accurately reproduced from its carrier. Reformatting a sound recording without compromising the authenticity of its content requires the use of well maintained and properly aligned playback machines; the correct stylus or playback head; equalization and other decoding mechanisms, such as noise reduction, as needed; and high-quality analog-to-digital converters to record uncompressed digital audio.

Carrier restoration for optimal playback, such as disc cleaning or tape baking, is often a necessary step in preservation reformatting and may already be part of conservation efforts. However, subjectively removing imperfections or interpolating lost material in the recording to optimize its sound quality is *restoration*, not preservation, and should be undertaken only after a true preservation copy has been made. Restoration processes such as hum removal, de-clicking, and noise reduction are helpful

A restored version of a sound recording cannot be considered a preservation copy.

for improving the usability of unintelligible audio recordings, but these processes also compromise the authenticity of the audio. A restored version of a sound recording cannot be considered a preservation master.

6.1 CONVERSION TO DIGITAL FILES

A digital preservation master should be encoded and stored in an uncompressed file format for two reasons: first, data reduction through the use of "lossy" (i.e., compressed) codecs will result in an irreversible loss of audio data; and second, it is unknown whether the lossy information will be decodable in the future. Pulse code modulation (or linear PCM) is the recommended encoding stream for digitized audio and is generally the default encoding scheme for WAVE (Waveform Audio File Format) .wav files.

The Broadcast Wave Format (BWF) .wav file is the de facto standard for digital archival audio. Like standard WAVE files, BWF files keep the .wav file extension. It is nonproprietary, and because BWF is limited to two file types of audio data (linear PCM and MPEG), it is interoperable with a wide range of applications and operating systems.

Advice on the naming of files may be found in chapter 7.

FILE USES

Three files are typically produced in the preservation reformatting process: the preservation master, access (or production) master, and access copy (Table 6.1). The preservation master is a digital surrogate for the original recording and should accurately capture all information in the source. This requires accurate playback of the source and high-resolution digital capture.

The access master, derived from the preservation master file, is typically a lower resolution, uncompressed BWF file from which all access copies—physical and file-based—are derived. Compact disc (CD) resolution (44.1 kHz sampling rate with a bit depth of 16 bits per channel) is common for access masters, as it allows for easy duplication of CDs and compressed MP3 files. However, if access masters are intended for use in a production environment, or for research and analysis, they should be created at a higher resolution than CD specifications. An access master may also be "restored," that is, optimized for sound quality and intelligibility to benefit the user. Audio levels might be adjusted, and digital signal processing such as de-noising and de-clicking applied as needed.

The access copy is the final deliverable to the user. It is commonly in the form of a compressed file, such as an MP3, for online streaming or download. An access copy may also be in a physical format, such as a CD.

Access masters and all copies derived from them can be efficiently created through batch processing tools found in most digital audio editing software or with standalone applications. Recommended storage practices for each of these file types are discussed in chapter 7.

Preservation Master	Access Master	Access Copy
High-resolution, uncompressed BWF	BWF derived from preservation master; possibly lower resolution	Physical copy or digital file derived from access master; may be compressed for online streaming
No signal processing	Signal processing allowed	
No edits other than trimming the beginning and end of file; may contain only a segment of the original recording if there are format changes or problems during the transfer	May be edited for content (e.g., remove long durations of silence; combine multiple files to create single intellectual unit; redact restricted information)	

Table 6.1: Characteristics of preservation master, access master, and access copy

SAMPLING RATE AND BIT DEPTH

In general, the accepted specifications for audio digitized from analog sources are a sampling rate of 96 kHz and a bit depth of 24 bits per channel. The sampling rate sets the range of the frequency spectrum of audio captured during the digitization process. The International Association of Sound and Audiovisual Archives (IASA) recommends a minimum sampling rate of 48 kHz, yet some projects may benefit from a sampling rate higher than 96 kHz (IASA 2009). When the appropriate conversion specifications are unclear, it can be helpful to develop a familiarity with the content and intended use of the material. Digitizing at a higher sampling rate facilitates removal of unwanted artifacts for access copies in the digital domain and the capture of sounds outside the human hearing range needed for research purposes, such as wildlife sounds.

Digital originals, such as optical discs, DAT, or MiniDiscs, should be kept at their native sampling rate and bit depth. There is no benefit in audio quality to up-sampling a digital recording that is fixed at a lower resolution, and it results in excessively large files that waste storage space.

6.2 METADATA FOR REFORMATTING

> We can make the highest quality transfers, with the finest equipment available, but unless we record and maintain the requisite metadata, essentially all we have is a bunch of files with an uncertain past and an even less certain future. (Casey and Gordon 2007, 62)

A digitized collection should be framed by descriptive, administrative, and structural metadata. Descriptive metadata are discussed in chapter 5 of this guide. The focus in this chapter will be on administrative and structural metadata as they pertain to audio preservation: their role in the preservation process, ways they can be created, and where they can be stored. Understanding these concepts can inform decisions about metadata workflows for in-house digitization and facilitate communication with a vendor about metadata needs.

ADMINISTRATIVE METADATA

Included in the administrative metadata is information that assists in the management of a digital file, such as how it was created, its provenance, its technical specifications, and any access restrictions that may be associated with it.

Technical Metadata. Understanding the object to be preserved, whether it is a reel of tape or a digital file, is essential to ensure proper care in the near term and to inform future migration. Technical metadata describe specific attributes of an audio object. For a physical source object to be digitized, some of these attributes include the following:

- Material composition (layer types, track configuration)
- Dimensions (disc diameter, tape gauge, unwound tape length, shape)
- Audio signal characteristics (playback speed, equalization, sound field)
- Condition (soft binder syndrome, delamination, deformation, contamination)

Common digital audio file attributes include the following:

- Sampling rate
- Bit depth
- Number of channels
- Data encoding type
- Duration
- File size
- File type
- Checksum value

Some of these metadata can be captured and stored automatically, although documenting unique physical audio objects tends to be more labor-intensive. As a collection manager, it is important to consider how such metadata will be used in the ongoing preservation process of your collections:

- What do I need to know to play back and capture the audio content now?
- What will I need to know to migrate the audio content in the future?

The notes written on a tape box, sometimes years ago—speed, tracking configuration, equalization, mono, or stereo—take away much of the guesswork surrounding proper playback of a recording by describing its basic attributes. These notes may have supported research by fieldworkers or interoperability in a broadcast environment in the short term, but they also provide future users with some guidance on accessing the content. Documenting digital file attributes in the preservation process will serve the same purposes.

Schemas for documenting audio object technical metadata provide guidance in preserving this information so that the recording, regardless of format, is usable. PBCore and *AES57-2011: Audio Engineering Society standard for audio metadata – Audio object structures for preservation and restoration* are two commonly used standards for describing technical attributes of audio objects. PBCore was developed by the public broadcasting community, but can be applied to audiovisual collections in any repository setting. It is based on the Dublin Core metadata element set and provides plenty of fields to sufficiently describe technical metadata. AES57-2011 is a vocabulary expressed as an XML schema designed specifically for the purpose of describing technical attributes of all audio formats. The schema is flexible in that there are few required elements: at a minimum one can simply indicate the format of an audio recording, or document detailed information about dimensions and material composition, digital file properties, playback and signal characteristics, or condition notes. Although AES57-2011 provides richer, more structured audio object metadata, it requires a thorough understanding of audio formats to use it effectively.

Technical metadata about digital audio files can be automatically extracted from the files and exported in a variety of formats including CSV or XML files using tools such as MediaInfo, BWF MetaEdit, or the PBCore Instantiationizer.

Digital Provenance. Sometimes called the process history, digital provenance describes the tools and processes used to create a digital file, the responsible entity, as well as when and where the process events occurred. Digital provenance metadata support both immediate workflow coordination and future auditing of digital surrogates. Examples of audio digitization events and tools are shown in Table 6.2.

Event	Tool
Playback of source recording	Playback machine and settings (speed, equalization, reproduction levels, outputs)
Digital conversion of source	Analog-to-digital converter and settings (sampling rate, bit depth, level trim, inputs)
Capture of digitized signal	Digital recorder and settings (sampling rate, bit depth)
Creation of derivative files	Software utilities and settings (sampling rate conversion, dither, other digital signal processing)

Table 6.2: Examples of audio digitization events and tools

The extent to which digital provenance metadata are captured will vary, depending on the scope of collection(s) to be digitized, digitization personnel, and equipment. The Library of Congress digiProvMD schema, though not widely used, is a useful template for recording process history.

Process history may also be annotated in other schemas, such as PBCore, or in a custom spreadsheet or database. The Audio Engineering Society has yet to publish its AES-X098C standard, which is an XML schema that captures every event, device, and configuration setting of the preservation process in minute detail. Basic digital provenance metadata may be embedded into a BWF file header (see Embedded Metadata, below).

Rights Management. Documenting the copyright status and any use restrictions in the preservation reformatting process will help collection managers and users make informed preservation and access decisions. Extra care should be taken to ensure that digitized recordings with restricted content are not disseminated in violation of copyright law or donor agreements. Rights information may be documented in descriptive metadata, a collection finding aid, or a Metadata Encoding Transmission Standard (METS) document; it may be embedded in the file header; or it may be noted in some combination of these.

STRUCTURAL METADATA

For digital audio files, structural metadata serve many purposes:

- Provide context for an audio file as part of a larger intellectual unit, e.g., Side B of LP "XYZ"
- Provide instructions for sequencing parts of a larger intellectual unit, e.g., the second of two audio files that make up the whole
- Allow users to navigate to points of interest within a single audio file or among multiple files, e.g., where individual songs begin and end within Side B
- Convey the relationships between master and derivative files, e.g., XYZ_B.mp3 is a derivative of XYZ_B.wav
- Convey the relationships between the audio and other related files, media, and metadata, e.g., XYZ_B_L.TIFF is the disc label of the B side of the LP

Types of structural metadata include the following:

- Directory structures and file names
- Project file exports, such as generic edit decision lists or AES31-3 Audio Decision Lists (Audio Engineering Society 2008)
- Track markers
- Time stamps
- METS document

A sound recording is often more than just one audio object. There may be multiple segments, associated notes, and images. METS not only supports the aggregation of metadata from one or more objects, but also expresses the relationships between objects. In addition, METS can be used as a wrapper for deposit into a digital repository or for dissemination.

EMBEDDED METADATA

Most simply, embedded metadata can be defined as metadata that are stored inside the same file, or container, that stores the essence to which the metadata refer. Chris Lacinak writes, "In many ways one can think of embedded metadata as the file-based domain's equivalent of labels, annotations, and written documentation stored inside of material housing, or even as 'in-program' annotations such as audio and video slates at the head of a recording" (Lacinak 2014, 1).

Every file format has distinct embedded metadata specifications and fields. For instance, the options for embedding metadata in WAVE files differ from those for embedding metadata in MP3 files (AudioVisual Preservation Solutions 2009; ID3). Embedded metadata are what enable the display of information, such as artist, album, and title in applications that play back audio files. The primary goal of embedding metadata for the purpose of preservation should be to identify the object when it is dissociated from its external metadata, identify the holding organization, identify the data source that holds information about the object, and identify the copyright status. The Federal Agencies Digitization Guidelines Initiative (FADGI) published guidelines that recommended the use of broadcast audio extension (BEXT) and list-info chunks, or data segments that comprise WAVE files, to store embedded metadata in files that result from the digitization process (Federal Agencies Audio-Visual Working Group 2012). Files that are acquired, rather than created through digitization, likely have existing embedded metadata that was generated by people, software, or hardware prior to acquisition. In the interest of maintaining the authenticity of the original object, these files should undergo a different process with regard to embedded metadata.

BWF File Header Fields. The BEXT chunk allows for embedding a rich set of important metadata fields in the BWF file header, including a unique source identifier (USID), description of file content, digital provenance, and time stamp for sequencing of files when necessary. Table 6.3 shows commonly used BEXT fields. The Federal Agencies Digitization Guidelines Initiative has published guidelines for embedding metadata in Broadcast WAVE files with additional usage examples.

BWF MetaEdit is an open source tool useful for embedding metadata in WAVE files. Some audio editing software also natively supports BWF metadata.[1] The European Broadcasting Union (2011) BWF specification provides further details on the use of the BEXT chunk. Ultimately, the use of these embedded metadata fields should most benefit the institution. For example, application of a metadata field need not follow European Broadcasting Union recommendations if the usage benefit to the institution outweighs any need for external interoperability (Figures 6.1 and 6.2).

Resource Interchange File Format (RIFF) INFO Chunk Fields. In addition to the BEXT chunk, the RIFF WAVE header provides an INFO chunk, which allows further opportunities for embedding descriptive and technical metadata, such as title (INAM), performer (IART), location (IARL), or copyright metadata (ICOP). (See Figure 6.3.) FADGI recommends the use of the IARL archival location field to repeat the value stored in the Originator field in the BEXT chunk, "which records the entity responsible for the creation, maintenance, [and] preservation" (Federal Agencies Audio-Visual Working Group 2012, 12). INFO chunk fields can be very useful for asset management, access, and discovery (Figure 6.4). Some applications can map INFO tags to ID3 tags in MP3 file access copies.

A discussion of preservation metadata and PREMIS appears in chapter 7.

---

[1] For a study on the support of embedded metadata in different audio recording software applications, see ARSC Technical Committee 2011.

BEXT Field	Explanation and Common Usage	Example Data
Description	Free text field (256 character limit) to store identifier information about the audio, such as title, file name and use, URL, or URI.	Friday performances at the 1993 Florida Folk Festival (Main Stage) (Tape 6)
Originator	Free text field (32 character limit) to indicate the creator of the digital audio file, usually the name of the institution or specific entity within the institution.	US, NPR/UMD
Originator Reference	Unique identifier that may be supplied by the institution or generated by a digital audio recorder or software.	USSDV47030511601510370008304801 Unique identifier generated by digital recorder
Origination Date	Date, in YYYY-MM-DD format, on which the digital file was created (a useful component of the file's provenance)	2015-01-01
Time Reference and Time Reference (Translated)	Time code in sample count. If the file is part of a multipart sequence, the Time Reference field should reflect its exact position in the sequence of audio files.	321332734 Time Reference value expressed in number of samples 00:27:53.607 Time Reference (Translated) value expressed in hours, minutes, seconds
Coding History	Signal chain from which the digital file was created, starting with the analog or digital source. There are six elements that can be included in the coding history: 1. A = coding algorithm (analog, PCM, etc.) 2. F = sampling frequency in Hz 3. B = bit rate (for MPEG only) 4. W = word length or bit depth 5. M = mode or sound field (mono, stereo) 6. T = free text to describe playback and capture equipment	Example syntax: A = [analog, PCM for digital], M = [mono or stereo], T = [playback or capture device; parameters; format information] A = ANALOGUE, M = stereo, T = Studer A810; SN6083; 7.5 ips; open reel tape A = PCM, F = 96000, W = 24, M = stereo, T = Lynx Hilo; SN3112122134; A/D The first line shows that a stereo open reel tape was played back on a Studer A810 with a serial number of 6083 at 7.5 inches per second. The second line shows that the audio was digitized to PCM at 96 kHz sampling rate and bit depth of 24 bits using a Lynx Hilo analog-to-digital converter with a serial number of 3112122134.

Table 6.3: Commonly used BEXT fields

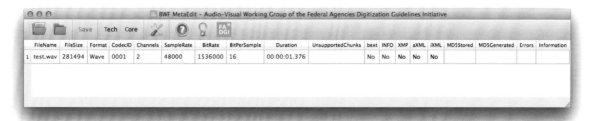

Fig. 6.1: BWF MetaEdit technical metadata fields

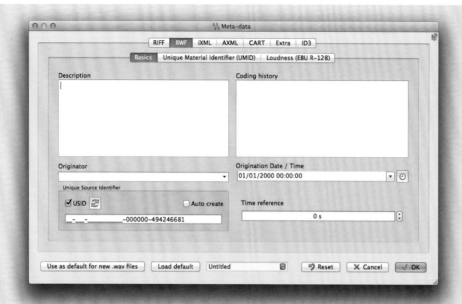

Fig. 6.2: BWF input screen in WaveLab

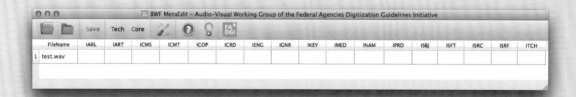

Fig. 6.3: BWF MetaEdit INFO fields

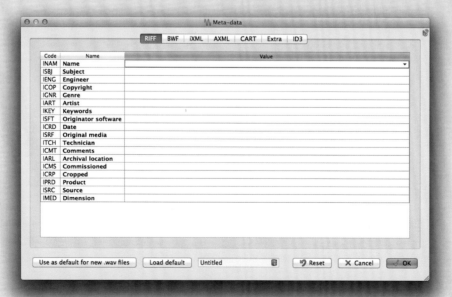

Fig. 6.4: RIFF INFO chunk input screen in WaveLab

6.3 DIGITIZATION: IN-HOUSE AND VENDOR OUTSOURCING

Once the materials to be digitized have been identified, your digital reformatting project is defined by its purpose and scope. Are you digitizing only for preservation, or will the project provide wide access to the material? Will the digitized audio need to be restored for intelligibility?

Before any digitization takes place, the items should be inventoried and reasonably described if they have not been already. Formats should be identified, and conservation issues noted. When you know how much of each format is in the collection, you can decide whether it is feasible to digitize in-house. If the collection is continually growing or the same few formats are regularly accessed, purchasing playback equipment may be justified for access and description as well as reformatting. The IASA 2009 guidelines and Casey and Gordon 2007 offer in-depth guidance and technical details about the necessary capabilities of an internal audio preservation infrastructure.

A project timeline is essential to meet budgetary, access, or other project deadlines. It is also important to define the project scope for both in-house and outsourced projects to ensure that the right personnel, equipment, and time are available when needed.

CONSIDERATIONS FOR IN-HOUSE DIGITIZATION

The availability of personnel, equipment, facilities, time, and funding are all critical in deciding whether to digitize recorded sound collections in-house.

Personnel. Preservation reformatting of audio material requires specialized skill sets in multiple fields that are not commonly found in many institutions. First, audio engineers with a knowledge of both legacy recording formats and their corresponding playback equipment, as well as the principles of digital audio, should be available to oversee the transfers. This expert supervision is a measure of quality assurance to ensure that the content of the recording will be properly preserved without the risks of improper handling that may cause unnecessary damage to the original carrier.

Second, it is helpful if an audio engineer, sometimes in collaboration with an electrical engineer, is available to see that equipment is properly installed and maintained. Equipment that is not properly installed and calibrated will lead to degradation in playback quality and may cause damage to original recordings. In addition, equipment must be well maintained over time; technicians may be needed not only to perform basic cleaning and alignment, but also to replace parts and to carry out advanced refurbishing with specialized tools and test equipment.

Finally, collaboration with your institution's information technology (IT) department will ensure successful maintenance of digitized content for the long term. IT personnel will be able to help estimate file storage needs and costs, allocate the appropriate storage systems, and

The availability of personnel, equipment, facilities, time, and funding are all critical in deciding whether to digitize recorded sound collections in-house.

implement a digital repository or asset management system if one is not in place already.

Equipment. Depending on the collections to be digitized, a wide range of equipment may be required. Most audio collections contain at least two or three formats, and in-house digitization requires the correct playback equipment for each format. In some cases, collections are accessioned along with playback equipment, which can be a huge benefit for formats such as DAT that are best reproduced on the machine on which they were recorded. By conducting a comprehensive survey of all audio holdings to be digitized, the collection manager can ensure that all proper playback equipment, converters, software, supplies, and maintenance items are available for the project to be successful.

In general, only modern, professional playback machines and converters should be used for preservation reformatting. Although this handbook is not meant to be a purchasing guide for audio equipment, there are a few basic qualities of professional-grade gear:

- *Transparency*: The source recording will be reproduced without any added noise, distortion, or other artifacts from the converter and playback machine.
- *Durability*: It is built to last; most playback equipment that will be used for legacy formats such as open reel tape is 30–40 years old already.
- *Reliability*: The likelihood of the component working below specification or completely failing is less than that of consumer audio products.

More detailed guidelines have been published in IASA-TC04 (IASA 2009); they address exact technical specifications necessary when building an audio digitization system.[2] All equipment should be fully tested and calibrated before being used to play unique archival recordings.

In addition to playback equipment and converters, supplies and accessories are required. Examples of these include splicing tape, leader tape, razors, a splicing block, cotton swabs, isopropyl alcohol, and a head degausser for open reel tape; spare cassette shells for rehousing damaged cassettes; and a variety of styli and disc-cleaning brushes and solutions for grooved discs. Some of these items present ongoing costs.

Facilities. The space available for audio transfer work is an important consideration for in-house digitization. Ideally, the space will be at least somewhat acoustically isolated so that the engineer can conduct his or her work without disturbing others, while also having the ability to listen critically when needed.

Time. Reformatting audio recordings often takes approximately three times as long as the run time of the recording. That is to say, a recording

---

[2] The Federal Agencies Digitization Guidelines Initiative (FADGI) A/V Working Group outlines different acceptable performance levels for audio digitization systems at http://www.digitizationguidelines.gov/guidelines/digitize-audioperf.html, and IASA 2009, chapter 2, outlines very specific technical specifications for analog-to-digital converters at http://www.iasa-web.org/tc04/key-digital-principles.

that is one hour in duration will take approximately three hours to digitize. The tasks that must be accomplished in those three hours include audio object inspection, alignment of playback equipment, signal extraction, and post-processing tasks, such as quality control, embedding of metadata, checksum calculation, and ingest into long-term storage. However, good workflow development can reduce time spent on reformatting processes. Throughput of signal capture can be increased through parallel transfer workflows, and post-digitization processes can be automated through scripting.

Funding. Developing an in-house audio digitization program involves much more than a one-time startup cost. You must plan for continual staffing, equipment maintenance, and supplies, as well as the ongoing storage, management, and potential migration of digital files and metadata. Although a grant may support some initial startup costs, it is necessary to budget for ongoing costs internally.

OUTSOURCING AUDIO DIGITIZATION

In many cases, it will be more cost-effective to outsource your collection to a digitization vendor. The learning curve for selecting a vendor is less complex than that for designing and building an in-house digitization program, but selecting the right vendor for your project still requires research.

Selecting a Vendor. Word of mouth from other institutions and private collection owners is a good place to start. All qualified vendors provide references from previous clients that you can contact.

The learning curve for selecting a vendor is less complex than that for designing and building an in-house digitization program, but selecting the right vendor for your project still requires research.

When reviewing vendor options, you will need to identify who will be transferring your audio assets; what their qualifications are; and what playback equipment, converters, and other treatments they will use. Many vendors make this information readily available online or in other informational literature. In addition to reviewing personnel and equipment, you should make sure that the vendor's facilities have the space and proper shelving to accommodate your collection. Storage facilities should be clean, secure, and climate-controlled, and a disaster preparedness plan should be in place.

Writing a Vendor Request for Proposal (RFP). While most vendors will work with you to develop project specifications, it is helpful to know what to expect. The client should include in the RFP submitted to vendors a project vocabulary, a project scope, and technical specifications. In addition, the client should provide the vendor with some history and context for the collection: the content type (e.g., music, spoken word, broadcast, field recordings), any known preservation issues, and recording format varieties and quantities.

In the statement of work included in the RFP, you must clearly define the purpose of the digitization project, whether it is for preservation, access, use in production or exhibition, or some combination of these. The purpose of the project will determine the types of digital files that are produced and their associated metadata. Also included within a statement of work is how and when the vendor will complete tasks during each phase of the project, from shipping of originals to return of the final deliverables. A model for an RFP for audio preservation can be found at Lacinak 2015.

Another factor to be considered in selecting a vendor is the estimated time for project completion. Some vendors may have a large backlog of work and will not be able to complete your project when you need it. Including a timeline in your RFP will help you select the right vendor to meet your needs and set realistic expectations for the project. An RFP timeline may include dates for the following:

- Bidder questions and client responses
- Proposal submission
- Award of contract
- Shipment of materials to vendor
- Submission of files to client
- Review of files and metadata by client
- Final project completion

Some technical specifications for audio reformatting include the following:

- Definitions of master and service copies
- Target file types for masters and derivatives
- Sampling rates and bit depths for audio files
- Directory structures, file names, and persistent identifiers
- Embedded metadata

Developing Project Specifications and Communication. Good communication and clear expectations of the project deliverables, starting with a well-defined statement of work, make for successful relationships with vendors. Before a project gets under way, you must establish appropriate communication channels and a point or points of contact within your institution. Establishing clear expectations for when and how communication should occur and adhering to those expectations will ensure that the project is completed on time and according to specifications. Typically, client and vendor communicate

- On the vendor's receipt of shipments from the client
- Prior to the vendor's shipping deliverables
- At predetermined intervals for regular project updates

Managing Quality Control and Rework. In an ideal scenario, all digital files and metadata arrive from the vendor properly named and with no ambiguity concerning the quality of the transfer work. Although reputable vendors have multiple quality control and quality assurance measures in place, you will need in-house metrics to verify that the job was done correctly. A familiarity with the collection, including durations, content, and overall fidelity of the source material will help you determine if the digital files are complete, named correctly, and transferred properly. Do not hesitate to ask questions or request that items be re-transferred if necessary.

Furthermore, the original media should also be reviewed. The vendor should provide documentation regarding both the restoration of the carrier used in the transfer process and any damage that may have occurred.

If the vendor completes the project satisfactorily, contracting the same vendor for future projects can strengthen quality assurance over time.

Controlling Costs. Whether done in-house or with an external service provider, digitizing audio is costly, and many collection holders are operating on a limited budget. Fortunately, there are ways to reduce costs while improving efficiency when working with a vendor. Many vendors offer discounts for high-volume projects. Once you know the minimum qualifications for a discount, start by identifying large quantities of single formats within your collections. It may be more cost-effective to expand your scope of items to be digitized, but a volume discount will not be worthwhile if the collections to be digitized are not of high value and your institution cannot support the long-term preservation and access responsibilities of the resulting digital assets.

There are ways to reduce costs while improving efficiency when working with a vendor.

Another option for obtaining a quantity discount is to collaborate with other institutions and combine collections under one vendor contract. For example, the cost-per-item for preserving a group of 200 audiocassettes, all with the same metadata requirements, will be significantly less than the cost-per-item for 20 cassettes. Collection managers should be encouraged to create partnerships with other institutions that hold like formats. If your institution is a member of LYRASIS, consider participation in its Digitization Collaborative.

Finally, completing any collection description, inventory, and carrier restoration in-house will reduce the amount of work the vendor must do and potentially save many hours billed to your organization. Providing as much metadata as possible about the collection is a good starting point; at the very least, it leads to more accurate cost estimates. Technical metadata, such as playback speed, equalization type, and tracking configuration, reduce the amount of guesswork by transfer engineers. Providing this information in a format compatible with that of your vendor will reduce the amount of data "housekeeping" required of your vendor and help control the cost of the preservation service. Similarly, historical documentation about the recordings, such as the type of equipment they were recorded on or their recording location, can help vendors make important judgments about the playback of the original and understand any anomalies that may be present in the source recordings. Collection inventories also aid the collection manager in making judgments on how to most effectively establish priorities and ship the items to be digitized. It will be cheaper to bundle like media together than to send collections of mixed formats separately. Chapter 5 offers recommendations on creating inventories for audio collections.

6.4 FUNDING FOR PRESERVATION INITIATIVES

Audio digitization often supports the mission of the holding institution, so requesting funds internally can be justified. Making the business case for audio preservation involves gathering support from a variety of stakeholders, including the upper level of administration. Creating user stories about the value of your recorded sound collections is an effective method for explaining the return on investment for preservation activities. Use cases should illustrate benefits to the institution:

- Research value, uniqueness, and user demand for the content
- Relevance to the institution's larger mission, goals, and vision
- How digitization will raise the institution's profile
- Cost of inaction if the collection is not digitized[3]

Much audio preservation reformatting work is funded by grants and donations. Grants are available from local, national, and international

---

[3] AVPreserve has developed an online "Cost of Inaction" tool that illustrates how preservation efforts will become more expensive over time. Available at https://coi.avpreserve.com/.

Building Your Constituency

Users of your recorded sound collections should be your supporters as well as your patrons. They can become your advocates and your publicists, informing other scholars of the riches in your collection and attesting to the value of your resources to your administrators. Recent years have witnessed a significant growth of scholarly interest in sound recordings among serious researchers, both as subjects themselves, notably in the emerging fields of sound studies and media studies, and as tools serving the study of political and cultural history, literature, historical music performance practice, folklife, and more. Managers of recorded sound collections should be aware of general trends in scholarship that relate to audio and the specific interests of the researchers that use their collections. Responding to these trends and needs will encourage greater use of the collections and prove to potential funders that their support of activities to maintain and preserve the collections serves an ever growing number of beneficiaries.

If your library or archives is part of an educational institution, efforts should be made to inform faculty members of resources in your collection that are related to their field of study or teaching. University faculty members are often uninformed of unique special collections of potential value to their work. You may find that your collections are of value to a faculty member or researcher in a way you never expected. For example, a linguist studying dialects might consult an oral history collection. Researchers might also be working in areas unknown to you and may present an unexpected but welcome acquisition opportunity. Keep in mind, too, that researchers as well as faculty members often welcome the opportunity to deliver lectures and develop public programs that relate to their work with your collections. Your relationships with your researchers can often be mutually beneficial.

The web and social media have become essential media to inform your existing constituency and the public at large of your services, programs, and old and new acquisitions. Excerpts from your collections can be featured in interpretive and educational website pages. The pages may be as simple as an annotated series of staff members' favorites or more sophisticated interactive presentations that incorporate excerpts from your collection to explore an issue, historical event, or musical genre.

Through these and other means your work can serve a wider audience, and potential funders will be assured of the broadest possible impact of their support.

sources. When applying for grants, make certain that your project meets the guidelines for the grant being offered.[4] Grants are generally limited to certain subject areas, geographic locations, or types of recipient. It is also important that you calculate cost estimates for digitizing your collections, either in-house or with a vendor, to ensure that you ask for the right amount of money and deliver the amount of content proposed in the application.

Funding from collection donors or other philanthropists can also support digitization efforts. If you are acquiring a collection of legacy format sound recordings, consider requesting money from the donor to fund digitization as part of the donor agreement. Donors may be willing to provide financial assistance to encourage broader access to the collection.

Funding opportunities from local or specialized institutions focused on specific areas of research may be available for digitization of a collection that supports the stated field of study. Similarly, crowdfunding sites can be enlisted to cover digitization costs. There are numerous options to choose from, so it will be important to review the administrative costs and restrictions associated with each crowdfunding platform and your own institution.

REFERENCES

All URLs are current as of May 1, 2015

ARSC Technical Committee. 2011. *A Study of Embedded Metadata Support in Audio Recording Software: Summary of Findings and Conclusions.* Association for Recorded Sound Collections. Available at http://www.arsc-audio.org/pdf/ARSC_TC_MD_Study.pdf.

Audio Engineering Society. 2011. *AES57-2011: AES standard for audio metadata–Audio object structures for preservation and restoration.* Available at http://www.aes.org/publications/standards/search.cfm?docID=84.

Audio Engineering Society. 2008. *AES31-3-2008 (r2013): AES standard for network and file transfer of audio-Audio-file transfer and exchange – Part 3: Simple project interchange.* Available at http://www.aes.org/publications/standards/search.cfm?docID=32.

AudioVisual Preservation Solutions. 2009. Federal Agencies Audio Visual Digitization Working Group. *Task 5.4: Assess Options for Embedding Metadata in WAVE Files and Plan the Audio Metadata File Header Tool Development Project. Assessment Report and Initial Recommendations.* Available at http://www.digitizationguidelines.gov/audio-visual/documents/AVPS_Audio_Metadata_Overview_090612.pdf.

BWF MetaEdit website. Available at http://sourceforge.net/projects/bwfmetaedit/.

---

[4] See Library of Congress and Foundation Center 2010.

Casey, Mike, and Bruce Gordon. 2007. *Sound Directions: Best Practices for Audio Preservation.* Trustees of Indiana University and President and Fellows of Harvard University. Available at http://www.dlib.indiana.edu/projects/sounddirections/papersPresent/sd_bp_07.pdf.

Cost of Inaction Calculator. Available at https://coi.avpreserve.com/.

European Broadcasting Union. 2011. E*BU-TECH 3285. Specification of the Broadcast Wave Format (BWF). A format for audio data files in broadcasting, version 2.0.* Geneva: European Broadcasting Union. Available at https://tech.ebu.ch/docs/tech/tech3285.pdf.

Federal Agencies Audio-Visual Working Group. 2012. *Embedding Metadata in Digital Audio Files. Guideline for Federal Agency Use of Broadcast WAVE Files*, version 2 (April 23, 2012). Available at http://www.digitizationguidelines.gov/audio-visual/documents/Embed_Guideline_20120423.pdf.

Federal Agencies Digitization Guidelines Initiative. n.d. *Guidelines: Embedded Metadata in Broadcast WAVE Files.* Available at http://www.digitizationguidelines.gov/guidelines/digitize-embedding.html.

IASA (International Association of Sound and Audiovisual Archives) Technical Committee. 2009. *Guidelines on the Production and Preservation of Digital Audio Objects*, second edition. (IASA-TC04). Kevin Bradley, ed. Aarhus, Denmark: International Association of Sound and Audiovisual Archives. Available at http://www.iasa-web.org/tc04/audio-preservation.

ID3 website. Available at id3.org.

Lacinak, Chris. 2015. *Guide to Developing a Request for Proposal for the Digitization of Audio.* New York: AVPreserve. Available at http://www.avpreserve.com/wp-content/uploads/2015/05/AVPS_Audio_Digitization_RFP_Guide.pdf.

Lacinak, Chris. 2014. *Embedded Metadata in WAVE Files. A look inside issues and tools.* New York: AVPreserve. Available at http://www.avpreserve.com/wp-content/uploads/2014/04/EmbeddedMetadata.pdf.

Library of Congress and Foundation Center. 2010. *Foundation Grants for Preservation in Libraries, Archives, and Museums.* Washington, D.C.: Library of Congress and Foundation Center. Available at http://www.loc.gov/.

Library of Congress digiProvMD schema. Available at http://www.loc.gov/rr/mopic/avprot/digiprov_expl.html.

LYRASIS Digitization Collaborative. Available at http://www.lyrasis.org/LYRASIS%20Digital/Pages/Digitization-Collaborative.aspx.

MediaInfo website. Available at http://mediaarea.net/en/MediaInfo.

METS website. Available at http://www.loc.gov/standards/mets/.

PBCore. Available at http://pbcore.org/.

PBCore Instantiationizer. Available at http://www.avpreserve.com/pbcore-instantiationizer.

CHAPTER 7

What to Do After Digitization

By Chris Lacinak

In the analog world, previous formats persisted over time. . . . But the default for digital information is not to survive unless someone takes conscious action to make them persist. (Besser 2000, 165)

This quote from Howard Besser may have you wondering why in the world you have been encouraged to digitize your physical legacy media. The quote is certainly true, but when put into an audiovisual context, there is another piece of the puzzle to consider. Audiovisual media is different in that, aside from its physical condition, the content must always be mediated through a system in order to be perceived—unlike that of a cuneiform tablet or printed page, which is visible to the naked eye. This system consists of a reproducer, reproduction expertise, and the medium itself—all in good working order.

With the passing of time, the manufacturing of audiovisual technology dwindles, the bank of expertise around maintenance and operation of technology erodes, and the media become less stable. If ignored, the combination of obsolescence and degradation will render content stored on physical audiovisual media inaccessible in the near term.[1]

To avoid loss, audio content stored on these media must be digitized, and the strategy necessary for managing the resulting digital files differs greatly from the strategy necessary for managing physical objects. Successful navigation of the digital preservation challenge requires mindfulness of the new problems, as well as the new opportunities and solutions inherent in this domain.

---

[1] See Casey 2015.

7.1 DIGITAL PRESERVATION AND ACCESS: PROCESS AND PRACTICE

Declaring something preserved is akin to declaring a lawn mown or an ocean tide risen. Preservation is not a single event, but rather an ongoing process that requires continual maintenance. In the physical domain, there is more latitude for less stringent management. The file-based domain requires rigorous management, but it also offers opportunities for efficiency gains such as automated processes that are not available in the physical domain.

Without active management, digital files and their associated content will disappear, either through media failure, human error, inaccessibility as a result of format obsolescence, or an inability to find what you are looking for because of poor metadata.

At the heart of preservation strategy is risk management. The objective is to remove barriers to access and mitigate identified risks to the greatest extent possible. At the same time, we must be mindful that every decision made in the administration of data for preservation has risk implications. Over time, risks and barriers to access change and shift, requiring ongoing monitoring to identify and respond to these events in a timely manner. Successful preservation strategies maintain as many options and as much flexibility for reacting to adversity as possible.

Two documents from the International Standards Organization (ISO) have served as the cornerstone for digital archiving and preservation systems to date:

Terminology Used for Referring to Media Objects

The terms *analog* and *digital* are often misused in discussions of media. People generally understand the intended meaning of these terms when they are used in day-to-day conversations. However, they can be too imprecise for detailed discussions, and it is important to note the distinction where needed.

Digital is often used to refer only to digital files. The reality is that some digital media objects are not files, but rather physical objects (e.g., digital audio tape [DAT] or compact disc [CD]-audio).

Physical is a term that can describe all analog audiovisual objects, but there are also some physical audiovisual digital objects in which the format and the media are inextricably bound. Because analog objects are always physical, this term becomes important primarily as a qualifying term for digital objects, as in *physical digital*.

Files refer to what people commonly think of when they talk about digital objects. Files end with extensions such as .wav or .mp3 and are stored digitally. To distinguish them from physical digital objects, the term *file-based digital* may be used. In this chapter, the term *digital preservation* refers only to the preservation of file-based digital materials, and not to physical digital materials.

Analog refers to media that store the audiovisual signal using analog encoding. Examples of this include analog open reel audio and audiocassettes.

Born digital describes items that are digitally encoded at the point of creation. Though people often use it to refer solely to file-based digital objects, technically it can refer to both physical digital and file-based digital objects.

- ■ *ISO 14721:2012, Space data and information transfer systems—Open archival information system (OAIS)—Reference model*[2]
- ■ *ISO 16363:2012, Space data and information transfer systems—Audit and certification of trustworthy digital repositories*

These standards offer comprehensive details on the makings of highly functional and robust digital archiving and preservation environments. Implementation of these standards is a major undertaking for organizations of any size, as it requires significant resources and cooperation from stakeholders across an organization. For the foreseeable future, it is likely that only large, well resourced organizations with a mandate to perform archiving and preservation will establish such environments.

What should smaller organizations or individuals do in practice? Some organizations partner with an archive that has a robust digital preservation environment and deposit materials on an ongoing basis. This option can support access while relieving the burden of preservation from the depositing organization, but it assumes that the content is of sufficient interest to the larger institution. For example, the Cunningham Dance Foundation partnered with the New York University Digital Library as part of the planning process in producing *Mondays with Merce*, a series created by the foundation to document the technique of choreographer Merce Cunningham. This partnership allowed the foundation to use its resources solely for content creation and distribution while ensuring that the preservation of the content was in good hands. Although useful, this type of arrangement may be available to relatively few.

For others, more traditional deposits, taking place either at the point of a big transition or as the organization prepares to close, are more likely. This still requires finding an institution with interest in the content and a suitable preservation environment.

Other institutions may have no plans to deposit their collections in an archive and may simply want to know how best to take care of their materials. If there is no mandate to archive and preserve their recordings—and these are not part of an organization's mission—then there is likely not a significant budget for such endeavors.

In these latter circumstances, there is a period in which digital information is under the care of organizations without a robust preservation environment. The question here becomes how an organization can responsibly care for its materials during this time. Despite their inability to conform to the aforementioned standards, organizations and individuals can still do a great deal to mitigate risk of loss.

---

[2] A similar, free document can be found at http://public.ccsds.org/publications/archive/650x0m2.pdf.

Interim and Long-term Storage

Preservation professionals are in near-unanimous agreement that, not only is there no permanent medium for digital information, there is never likely to be one. An actively managed digital storage system is the only way to ensure that digital files remain viable over the long term. Even when you are storing files just for the short term, it is imperative that you never maintain only a single copy. If you are temporarily storing your preserved digital files on physical media exclusively, be sure to make several copies of the same set of files and store those copies in different geographic locations. Above all, do not consider your files on CD-Rs, flash drives, your internal hard disc, or your portable backup drive "preserved." They are not.

This chapter of the guide examines an in-house and a cloud option for long-term preservation of digital files. These are but two examples among the many options available to libraries and archives. The cost to use digital storage systems will decrease in coming years as new options become available and fees for digital storage decline. However, it is important to weigh the continually decreasing costs against the increasing risk of loss that accompanies storing files on a high-risk storage media or in an unmanaged system.

PRIORITIZATION AND PHASING

> Another misleading perception about digital preservation investments is that . . . choices are binary: either we implement intensive preservation . . . immediately and forever; or we do nothing . . . a relatively small investment may be enough to preserve the option of making larger commitments in the future. (Blue Ribbon Task Force 2010, 99)

Approaching digital preservation as a whole can be intimidating and overwhelming. It is important to set priorities and to plan in phases. Instead of thinking about preservation in terms of forever, think in terms of 5- or 10-year increments. At the end of each period, you have the option to reconsider and decide what to do in the next 5 or 10 years. You can choose to do nothing, do the minimal amount necessary to maintain the option to reconsider again later, or pursue a more robust solution, in whole or in part. Avoid falling into the pitfall of thinking in binary terms and begin taking some action as soon as possible to ensure flexibility and options in the future.

The National Digital Stewardship Alliance (NDSA) Levels of Digital Preservation provides a useful framework for thinking about how to set priorities for digital preservation infrastructure. The NDSA refers to these levels, 1 through 4, as protecting, knowing, monitoring, and repairing your data.

As seen in Table 7.1, the framework also identifies five functional areas that traverse all levels to form a matrix: (1) storage and geographic location, (2) file fixity and data integrity, (3) information security, (4) metadata, and (5) file formats.

This framework is intended to help institutions think about planning, assessing, and implementing digital preservation environments. The framework does not dictate that systems be built progressively and that all functional areas for Level 1 preservation be completed before starting on Level 2. However, it sets priorities by level, beginning with Level 1 as the most critical.

The framework can be approached in several ways. One option is to commit to a certain level of preservation across collections. For instance, if an organization wants to create a uniform foundation for its entire collection of digital materials, it can provide Level 1 attention across the five functional areas for all assets.

	Level 1 (Protect your data)	Level 2 (Know your data)	Level 3 (Monitor your data)	Level 4 (Repair your data)
Storage and Geographic Location	• Two complete copies that are not collocated • For data on heterogeneous media (optical discs, hard drives, etc.), get the content off the medium and into your storage system	• At least three complete copies • At least one copy in a different geographic location • Document your storage system(s) and storage media and what you need to use them	• At least one copy in a geographic location with a different disaster threat • Obsolescence monitoring process for your storage system(s) and media	• At least three copies in geographic locations with different disaster threats • Have a comprehensive plan in place that will keep files and metadata on currently accessible media or systems
File Fixity and Data Integrity	• Check file fixity on ingest if it has been provided with the content • Create fixity information if it wasn't provided with the content	• Check fixity on all ingests • Use write-blockers when working with original media • Virus-check high-risk content	• Check fixity of content at fixed intervals • Maintain logs of fixity information; supply audit on demand • [Have] ability to detect corrupt data • Virus-check all content	• Check fixity of all content in response to specific events or activities • [Have] ability to replace or repair corrupted data • Ensure no one person has write access to all copies
Information Security	• Identify who has read, write, move, and delete authorization to individual files • Restrict who has those authorizations to individual files	• Document access restrictions for content	• Maintain logs of who performed what actions on files, including deletions and preservation actions	• Perform audit of logs
Metadata	• Inventory of content and its storage location • Ensure backup and non-collocation of inventory	• Store administrative metadata • Store transformative metadata[3] and log events	• Store standard technical and descriptive metadata	• Store standard preservation metadata
File Formats	• When you can give input into the creation of digital files, encourage use of a limited set of known open formats and codecs	• Inventory of file formats in use	• Monitor file format obsolescence issues	• Perform format migrations, emulation, and similar activities as needed

Table 7.1: NDSA Levels of Digital Preservation progression

[3] Information documenting events that have resulted in changes in objects.

Another option is to be very selective about the materials being preserved and provide a more robust environment for those materials. Figure 7.1 conveys this idea, where a few materials receive attention at all levels and across all functional areas. This approach represents a choice to take maximum action with very high priority materials.

These strategies are not mutually exclusive. The optimal cost-benefit is often found using a hybrid approach, conveyed in Figure 7.2.

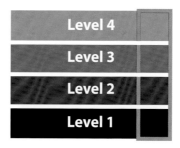

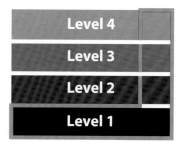

Fig. 7.1: Prioritize set of assets and provide full NDSA Preservation Level support

Fig. 7.2: Focus on fulfilling NDSA Level 1 across a collection and allocating resources to a subset of material that will reap the benefits of Levels 1 through 4

FIXITY

In the context of digital preservation, fixity is the unchanged state of a digital file. When a digital file is placed into a digital preservation environment, you may think it will remain unchanged forever; however, there are myriad reasons why a file might be altered, intentionally or unintentionally. Fixity information helps you track whether files have been changed and manage your response accordingly.

Organizations charged with maintaining the archival record use fixity information as a way to authenticate a digital object in their care and ensure that the integrity of that object has not been compromised. Aside from confirming authenticity, fixity is important because it has a direct impact on a digital object's quality and accessibility. For instance, an audio file that has been corrupted is likely either to play with artifacts or not to open at all.

Files can become altered over time in many ways. Stored bits may become corrupted, resulting in what is commonly called "bit rot." Or system malfunctions may result in data being written incorrectly. Data corruption can also occur during the transfer of files over networks or to other removable media. Resultant errors can range from subtle problems to complete inaccessibility and loss.

More common than these technological causes are human causes. Unintentional changes may be made while staff are managing or working with files, or changes may be intentional malicious acts.

Mitigating fixity risks and responding to issues appropriately is a matter of both systems and policy. Under any circumstance, the ability to recognize when problems do occur is fundamental to successfully managing file-based collections over time.

Of course, there are also many legitimate reasons for an organization to alter its files. For instance, it may be necessary to migrate data from one format to another or to update a rights statement embedded in a file. Both actions would affect the fixity of a file. In such scenarios, where changes are planned and controlled, fixity should be verified immediately before the change is made, and new fixity information should be generated after the change is made.

The primary mechanism for managing the fixity of digital files is a checksum: a small, alphanumeric text string that is generated by a checksum application. The application analyzes a file using an algorithm that generates a checksum representing a unique signature of that file. If a file remains unchanged, every analysis by a checksum application will generate the same checksum. If a file is changed, even in seemingly insignificant ways, the analysis will produce a different checksum.

Applications that use checksum algorithms to generate checksum values are referenced by the name of the checksum algorithm. The two most common types of checksum algorithms used in digital preservation environments are MD5 and SHA-256, and their checksum values are 32-digit and 64-digit alphanumeric strings, respectively.

Generating checksums is relatively straightforward. Validating your checksum is an important part of the fixity process and often the most overlooked. Validation simply means regenerating the checksum on a specified file or directory and making sure that it is identical to the original hash value. Validation should be performed at specific points, such as file transfers over networks or to new drives, or before purposeful changes; more generally, it should take place on an ongoing and routine basis.

While the checksum is the primary mechanism for monitoring fixity at the file level, the fixity of a collection of files is monitored through file attendance. Whereas checksums indicate whether a file has changed, file attendance indicates whether a file is new, removed, moved, or renamed. Tracking and reporting on file attendance is a fundamental component of file-based collection management and fixity.

In an ideal digital preservation system, the fixity checking and repair is automated, frequent, and distributed (Bailey 2012). Fixity repair refers to replacing the corrupted file with a "clean" or non-corrupt copy from a secure backup.

In addition to checksums, each storage solution often has optional or built-in mechanisms for monitoring the health of the media and the data on the media. These are also useful in the context of fixity and should be used where available.

Data integrity presents a challenge to many organizations lacking the resources to set up sophisticated systems and workflows. Lacking a robust information technology infrastructure, organizations can turn to less resource-intensive solutions, such as the free and open source tool aptly named Fixity. Created with smaller and less affluent organizations in mind, Fixity is a simple application that facilitates automated checksum and file attendance monitoring and reporting.

Monitoring and proactive planning around obsolescence are important aspects of a solid digital preservation strategy.

OBSOLESCENCE MONITORING

Over time, technologies and formats become obsolete, making information stored within them inaccessible if no action is taken to migrate the data to a current technology or format. Monitoring and proactive planning around obsolescence are important aspects of a solid digital preservation strategy.

Obsolescence can occur in multiple places within a system, including in the

- File wrapper
- File codec[4]
- Storage system
- Application
- Operating system

Maintaining awareness of obsolescence and preparation to prevent it can avert loss of content and needless expenditure of resources on responding to emergency situations.

At the file level, obsolescence monitoring should be ongoing. Typically, it begins with a scan of a storage location using a tool such as MediaInfo to report on all files and their technical attributes. This is followed by a review of the results of the report and assessment of the many factors that might foretell how long the format will be supported. These factors include the following:

- The proven ability to properly reproduce a file with particular technical attributes using software or hardware that is owned or accessible internally
- The number of software/hardware manufacturers creating current and supported products that have been proven to properly reproduce a given file with particular technical attributes
- The number of organizations holding significant quantities of the same format with the same technical attributes
- The number of similar organizations holding significant quantities of the same format with the same technical attributes
- Internal trends in use over time indicating a phasing out of a format or a given set of technical attributes
- Trends in use at other organizations over time indicating a phasing out of a format or a given set of technical attributes
- Trends in use at other similar organizations over time indicating a phasing out of a format or a given set of technical attributes

Routinely reviewing your files, conferring with colleagues, learning about formats in use, and understanding the issues that other organizations face will serve as the best available strategy for ongoing obsolescence monitoring of files. For considerations related to hardware and software, being in touch with manufacturers' technology roadmaps (e.g., release of new products and discontinuation of existing products and product lines) and conferring with colleagues at similar organizations will be helpful in obsolescence monitoring and planning. Hardware as well as file formats

---

[4] Recommendations for codec selection and management are available at Lacinak 2010.

are often at risk of becoming obsolete. Being aware of emerging trends will assist in preparing for future needs.

REFRESHING AND MIGRATION

The independence and persistence of essence and metadata over time and through multiple technological landscapes is at the heart of preservation. When the risk of loss from format obsolescence becomes too great, the primary mechanisms for escaping the threat and maintaining independence and persistence are refreshing and migration.

Refreshing refers to the transfer of files, metadata, or both from one system to another. It may consist of copying a collection of files from an obsolete server to a new server, or it may consist of copying metadata from an obsolete database to a new database. Great care must be taken during these processes to ensure that all data are transferred without loss and that the integrity of files and metadata is verified.

Migration refers to the transfer of essence and metadata from one format (wrapper, codec, or both) into another. It may consist of transferring the audio from one wrapper to another wrapper without changing the audio codec, or it may consist of transcoding the audio and placing it in a new wrapper. It may involve migration from an obsolete audio codec and wrapper to a new codec and wrapper.

Because obsolescence can happen at many levels, refreshing and migration plans must consider hardware (e.g., servers); software (e.g., digital asset management [DAM], video platform, codecs); databases (e.g., discovery systems, collection management systems); and other system components (e.g., intermediary scripts that enable information exchange and publishing).

Consideration of the future format of all files and system components is critically important to preservation planning. When selecting new file formats and systems, you should always think about ways to ensure a lossless path into the next file format or system.

Target Format Selection and Sustainability

In choosing target formats for digitization, consider obsolescence as a primary factor. The Library of Congress Sustainability of Digital Formats website provides guidance on the selection of file formats that are suitable for preservation. In the audio domain, there has been overwhelming consensus around the use of uncompressed pulse code modulation (PCM) data wrapped in the Broadcast Wave File format as the target preservation format. When you have control to specify the target formats, conforming to these specifications will help to proactively combat obsolescence.

REDUNDANCY AND GEOGRAPHIC SEPARATION

Maintaining multiple geographically dispersed copies of your data is a fundamental practice for preservation, whether in the physical domain or in the file-based domain, and across all types of storage infrastructures. A single instance of data is extremely vulnerable to a wide range of threats, and two copies of data in a single location are nearly as vulnerable. You should maintain at least three copies of digital assets to protect against disaster, hardware or software failure, and human error (Phillips et al. 2013). Make sure that these copies are in geographically disparate storage locations/systems to reduce the likelihood of loss from a major or minor disaster or service interruption.

The following factors should be considered when thinking about implementing redundancy and geographic separation.

- **Recovery point objective (RPO):** The RPO is the longest period in which the files do not exist in redundant locations, or the greatest amount of time that data are vulnerable to nonrecoverability in case of an incident. If you run a nightly routine to copy all new files to redundant storage locations, then your effective RPO is one day plus the time it takes to replicate to the redundant locations.
- **Recovery time objective (RTO):** The RTO is the maximum amount of time you are willing to allow for recovery of data from a redundant storage location if there is an incident. If the redundant storage locations consist of offline media, then the RTO will be the time it takes to get the media in hand, along with any associated drives that are necessary (e.g., LTO tape drive), and transfer all the data from the media to a new storage device. If the redundant storage locations are nearline or online (see sidebar, p. 141), then the time it takes to recover may consist of simply accessing the data on those secondary devices until the data are copied back to a new primary storage device.
- **Mirroring and replication:** Mirroring means that all storage locations contain exactly the same data. If a file is added to the primary storage location, it will be added to the secondary storage location as well. If a file is deleted from the primary storage location, it will be deleted from the secondary location as well. If a file is altered on the primary storage location, it will replace the unaltered version on the secondary storage location. The primary purpose of mirroring and replication is to provide an exact copy that can serve as an almost instant replacement if your primary storage system goes down.
- **Backup:** Similar to mirroring, backup involves copying data from a primary storage location to a secondary storage location. With backup, however, when files are removed from the primary storage location, they are not removed from the secondary storage location. When files are altered on the primary storage location, they are copied to the secondary storage location, but the prior version is kept as well. Backup policies dictate the length of time that deleted files and previous versions are kept.

PRESERVATION METADATA

The information necessary to support management and the long-term usability of an object make up the preservation metadata. It may include information on the storage and management of fixity information; auditing logs to identify who has interacted with an object and when; obsolescence monitoring information; and provenance information to support the authenticity of an object.

The primary reference for preservation metadata is the *Preservation Metadata: Implementation Strategies (PREMIS) Data Dictionary* and associated documentation, which the Library of Congress maintains as a standard.

According to the *Data Dictionary*, preservation metadata

- Support the viability, renderability, understandability, authenticity, and identity of digital objects in a preservation context;
- Represent the information most preservation repositories need to know to preserve digital materials over the long-term;
- Emphasize "implementable metadata": rigorously defined, supported by guidelines for creation, management, and use, and oriented toward automated workflows; and
- Embody technical neutrality: no assumptions made about preservation technologies, strategies, metadata storage and management, etc. (PREMIS Editorial Committee 2012, 1)

Aside from using the *PREMIS Data Dictionary* to identify which metadata fields to capture, it is important to have a mechanism for the acquisition, storage, and management of these data. You need to consider such a mechanism when thinking through workflows, outputs from processes and applications in use, and database applications being used for managing files. Answering the following questions can be helpful in planning:

- Which information will I be unable to capture at a later date if I pass up the opportunity to capture it in the present?
- Where in the workflow can I capture this information?
- What is the method or mechanism for capture? For example, will I export the information from an audio application, will I enter it manually, or will I use a script to generate it automatically?
- Where is the best place to store and manage this information?
- How will I use this information on an ongoing basis?

A preservation metadata spreadsheet, available at the AVPreserve website,[5] provides one example of the fields that smaller organizations with less sophisticated systems may capture. Where applicable, references to the *PREMIS Data Dictionary* are identified. This does not imply conformance with PREMIS, but is intended to identify a loose reference.

After deciding which fields to capture you must decide how to model and

---

[5] Spreadsheets are available at
http://www.avpreserve.com/wp-content/uploads/2015/04/AVPS_Audio_RFP_Guide_Metadata_Appendix_1.xlsx and
http://www.avpreserve.com/wp-content/uploads/2015/04/AVPS_Audio_RFP_Guide_Pricing_Appendix_2.xlsx.

Scenario:
Reformatted audiocassette, resulting in 1 BWF file for each side of the audiocassette.

TAPE/ITEM LEVEL FIELDS: Field Name	Object Identifier Value	Analog/Digital	Format				Sound				
Subfields/ elements			Format Name	Specification version (if applicable)	Size (MB)	Date created	Number of channels	Sound field	Noise Reduction	Mix type	Sampling rate (Hz)
	298494	Analog	Audiocassette	NA	NA	1994-12-01	2	stereo	Dolby B	field recording	NA
	574033	Digital File	BWF	2	1059.3	2014-09-03	2	stereo	NA	field recording	96000
	349503	Digital File	BWF	2	1129.9	2014-09-03	2	stereo	NA	field recording	96000

Fig. 7.3: Portion of "Reformatting Example" spreadsheet

Tips on File Naming

Do not develop a file name dependency

File names are not actually part of the file, but rather part of the file system. Therefore, do not count on their persistence over time and across systems. The unique identifier (UID) assigned to the object should be the constant identifier used to track and maintain the provenance of the file. The UID may be the same as the file name, but whatever the case, be sure to embed the UID inside the file in an appropriate and documented place.

Do not overthink

Whether the file name is a randomly generated value or not, be systematic. Think, "Is this logical? Can I spell out the rules easily enough to do batch renaming?" In trying to create the perfectly contained and expressed file name or UID structure, it is often tempting to overthink the name or structure to the point that it becomes nonsystematic or too idiosyncratic to be logically parsed. If a naming structure is not systematic enough to have a piece of software perform a series of logical renaming steps, many manual hours will be spent retyping names if a mass renaming of files is required in the future.

Do not use file names as database records

File names are not the place for descriptive and structural information. That is what databases are for. All we require from a file name and identifier is that they act as a link to the database record for that unique object. Trying to cram excessive descriptive information into a file name creates unwieldy names and is often futile because conditions or conventions change and new scenarios arise over time. File names that are tied too closely to specific scenarios create inflexible structures that require nonsystematic revision when situations change. This puts you in the same predicament that overthinking does.

Make sure that file names are machine-readable

A file-naming structure must be decodable not only by humans, but also by computers. Avoid characters that are not URL-compatible, that require escape characters, or are reserved by operating systems. Limit options to numbers, letters, periods, and underscores. Avoid the use of periods, spaces, and special characters (e.g., ~ ! @ # $ % ^ & * ( ) ` ; < > ? , [ ] { } ' " and |).

Do not assume you are the first person to name the file

When establishing file-naming conventions for a collection, most people think in terms of newly derived files reformatted from other sources. In reality, archives receive more and more born-digital files that already have names. In some cases, these can be renamed to fit the archive's naming structure with no loss of information, but at other times, such as with files generated through a recording and editing application (e.g., ProTools), the inherited naming scheme refers to file and directory structures that must be maintained to preserve relationships on which the application depends. Naming structures should be flexible enough to recreate any necessary naming conventions.

store the data. This means figuring out the most effective way of organizing fields and values and defining their relationships. A spreadsheet is not the most effective way to capture and store data because it requires creating a flat table. Databases, in contrast, provide multiple tables and a more sophisticated way of relating them to each other. For instance, in the spreadsheet's "Reformatting Example" tab (a portion of which is shown in Figure 7.3), rows 5, 6, and 7 contain information for the original physical item as well as for digital files produced through digitization. As you look across the columns, you see that there are fields that may or may not apply to all rows, and that certain fields are repeated across all of the rows.

The data could be modeled in alternate ways. The original and its digital derivatives could all be documented in one row instead of three separate rows. Or there could be one sheet that is dedicated to the originals and another that is dedicated to the files. There are pros and cons to all of these, and this begins to show the importance and challenge of data modeling. It also shows that performing the metadata modeling necessary to support effective management and efficient data entry requires more capability than spreadsheets offer. For these reasons and others, it is highly recommended that metadata be stored and managed in a database rather than in a spreadsheet.

SECURITY

It is necessary for an organization to control which users access and manipulate data in a digital preservation environment. Creating, assigning, logging, and managing permissions and restrictions in a system are critical in mitigating the risk of intentional or unintentional data corruption and misuse of content. As the NDSA levels of digital preservation show, there is an array of mechanisms for acting on security. Level 1 of information security begins with identifying who has read or write permissions and restricting access to identified assets. As the levels ascend, there is the addition of logging who accesses the files and the actions taken, followed by auditing of the generated logs.

Additionally, an organization should be concerned about protecting the digital preservation environment from external threats, in particular, storage devices that are connected to networks and the Internet. All network-attached storage devices with public Internet protocol (IP) addresses are constantly under attack by automated bots scanning the Internet and trying to log in to systems using standard default usernames (e.g., admin) and passwords (e.g., password). At minimum, make sure that access to these devices is protected with unique, high-strength passwords that are changed routinely.

If you access the network-attached storage device or replicate data over the Internet, you can take some precautions to help secure the system. Obtaining an X.509 certificate and using Hypertext Transfer Protocol Secure (HTTPS) enables authentication of websites and servers, as well as encryption of data being sent over the Internet. If using File Transfer

Protocol (FTP) to upload and download files, use a secure form of FTP (i.e., SFTP) instead of standard FTP. Many services (e.g., Secure Shell [SSH], FTP, replication) that are available on network-attached storage devices use specific ports for getting data in and out of the device. These are generally standard across devices, which makes them vulnerable to some extent. Disabling any ports that are not being used limits the points of possible entry. It is also recommended that your device be placed behind a firewall for an added layer of security.

From a different perspective, it is equally important to make sure that protection mechanisms are not so aggressive that they put the content at risk. For instance, encryption on the storage device or overly restrictive permissions could prove to be a significant risk and obstacle to access and preservation if encryption keys or passwords are misplaced.

Files that are brought into the system from external sources should be scanned for viruses to avoid ingesting viruses into your digital preservation environment. If you are performing digitization internally and have full control over the files being created, the risk of a virus is less. Virus scanning should also be performed routinely in the digital preservation environment as an added precautionary measure. However, antivirus utilities should not be enabled on a digital audio workstation (DAW) being used for digitization, as they can cause errors in the digitization process. If an antivirus utility is installed on the DAW, be sure to turn it completely off before digitization begins.

7.2 STORAGE INFRASTRUCTURE

Although capacity and cost tend to be the focus of discussion when it comes to storage, preservation and performance must be considered if planning and implementation of a storage environment are to be successful. These considerations include factors such as class of storage (e.g., level of reliability, uptime), types of content being stored, number of users, types of users, bandwidth requirements, redundancy, and permissions.

Storage options can be local or outsourced (also known as cloud storage). Every organization has different requirements for the storage and use of its assets, which influences the storage architecture.

Regardless of the type of storage, thinking through your organizational requirements, implementing the best practices discussed earlier, and considering the NDSA levels of digital preservation are extremely useful in the analysis and planning of a storage infrastructure. This approach makes it clear that access to files is extremely important, because it allows the performance of automated routines on an ongoing basis that benefit digital preservation efforts. The difference in the level of effort and risk between having your digital data in a preservation environment online and having them stored offline on removable media is significant.

> ## Online, Nearline, and Offline Storage
>
> The terms *online*, *nearline*, and *offline* are often used in discussions about storage architectures. These terms speak to the ease and speed with which data can be retrieved from a particular storage solution.
>
> **Online storage**: In this context, online has nothing to do with the Internet; it simply means that the data are immediately available to users of a storage system. An example is a spinning disk server.
>
> **Nearline storage**: The data are available to users with some lag time, but without human intervention. An example is magnetic tape libraries.
>
> **Offline storage**: The data are stored on a medium in a location where retrieval requires human intervention. An example is an LTO tape stored in a physical storage facility that must be retrieved and placed in an LTO deck before the data can be retrieved.

STORAGE MEDIA

Removable media, such as portable hard drives, portable flash drives, or CDs and DVDs stored on shelves, are not viable as part of a preservation strategy. These media are highly susceptible to failure. Monitoring them for errors is resource-intensive, and in the event of complete data loss, data recovery procedures are expensive. They also don't provide the necessary accessibility to routinely perform all of the best practices discussed in this chapter. Although it is technically possible to perform all of the best practices using removable media, in reality it does not happen because it is too onerous. As a result, the use of removable storage media places files at risk of loss and impedes ongoing monitoring of their integrity. There are library devices for optical media that will allow the use of collections of CDs and DVDs in a nearline mode, improving the functionality and performance when compared with storing media offline, but these are costly and would need to be weighed against solutions such as data tape libraries and network-attached storage (NAS) devices.

The following are a few predominant types of media that underlie storage infrastructures:

- **Spinning disk storage** in the form of NAS devices is commonly used in digital preservation storage environments. They offer better functionality and performance than data tape, but come at a higher cost.
- **Magnetic data tape** is typically used either for nearline (e.g., in a data tape library) or offline (e.g., stored on a shelf) storage, but entails compromises. A nearline tape library solution requires human and facility resources akin to those required by spinning disk storage. However, retrieval of content from magnetic data tape is somewhat slower than retrieval from a spinning disk. Storing LTO tape offline reduces the human and facility resources required, but also greatly inhibits access and implementation of best preservation practices. As with storing portable drives

and optical media offline, there is a loss of functionality and performance. However, data tape is less prone to failure than portable drives and optical disc media.

- **Optical media,** like data tape, can be used with library systems to provide a nearline storage environment. Organizations such as Facebook and services such as Amazon Glacier reportedly use Blu-Ray discs as a main component of their storage infrastructure, albeit with highly sophisticated automation and systems in place that exceed standard optical media library systems and come at a great cost.

Although selection of the proper storage technology is an important consideration of storage planning, it is only one element of the infrastructure required. Discussions of cost commonly focus on the purchase price of storage (i.e., cost per gigabyte). A better and more meaningful metric is the total cost of ownership (TCO), which takes into account all of the media, labor, and overhead costs that go into installation, ongoing management, and exiting from a given storage solution within the context of your envisioned use cases. Ongoing management is often the greatest cost, as increased staff expertise and greater resources may be needed to manage, troubleshoot, and properly plan for the inevitable replacement of the technology over time. Thus, it is important to determine whether the staff have the necessary expertise to support a given storage solution or whether additional staffing will be required.

Recognition of the total cost of ownership and the resources needed to manage a local storage infrastructure has led many organizations to look at outsourcing their storage. Many providers offer such services, commonly referred to as cloud storage. Although some service providers offer features that are useful to preservation, it is essential to remember that you are outsourcing only storage—not preservation. As Seth Anderson points out in *Feet On The Ground: A Practical Approach To The Cloud. Nine Things To Consider When Assessing Cloud Storage*:

> Cloud storage may be suitable to fulfill one or more aspects of an integrated digital preservation environment consisting of systems, storage, policies, and people. It is then necessary to understand exactly what role a third-party service will play, what services the service will not provide (e.g., SIP validation, data integrity validation, file characterization, among others), and how it may integrate with other technology prior to researching and vetting potential solutions. (Anderson 2014, 1)

Anderson rightly identifies preservation as an ecosystem of technology, policy, and people, and notes that providers of these types of services often offer only part of the solution. In an outsourcing scenario, you must be clear on the allocation of roles and responsibilities, and you must be diligent both in fulfilling your own obligations and in auditing the compliance of the service provider.

Outsourcing storage may provide relief from the staff expertise required or the TCO of a local storage infrastructure, but an upfront investment in vetting the service provider and its offerings is imperative to determine the service that is the best fit. Cloud storage providers are not identical; their services, features, and performance levels vary according to their target market and intended use (e.g., offline deep storage, low-latency high-speed hosting). Due diligence must be performed to ensure that services provide appropriate data security measures, geographic separation, disaster recovery and backup mechanisms, and service termination and migration policies in a cost-effective way.

It may be tempting to place collections in "the cloud" and assume that the job of preservation is done, especially if you know someone else who is happy with the service or if it reportedly provides an array of beneficial services. To avoid entering into an agreement that ultimately fails to support your digital preservation and access needs, and to properly calculate the TCO of each solution, it is recommended that you fully evaluate each service provider you are considering by using the best practices described in this document and examining your particular requirements and envisioned use cases.

To help navigate these realities, Anderson followed up his publication of *Nine Things To Consider When Assessing Cloud Storage* (2014a) with *Comparing NDSA Levels Rankings Across Cloud Storage Vendors* (2014b) and *Cloud Storage Vendor Profiles* (2014c). Anderson's comparison of NDSA rankings across cloud storage vendors is summarized in Table 7.2.

Provider	Service	Infrastructure	Cost	NDSA Category	Level 1	Level 2	Level 3	Level 4
Chronopolis	Deep Storage	Partnership	High	Storage				
				Data Integrity				
				Security				
Dternity	Deep Storage	Wholly Owned	High	Storage				
				Data Integrity				
				Security				
DuraCloud	Deep Storage, Streaming	Contracted	High	Storage				
				Data Integrity				
				Security				
EVault	Deep Storage, Production	Wholly Owned	Low	Storage				
				Data Integrity				
				Security				
Glacier	Deep Storage	Wholly Owned	Low	Storage				
				Data Integrity				
				Security				
Preservica	Deep Storage, Production, Streaming	Contracted	High	Storage				
				Data Integrity				
				Security				
Rackspace	Production, Streaming	Wholly Owned	Medium	Storage				
				Data Integrity				
				Security				

Table 7.2: Comparison of NDSA level rankings across cloud storage vendors. Green, yellow, and pink shading indicate full, partial, or no adherence respectively.

The importance of comprehensive planning and comparison of storage types cannot be overstated. Table 7.3 outlines key considerations for decisions about cloud and local storage.

	Cloud	Local
Cost	Change in cost of services over time is unknown. Pricing is frequently akin to that for early cell phone plans—many unknowns until use has begun. Users pay as they go. Required internal increase in incoming/outgoing bandwidth must be taken into account. Amount of administrative cost required is typically unknown up front.	Most storage systems last 5–7 years. The cost of replacement must be taken into consideration. A significant portion of costs are up front. Cost of support is the least reliable cost. If the organization needs more than estimated, cost will go up.
Performance	Performance is largely based on available bandwidth. Performance can be scaled to fit needs within reason.	Performance must be significantly overestimated to anticipate future needs. Higher performance demands are better suited to local infrastructure.
Staffing	Internal staffing would focus on configuration, troubleshooting (enough to have conversations with tech support), and the provision of in-house support for those with problems. The staffing burden would be less than that for local storage.	Some staffing must be dedicated to supporting the infrastructure and its users. As an alternative to dedicated staffing, a contractor may be used, although this may increase time for issue resolution and has an unpredictable cost associated with it.
Infrastructure of Provider	Providers may have infrastructure that is reportedly robust and impenetrable, but remains largely untested.	Larger storage systems may be acquired and installed by an integrator, who also offers a support contract. This arrangement may create a dependency on the integrator.
Support	Support may not be reliable from large service providers. It is hard to generalize. If you are having a problem, someone else is probably experiencing it, too, which attracts more attention to the problem. But it may be a disadvantage to be a small customer that is one of thousands.	Support is provided either directly by the storage manufacturer or through your storage integrator. The quality of customer service and support to be expected from the provider you are using should be examined as part of the vetting process.
Transition Risks	There are concerns about data being "trapped" in cloud services and organizations having to pay exorbitant fees to perform a mass migration. Costs are substantially lessened if recovery of data takes place over a longer period of time, although a slow recovery may not meet your need to recover your data. For instance, disaster recovery is a very different scenario from a planned migration.	There is a clear exit path that is straightforward, although it requires more logistical planning and coordination on the organization's part.
Scalability	Cloud storage is more easily scalable.	Local storage is typically scalable, but less so than cloud storage.
Future	Storage and computing in general are trending toward the cloud, providing some potential advantages.	It may be wise to take a "wait and see" approach with cloud storage, allowing more time for better insights into the true nature of cloud storage and computing as it matures and is tested over time.
Sustainability	"Pay as you go" provides for more predictable financial planning over a longer period of time, but requires continual investment. If funding ends, there are few options for dealing with the stored content.	Certain funders may find capital investments more attractive. More significant funding is required at particular points, but little to no funding is needed for storage in between these points. If funding ends suddenly, you have an infrastructure that may buy you time and give you more options.
Biggest Risk Factors and Prospective Impact	Poor performance may cause dissatisfaction and lead to the formation of alternative bad habits that undermine preservation. Cloud providers are still relatively untested, and it is debatable whether cloud storage is more or less trustworthy and dependable than in-house storage.	Inability to provide appropriate expertise and resources may result in loss of data. Storage demands may exceed all expectations significantly, and the need to scale may require greater cost and effort than anticipated.

Table 7.3: Comparison of cloud and local storage

POTENTIAL STORAGE SCENARIOS

Individually, each storage mechanism has its own functional and financial implications, and organizations often find value in building a multitier and distributed storage architecture. The architecture may consist of local storage, cloud storage, or a combination of the two. The appropriate choice depends on your unique use cases and sensitivities, as well as on performance and costs.

For instance, different file types serve different purposes and have varying performance requirements that dictate storage and bandwidth needs. The scenarios in Table 7.4 represent different approaches to a multitiered, distributed storage architecture with the rationales for their potential use.

Scenario	Access Copy	Access Master	Preservation Master	Rationale and Implications
1	Stored locally in online spinning disk	Stored locally in nearline data tape library	Stored locally in nearline data tape library; additional copies stored offline in offsite location	Storage is managed internally to ensure the security of sensitive collection materials. Access masters are kept on nearline storage for editing materials in new productions. The creation of multiple copies increases the storage requirements, and in-house storage increases the total cost of ownership.
2	Stored locally in online spinning disk	No access master	Stored locally in offline data tape library; additional copies stored on deep cloud storage (e.g., Amazon Glacier)	Scenario assumes consistent access of low-resolution copies for browsing. Preservation masters are rarely accessed on low-cost cloud service and offline data tape, lowering the total cost of ownership on day-to-day basis, but increasing effort required in larger-scale efforts such as migration and reformatting. Fixity and redundancy are dependent on cloud storage provider, so provider must be vetted and capabilities confirmed. Collection management activities may be difficult or impossible, depending on level of access and cost for retrieving files.
3	Stored in low-latency cloud service (e.g., Amazon S3)	No access master	Stored on deep cloud storage (e.g., Amazon Glacier) and replicated to similar cloud service	Scenario is similar to above. Cloud service is used for high-speed delivery of access copies instead of local storage, potentially decreasing total cost of ownership but raising security and exit path concerns. Fixity and redundancy are dependent on cloud storage provider, so provider must be vetted and capabilities confirmed. Collection management activities may be difficult or impossible, depending on level of access and cost for retrieving files.
4	Stored on local high-performance disk storage and mirrored to another locally managed, but geographically separate disk facility	No access master	Stored on local high-performance disk storage and mirrored to another locally managed, but geographically separate, disk facility; backup copy stored in local offline tape library	This scenario may be chosen to meet high-performance requirements involving regular, secure access to preservation masters. It represents a high total cost of ownership for design, installation, and management of two local disk storage environments, but offers high performance and control.

Table 7.4: Scenarios for multitier storage architectures

There are many more potential combinations of multitier storage architectures. The scenarios in Table 7.4 are meant as examples of the requirements-based approach to determining the appropriate architecture. As stated earlier, each organization will encounter different requirements and use cases for their collections that will influence the selection and use of storage media. It is imperative to understand your own requirements and use cases and to plan accordingly.

Example 1 Description: 10TB, local and outsourced	
Data capacity requirement	10TB
Architecture	The organization maintains one network-attached storage (NAS) device locally, which is replicated to an offsite NAS device and to Amazon Glacier.
Management resources	The organization hired an IT consultant for 8 hours to set up and configure the NAS and Amazon Glacier. It retains the consultant for 2 hours per month to monitor and maintain the systems. Technical support is obtained as needed through the NAS manufacturer.
Hardware configuration	The organization purchased (2) Qnap TS-669L 6-Bay Turbo NAS devices, populated with (6) Western Digital WD40EFRX 4TB drives, totaling 24TB of raw capacity. Each NAS device was configured as RAID 6. After accounting for RAID 6 configuration and storage overhead, actual usable capacity is approximately 14.9TB. This capacity allows storage of 10TB with a healthy margin of 33 percent additional storage. One NAS device is kept in one office location, and the other is kept in a geographically separate office location.
	The NAS devices are connected to their existing gigabit Ethernet switches by Cat6 cables, and they are accessible over the local area network. Access to the NAS device is controlled through login authentication and permissions.
	A computer is dedicated to fixity monitoring and reporting at each office location. This computer has a gigabit Ethernet port and is also plugged into the gigabit Ethernet switches by means of Cat6 cabling.
Software configuration	The organization uses the QNAP browser-based administrative interface, QTS, to configure and administer the NAS devices. Within this interface, many applications are available for use.
	There are two applications used to enable redundancy of data. One is called Backup Station; it has a utility called Remote Replication, NAS to NAS. It is configured to replicate daily to the other NAS device. The other application is called Glacier and allows the transfer of data to Amazon Glacier from the NAS device. Among the other available applications is one called Antivirus, which runs monthly antivirus scans on the NAS devices.
	The organization uses its computers dedicated for fixity to run the AVPreserve application, Fixity. It is set up to run weekly and to email reports to the staff and their IT consultant.
	All of these applications were free to use.
Cloud storage configuration	It would take a significant amount of time to transfer 10TB to Glacier using the Internet, Therefore, the organization uses Amazon's import service, which allows for delivering files via hard drive.
	There is a monthly fee for Amazon Glacier storage. If it were necessary to retrieve the organization's data from Glacier, the staff calculate that the retrieval would cost approximately $1,475 using the slowest retrieval option. They will only need to retrieve data from Glacier if both NAS devices fail catastrophically.

DETAILED STORAGE EXAMPLES

The scenarios at the bottom of these pages and on p. 148 offer a look into more specific implementations and prospective costs of storage solutions. Keep in mind that costs are constantly changing when it comes to storage systems and that these examples offer only a snapshot.[6]

Example 1 Budget: 10TB, local and outsourced			
Item	Quantity	Unit Cost	Total Cost
Consulting Costs			
Setup and Configuration	8	$150	$1,200
Annual Retainer	24	$150	$3,600
Total Consulting Costs			$4,800
Hardware Costs			
Qnap TS-669L 6-Bay Turbo NAS	2	$730	$1,460
Western Digital WD40EFRX 4TB drives	14*	$163	$2,282
HP All-in-One Desktop Computer (for fixity)	2	$350	$700
Total Hardware Costs			$4,442
Cloud Storage Costs			
Amazon Glacier Hard Drive Import Fee	1	$167	$167
Annual Cost of Glacier Storage	12	$103	$1,236
Total Year 1 Cloud Storage Costs			$1,403
TOTAL YEAR 1 BUDGET			$10,645
TOTAL YEAR 2 BUDGET**			$4,836
TOTAL YEAR 3 BUDGET**			$4,836
TOTAL COSTS OVER THREE YEARS**			$20,317

* The two additional drives are a spare drive for each NAS in case of drive failure.

** This includes $3,600 annual retainer for consulting and $1,236 annual cost of Glacier storage. This does not account for likely reduction in storage costs, possible increase in consulting fees, or cost of any potential necessary repairs. QNAP unit comes with two-year warranty.

---

[6] These data were generated in January 2015.

Example 2 Description: 10TB outsourced	
Data capacity requirement	10TB
Architecture	The organization uses DuraCloud Enterprise Plus, which enables redundancy of data, between either Amazon S3 and Glacier or Amazon S3 and San Diego Super Computer cloud service. The organization prefers to store its data with two different service providers to avoid the risk of dependency on a single service provider. They use no local storage.
Management resources	The support provided by DuraCloud and the lack of any internal storage infrastructure alleviates the need for any additional information technology resources for management.
Hardware configuration	The lack of any internal infrastructure alleviates the need for hardware configuration.
Software and cloud storage configuration	The organization utilizes the administrative user interface that DuraCloud provides for managing, tracking, and reporting. User management, permission, and access controls to the data are configured through the administrative user interface.
	As part of its service, DuraCloud offers replication between the two cloud service providers, as well as fixity monitoring and reporting. A file found to be corrupt is automatically replaced with a known good copy from the other service. Downloading of data is included in the price.

Example 2 Budget: 10TB outsourced	
Item	**Total Cost**
Cloud Storage Costs	
Annual DuraCloud Enterprise Plus for 10TB	$17,300
TOTAL YEAR 1 BUDGET	$17,300
TOTAL YEAR 2 BUDGET*	$17,300
TOTAL YEAR 3 BUDGET*	$17,300
TOTAL COSTS OVER THREE YEARS*	$51,900

* Not accounting for any potential reduction in storage costs.

CONCLUSION

Understanding and accepting that audio preservation is an ongoing process may be challenging, if not intimidating. It is important to remember that setting priorities is central to a successful preservation strategy. Avoid thinking in black-and-white, all-or-nothing terms. This chapter provides an overview of the basics of digital preservation. Use this chapter, the NDSA Levels of Digital Preservation, and other referenced resources to think critically about how best to set priorities and take a phased approach to digital preservation for you or your organization. There are paths to digital preservation for organizations of almost all types and sizes.

Although much of this chapter and the guide as a whole focuses on reformatted analog media, the creation of audio today is almost exclusively file-based digital. The methodologies outlined in this chapter are equally relevant to today's born-digital creations.

It is also important to remember that the outcome of digital preservation is long-term access and use. The practices outlined in this chapter form a foundation not only for preserving your audio content, but also for being able to use it in ways that surpass the possibilities of yesterday's analog domain and outpace what we can imagine lies ahead. Whether the use is focused on education, scholarship, broadcasting, marketing, or sales, it is digital preservation that will enable the fulfillment of that goal today and over the long term.

REFERENCES

All URLs are current as of May 1, 2015

Anderson, Seth. 2014a. *Feet On The Ground: A Practical Approach To The Cloud. Nine Things To Consider When Assessing Cloud Storage.* New York: AVPreserve. Available at http://www.avpreserve.com/wp-content/uploads/2014/02/AssessingCloudStorage.pdf.

Anderson, Seth. 2014b. "Comparing NDSA Levels Rankings Across Cloud Storage Vendors" (blog, July 18). Available at http://www.avpreserve.com/blog/comparing-ndsa-levels-rankings-across-cloud-storage-vendors/.

Anderson, Seth. 2014c. "Cloud Storage Vendor Profiles." Available at http://www.avpreserve.com/papers-and-presentations/cloud-storage-vendor-profiles/.

Bailey, Jefferson. 2012. "File Fixity and Digital Preservation Storage: More Results from the NDSA Storage Survey" (blog, March 6). *The Signal: Digital Preservation.* Available at http://blogs.loc.gov/digitalpreservation/2012/03/file-fixity-and-digital-preservation-storage-more-results-from-the-ndsa-storage-survey/.

Besser, Howard. 2000. *Digital Longevity. Handbook for Digital Projects: A Management Tool for Preservation and Access,* edited by Maxine Sitts, 164–176. Andover, Mass.: Northeast Document Conservation Center.

Blue Ribbon Task Force on Sustainable Digital Preservation and Access. 2010. *Sustainable Economics for a Digital Planet: Ensuring Long-Term Access to Digital Information.* Available at http://brtf.sdsc.edu/biblio/BRTF_Final_Report.pdf.

Casey, Mike. 2015. "Why Media Preservation Can't Wait: the Gathering Storm." *International Association of Sound & Audiovisual Archives Journal* 44. Available at http://www.avpreserve.com/wp-content/uploads/2015/04/casey_iasa_journal_44_part3.pdf.

Fixity. Available at http://www.avpreserve.com/tools/fixity/.

Lacinak, Chris. 2010. *A Primer on Codecs for Moving Image and Sound Archives & 10 Recommendations for Codec Selection and Management.* New York: AudioVisual Preservation Solutions. Available at http://www.avpreserve.com/papers-and-presentations/a-primer-on-codecs-for-moving-image-and-sound-archives/.

Library of Congress. *Sustainability of Digital Formats. Planning for Library of Congress Collections.* Available at http://www.digitalpreservation.gov/formats/sustain/sustain.shtml.

MediaInfo website. Available at http://mediaarea.net/en/MediaInfo.

Mondays with Merce. Available at http://www.mercecunningham.org/film-media/mondays-with-merce/.

National Digital Stewardship Alliance. n.d. *NDSA Levels of Preservation.* Available at http://www.digitalpreservation.gov/ndsa/activities/levels.html.

Phillips, Megan, Jefferson Bailey, Andrea Goethals, and Trevor Owens. 2013. "The NDSA Levels of Digital Preservation: An Explanation and Uses." Available at www.digitalpreservation.gov/ndsa/working_groups/documents/NDSA_Levels_Archiving_2013.pdf.

PREMIS. Available at http://www.loc.gov/standards/premis/.

PREMIS Editorial Committee. 2012. *PREMIS Data Dictionary for Preservation Metadata*, version 2.2. Available at http://www.loc.gov/standards/premis/v2/premis-2-2.pdf.

ADDITIONAL RESOURCES

AVPreserve. 2014. *Mapping Standards for Richer Assessments: NDSA Levels of Digital Preservation and ISO 16363:2012.* Available at http://www.avpreserve.com/papers-and-presentations/mapping-standards-for-richer-assessments-ndsa-levels-of-digital-preservation-and-iso-163632012/.

Bailey, Jefferson, Andrea Goethals, Trevor Owens, and Megan Phillips. 2013. "Putting the NDSA Levels of Digital Preservation to Work for Your Organization." Presentation at Digital Preservation 2013. National Digital Stewardship Alliance. Available at http://www.digitalpreservation.gov/meetings/documents/ndiipp13/NDSA-Levels-DigitalPreservation-NDSA-2013.pdf.

BWF MetaEdit website. Available at http://sourceforge.net/projects/bwfmetaedit/.

Duryee, Alex. n.d. *Fixity and Filesystems: Enhanced System Monitoring via Inodes.* Available at http://www.avpreserve.com/wp-content/uploads/2014/07/FixityAndFilesystems.pdf.

European Broadcasting Union. 2011. E*BU-TECH 3285. Specification of the Broadcast Wave Format (BWF). A format for audio data files in broadcasting, version 2.0.* Geneva: European Broadcasting Union. Available at https://tech.ebu.ch/docs/tech/tech3285.pdf.

Federal Agencies Audio-Visual Working Group. 2012. *Embedding Metadata in Digital Audio Files. Guideline for Federal Agency Use of Broadcast WAVE Files*, version 2 (April 23, 2012). Available at http://www.digitizationguidelines.gov/audio-visual/documents/Embed_Guideline_20120423.pdf.

Federal Agencies Digitization Guidelines Initiative. 2013. *Guidelines: Embedded Metadata in Broadcast WAVE Files* (last updated June 17, 2013). Available at http://www.digitizationguidelines.gov/guidelines/digitize-embedding.html.

Lacinak, Chris, 2014. "The Cost Of Inaction: A New Model And Application." *International Association of Sound & Audiovisual Archives Journal* 43. Available at http://www.avpreserve.com/papers-and-presentations/the-cost-of-inaction-a-new-model-and-application/.

Lacinak, Chris, and Walter Forsberg. 2011. *A Study of Embedded Metadata Support in Audio Recording Software: Summary of Findings and Conclusions.* Association for Recorded Sound Collections (ARSC) Technical Committee. Available at http://www.arsc-audio.org/pdf/ARSC_TC_MD_Study.pdf.

NDSA Infrastructure & Standards Working Groups. "Checking Your Digital Content: How, What, and When to Check Fixity?" Draft Fact Sheet. Available at http://blogs.loc.gov/digitalpreservation/files/2014/02/NDSA-Checking-your-digital-content-Draft-2-5-14.pdf.

Owens, Trevor. 2014. "Check Yourself: How and When to Check Fixity" (blog, February 7). *The Signal: Digital Preservation.* Available at http://blogs.loc.gov/digitalpreservation/2014/02/check-yourself-how-and-when-to-check-fixity/.

CHAPTER 8

Audio Preservation: The Legal Context

By Brandon Butler

Several legal rules may affect whether and how audio recordings can be copied, distributed, and performed. Although laws regarding privacy, publicity, and contracts can come into play in particular cases, by far and away the most important set of legal rules governing audio works is copyright. Institutions, professionals, and collectors working to preserve and provide access to audio works that make up our collective cultural heritage need to understand the basic outlines of copyright law.

8.1 COPYRIGHT

Copyright is a complex body of law that awards authors limited rights to control and monetize creative works. The ultimate goal is to encourage cultural progress by providing an incentive for the production and distribution of new creative works. Indeed, since the very first copyright statute, England's Statute of Anne in 1709, the purpose of copyright has been characterized in terms of the benefit to society in general and especially the benefit to education and progress that is achieved by giving a limited bounty to authors.[1] Thus, although the rights of authors are an essential part of the copyright regime, the complementary rights granted to other parts of the cultural ecosystem are equally important. When libraries,

---

[1] Most importantly, the U.S. Constitution directs Congress to make laws regarding intellectual property "to promote the Progress of Science and the useful Arts." U.S. Const. Art. I § 8, cl. 8. The first copyright law passed by the U.S. Congress, the Copyright Act of 1790, was subtitled "an act for the encouragement of learning."

NOTE: *This chapter is provided for informational purposes only and is not intended as legal advice. If you need legal advice and cannot afford a lawyer, one of the many intellectual property law clinics around the country may be able to help. For example, see http://ipclinic.org for more information about the clinic where I work, the Glushko-Samuelson Intellectual Property Clinic at American University Washington College of Law in Washington, D.C. The views and opinions expressed here are mine and do not necessarily represent the views and opinions of the U.S. Government, the Library of Congress, the Association for Recorded Sound Collections, or the Council on Library and Information Resources.*

When libraries, archives, and museums exercise their legal rights to preserve and facilitate access to information, they are furthering the goals of copyright.

archives, and museums exercise their legal rights to preserve and facilitate access to information, even without permission or payment, they are furthering the goals of copyright.

Although most copyright law is contained in a single federal law,[2] state laws also play an important role. In the special case of sound recordings made prior to February 15, 1972, state law protection looms large. Most of the discussion in this chapter addresses the federal copyright scheme, but given the importance of older recordings, the status of pre-1972 works is discussed at some length in a separate section.

RIGHTS

Copyright gives the author of an original work the exclusive right to do any of the following:

- Reproduction (the right to make copies of the work)
- Preparation of derivative works (to create new works based on the underlying work, such as a translation or film adaptation)
- Distribution (the right to transfer physical copies to others)
- Public performance (the right to play or perform a work to the public)
- Public display (for images and other still visual works, to show the work to the public)
- In the case of sound recordings, to perform the copyrighted work publicly by means of a digital audio transmission[3]

These rights cover a wide variety of activities that owners of a recorded sound collection may want to pursue, making them subject to the copyright holder's permission unless a limitation or exception (discussed at length below) applies. The most familiar of these rights is the right to control making and distributing copies of works, including portions of works, unless the use is fair or the portion is so small that a court might consider it *de minimis* (i.e., so small that the law should not concern itself with the use). Less well known is the copyright holder's right to control public performance or display of the work. This control covers in-person performances (such as concerts) as well as transmissions (such as those over the Internet). Private performances—listening to a work among friends and family, for example—do not involve copyright and can be made without payment or permission. The derivative works right is another complex right that covers the creation of new works based on an existing work (such as an adaptation of a radio documentary into a television drama, a translation, or a new arrangement of an opera) where the new creation is not a fair use.

---

[2] The Copyright Act of 1976, which has been amended many times in the intervening years, can be found at Title 17 of the U.S. Code, available online at http://www.copyright.gov/title17/.

[3] See 17 U.S.C. § 106. Section 106(6) may be particularly important (and confusing) for audio collectors. Copyright protects both the sound recording (e.g., one performer's rendition of a song) and the underlying work that is performed on the recording (e.g., the lyrics and music of the song itself). Only the owner of the second work (e.g., the musical composition) has a public performance right. The owner of a sound recording controls public performances only in certain digital contexts.

In the first instance, these rights belong to authors. However, they are often sold to media companies or licensed through collecting societies that further assign and divide them in a variety of ways. In the music realm, collecting societies like the American Society of Composers, Authors, and Publishers (ASCAP) and Broadcast Music Incorporated (BMI) can sell blanket licenses to publicly perform large catalogs of musical works. SoundExchange licenses digital transmission of sound recordings. The U.S. Copyright Office maintains a registry of copyrighted works that can serve as a starting point for a search for individual copyright holders when permission is needed.[4]

These rights may seem broad, and the search for copyright holders can be daunting, but copyrights are "subject to" the exceptions and limitations in the rest of the Copyright Act, including the first sale doctrine, fair use, and the special protections for libraries and archives.

OVERLAPPING RIGHTS

Copyright law allows for multiple overlapping rights to exist in a single work, such as a sound recording. For example, sound recordings of musical works are typically covered by at least two rights: The songwriter or publishing company may own rights in the composition itself (Dolly Parton wrote and owns the copyright for the words and music for "I Will Always Love You"), but a record company typically owns the rights to a particular sound recording of a performance of the song (RCA Music Group, which is the successor to Arista Records, owns the rights to the Whitney Houston recording of "I Will Always Love You"). This overlap of rights in a work on one hand and rights in a particular recorded performance of that work on the other can occur in several other contexts, such as radio performances of dramatic works like plays, or audio versions of literary works such as poetry or novels.

The overlap or multiplicity of rights holders can be an issue for sound recordings in many contexts.

The overlap or multiplicity of rights holders can be an issue for sound recordings in many contexts. A recorded interview or oral history, for example, may be co-authored by the interviewer and the subject. A careful interviewer will obtain necessary permissions or copyright transfer from the subject, but these documents may be lost or poorly drafted, leaving a downstream audio collection with uncertain rights. The sound engineer may be the sole author of some field recordings (e.g., in the case of nature recordings), but an engineer's recorded subjects may be co-authors in many other cases (e.g., recordings of musicians or other human performers who contribute creatively to the recording).[5]

---

[4] Works registered since 1978 can be searched online at the U.S. Copyright Office's website, http://www.copyright.gov. Older works can be searched only in person at the Copyright Office in Washington, D.C. However, other institutions maintain useful information about copyright ownership. The University of Pennsylvania has collected some other search resources at The Online Books Page, http://onlinebooks.library.upenn.edu/cce/. Despite the website's name, many of the resources collected there pertain to works other than books.

[5] While the presence or absence of an "author" credit in connection with a work can be a factor in determining who is an author for legal purposes, it is not determinative. And, as has been described above, authors frequently assign their rights to third parties, often immediately upon creation of the work. In some limited circumstances, however, authors may reclaim their rights after an assignment.

The phenomenon of overlapping rights has several important consequences for sound recording collections. One is that when permission is needed for access and use, it may be necessary to seek permission from multiple rights holders—the songwriter and the record label, for example, or the author and the audiobook publisher. Another consequence is that recordings of performances of works in the public domain—a play by William Shakespeare, for example, or a symphony by Mozart—may be subject to copyright protection because there is a separate right in the particular recorded performance. To determine whether some audio works are in the public domain, you may need to know both when the underlying work was written and when this particular performance was recorded or published.

DIVISIBILITY

Any of the rights in a sound recording (e.g., reproduction, distribution, public performance) may be divided and licensed to different entities in an almost infinite variety of ways. Customarily, these rights are divided geographically (rights to stream a recording in the United States versus in the United Kingdom, for example), temporally (original release versus re-release, for example), or by media (streaming rights versus physical distribution, for example). Whenever possible, it is best to obtain the entire copyright rather than a license.

TERM, PUBLICATION, AND FORMALITIES

Although copyright term has grown longer and longer in recent years, it is still finite, and when a work's copyright term expires it becomes part of the public domain, free for all to use however they like. The details of copyright term can be quite complicated; they vary according to when a work was made, the nature of its author, and whether (and how) it was published. For works made after 1978, the general rule is that copyright lasts for the life of the author plus 70 years. For works whose owners are anonymous, pseudonymous, or corporate (for example, works made for hire by employees of radio or television networks), the term is typically 95 years from publication. For works made before 1978, a series of complicating factors apply. Works published before 1923 are very likely to be in the public domain, with a few exceptions.[6]

Before 1978, different rules applied to published and unpublished works. Federal copyright law protected only published works, while a patchwork of state laws protected unpublished works. Works created after 1977 are automatically protected by copyright as soon as they are created.

To obtain copyright protection, works published prior to January 1, 1978, had to include proper notice—the symbol © and the year of publication, among other things. Between January 1, 1978 and March 1, 1989, use of a copyright notice was still necessary, but omission of notice could be cured within a very generous grace period of five years after

---

[6] For more detailed information about copyright term and how to determine whether a work is in the public domain, see Hirtle 2015 and Mannapperuma et al. 2014.

first publication. After March 1, 1989, notice became purely optional. Although a 1996 law reinstated protection for some foreign works, George Romero's American classic 1968 zombie movie *Night of the Living Dead*, for example, is in the public domain because it was first published without adequate copyright notice.[7] Prior to 1989, rights holders had to file renewal paperwork with the U.S. Copyright Office in order to obtain the full term of protection; copyright in many works was not renewed,[8] and those works entered the public domain at the expiration of their initial term of protection, which was 28 years.

This tangle of formalities, publication, registration, renewal, and so on can make it difficult to determine whether a given work is even protected by copyright. Identifying and locating rights holders in older works can also be costly and difficult.[9] It is therefore important to obtain the broadest possible grant of copyright at the time of acquisition, when possible, and to understand the provisions in the law that allow preservation and access without permission.

LIMITATIONS AND EXCEPTIONS GENERALLY

The rights granted to authors are balanced by a series of limitations and exceptions favoring the public, including provisions specifically favoring libraries and archives. When one of these exceptions applies, neither payment nor permission is required for access and use. The three most important copyright limitations and exceptions are the first sale doctrine, fair use, and the library and archives provisions.

The First Sale Doctrine. Also known as *exhaustion*, the first sale doctrine allows owners of a particular lawfully made copy of a copyrighted work to sell or otherwise dispose of the copy they own.[10] In other words, the copyright holder's control over a particular copy of a work is "exhausted" after the "first sale" of that copy. Subsequent owners are free to lend, sell, rent, or otherwise use their particular copy.[11] It is the first sale doctrine that allows libraries to lend books despite the copyright holder's right to control distribution of protected works. There is an important caveat here for sound recordings, which may not be rented, leased, or loaned for direct or indirect commercial advantage, even after the first sale.[12] Nonprofit libraries and educational institutions may still lend sound recordings for nonprofit purposes, however. The requirement that copies be "lawfully made" can also come into play for copies that have dubious origins, such as pirate editions or bootleg recordings.

---

[7] See Rapold 2014.

[8] A study by the U.S. Copyright Office found that, overall, less than 15 percent of the copyrights examined were renewed after their initial term of protection. However, musical works were renewed at a much higher rate than other categories—more than one-third of musical works registered in 1931–1932 were renewed, compared with 7 percent of books and 11 percent of periodicals (Ringer 1961, 220).

[9] See, e.g., Dickson 2010. Fourteen weeks of full-time searching by a professional archivist located only a handful of rights holders in an archival collection.

[10] See 17 U.S.C. § 109.

[11] So far, courts have not interpreted the right of first sale to allow rental or resale of digital files because "transfer" of digital objects (such as .mp3 files) from one digital device to another requires the creation of a new copy. For now, it looks like a change in this area will require legislative action.

[12] See 17 U.S.C. § 109(b)(1)(A).

Fair Use. The most flexible, and the most powerful, limitation to copyright is the fair use doctrine. Some right of fair use has been a part of copyright since the Statute of Anne. The current version of the doctrine provides that fair use for purposes such as criticism, comment, news reporting, teaching, scholarship, or research is not an infringement.[13] To determine whether a particular use is fair, courts weigh four factors:

1. The purpose and character of the use
2. The nature of the work(s) used
3. The amount and substantiality of the work(s) used
4. The effect on the market for the works used

Over the last two decades, courts have increasingly focused on the first factor. If the courts find that a use is "transformative," by which courts generally mean that the use is for a new and socially beneficial purpose rather than merely displacing and competing unfairly with the original work, and that the amount used is appropriate given that purpose, they overwhelmingly find the use to be fair.

Rules of thumb about particular quantitative limits to fair use are as common as they are baseless.

Many myths and misconceptions have grown up around fair use. Rules of thumb about particular quantitative limits to fair use (e.g., 30 seconds, 10 percent) are as common as they are baseless. Copying even smaller portions of a work can be found infringing if the purpose is merely to compete with the original,[14] but use of entire works has been found fair when the court finds the amount is appropriate in light of the user's legitimate purpose.[15] Several fair use guidelines have been created and promulgated with the appearance of government authority,[16] but none have the force of law; further, the limited view of fair use that they reflect (which predates the courts' turn to transformativeness as the key to fairness) has become obsolete.[17]

---

[13] See 17 U.S.C. § 107.

[14] See, e.g., Harper & Row v. Nation Enters. Inc., 471 U.S. 539 (1985) (finding *The Nation* magazine infringed copyright in President Gerald Ford's memoir by publishing leaked excerpts that made up the commercial "heart" of the work, even though the excerpt made up a small percentage of the total memoir).

[15] See, e.g., Swatch Mgmt Grp. v. Bloomberg L.P., 742 F.3d 17 (2d Cir. 2014) (finding fair use where a news organization distributed full audio recording of earnings call as part of news reporting on the contents of the call).

[16] The 1976 *Agreement on Guidelines for Classroom Copying in Not-for-Profit Educational Institutions*, for example, is often misrepresented as an expression of legislative intent, but in fact it was negotiated between private parties and was immediately repudiated by some educational groups as too restrictive. The guidelines are clearly described as a "safe harbor" and "minimum" standard, but publishers and others have portrayed them as the outer limit of what fair use allows.

[17] In a recent case involving fair use for teaching, publishers sought to enforce the 1976 *Classroom Guidelines* as the outer limits of fair use. Both the district court and the appellate court roundly rejected this effort. Judge Evans of the district court characterized their restrictive limits as "undermin[ing] the educational objective favored by §107." Cambridge Univ. Press v. Becker, 863 F.Supp.2d 1190, 1234 (N.D. Ga. 2012). Judge Tjoflat in the appellate court warned that "to treat the Classroom Guidelines as indicative of what is allowable would be to create the type of 'hard evidentiary presumption' that the Supreme Court has cautioned against." Cambridge Univ. Press v. Patton, 769 F.3d 1232, 1273 (11th Cir. 2014). The Consortium of College and University Media Centers (CCUMC), which promulgated the *Fair Use Guidelines for Educational Multimedia* in 1996 in conjunction with most of the major rights holder trade groups, has since retired those guidelines as no longer reflecting the realities of fair use law. Instead, CCUMC has endorsed the *Code of Best Practices in Fair Use for Academic and Research Libraries* (Association for Research Libraries and American University, 2012) available at http://www.arl.org/fairuse.

The most powerful tools for understanding fair use in contemporary context are the best practices statements that several professional groups have developed over the last decade.

Arguably the most powerful tools for understanding fair use in contemporary context are the best practices statements that several professional groups, such as documentary filmmakers, dance archivists, and academic and research librarians, have developed over the last decade.[18] With help from community leaders and legal scholars, these community best practices eschew arbitrary quantitative limits and negotiated stalemates to focus instead on which community practices are sufficiently distinctive and central to the unique social role of the community to qualify as transformative in the way judges have used that term. The Association of Research Libraries' *Code of Best Practices in Fair Use for Academic and Research Libraries* and the *Statement of Best Practices in Fair Use of Collections Containing Orphan Works for Libraries, Archives, and Other Memory Institutions* (Center for Media & Social Impact 2014) may be of particular interest to readers of this guide. Appendix A describes some of the ways that existing fair use principles could be applied to recurring copyright challenges faced by sound recording collections.

There have been very few cases where courts have ruled on whether preservation constitutes fair use, but decisions in the cases that have been resolved are encouraging. In *Sundeman v. Seajay Society*, for example, the court found that it was fair use to provide a scholar with a complete copy of a fragile unpublished manuscript to avoid damage to the original.[19] In the 2014 decision in *Authors Guild v. HathiTrust*, the appellate court seemed to bless preservation, saying, "By storing digital copies of the books, the HDL [HathiTrust Digital Library] preserves them for generations to come, and ensures that they will exist when the copyright terms lapse."[20]

The legislative history of the Copyright Act is equally encouraging. One of the few references to a particular practice that members of the U.S. Congress believed to be fair involves preservation of decaying film. The House Judiciary Committee's report on the Copyright Act concludes: "The efforts of the Library of Congress, the American Film Institute, and other organizations to rescue and preserve this irreplaceable contribution to our cultural life are to be applauded, and *the making of duplicate copies for purposes of archival preservation certainly falls within the scope of 'fair use.'*"[21]

Congress further signaled its approval of fair use by nonprofit educational institutions and broadcasters by including special protection in the statute for their employees who reasonably believe their uses to be fair, barring the astronomical fines that can sometimes accompany copyright

[18] See, generally, Center for Media and Social Impact 2014, and Aufderheide and Jaszi 2011.
[19] Sundeman v. Seajay Society, Inc., 142 F. 3d 194, 206 (1998). "It would severely restrict scholarly pursuit, and inhibit the purposes of the Copyright Act, if a fragile original could not be copied to facilitate literary criticism." As a private club, the Seajay Society relied on fair use, but as discussed later, a qualified library or archive could also rely on Section 108(d) to make such a copy.
[20] Authors Guild v. HathiTrust, 755 F.3d 87, 103 (2d Cir. 2014). The appellate court did not rule on the HathiTrust practice of making replacement copies for lost or damaged books, but suggested the publisher plaintiffs may not have standing to challenge the practice unless they can demonstrate that their works in particular were in danger of being copied for replacement under the HathiTrust policy.
[21] H.R. Rep. No. 94-1476, at 73 (1976) (emphasis added).

Does Copyright Law Treat Individual Collectors and Institutions Differently?

In general, copyright law is indifferent to whether a user is an individual or an institution. Fair use, for example, is concerned primarily with the nature of the use, not the user. However, some libraries and archives may have a few advantages that are not necessarily available to individuals.

First, although the terms *library* and *archive* as used in Section 108 are not defined, institutions will certainly have an easier time claiming protection under that provision than an individual collector might.

Second, institutions affiliated with states (such as public universities) are protected by state sovereign immunity and cannot be sued for monetary damages under federal law. This protection may not apply to state law claims, however.

Finally, federal law grants immunity from statutory damages to any employee of a nonprofit educational institution (public or private) or broadcaster who had a reasonable good faith belief that his or her activities constituted fair use.

So, although the law does not distinguish categorically between individuals and institutions, it favors the latter in several ways.

lawsuits.[22] This protection applies even if the court decides that the employee was mistaken and the use was not fair, so long as the employee's belief at the time was reasonable.

One final issue merits discussion: the relationship between fair use and other limitations. In recent lawsuits, rights holders have claimed that other limitations should act as ceilings to fair use (i.e., that when a use exceeds the limits of a specific exception, it cannot be fair use). This view is inconsistent with express provisions in the law,[23] and courts have consistently rejected it. In reality, fair use acts as a supplement to the specific exception, and "near miss" scenarios that roughly resemble those favored in specific exceptions should generally be favored in the fair use calculus.[24]

Section 108: Reproduction by Libraries and Archives. For libraries and archives whose collections are either "open to the public" or open to researchers who are "not affiliated with the institution" and copies are not made with any purpose of commercial advantage, Section 108 describes a series of specific scenarios in which works can be reproduced for patrons' use, for interlibrary loan, or for preservation. For preservation of unpublished works, Section 108 allows creation of three copies. Copies in digital formats cannot circulate "to the public" beyond the "premises" of the library.[25]

---

[22] 17 U.S.C. § 504(c)(2).

[23] 17 U.S.C. § 108(f)(4) states that, "Nothing in this Section… in any way affects the right of fair use …."

[24] See Band (2012). The Court of Appeals for the Second Circuit used this approach in finding that fair use allowed HathiTrust to provide access to print-disabled patrons, citing other exceptions favoring the blind as proof of a general policy favoring access.

[25] These two elements of the limitation on digital access are open to interpretation and provide more flexibility than is sometimes acknowledged. Libraries and archives have some room to determine for themselves what constitutes the "premises" of their institution, for example. The limitation to the "premises" applies only to "the public," leaving open the

For replacement copies of published works, Section 108 again allows making three copies, but requires that the original be "damaged, deteriorating, lost, or stolen" or stored on an obsolete format. Critics have observed that once a library's copy qualifies for replacement, the very condition that qualifies it (e.g., damage, loss) will make it difficult or impossible to use the library copy to create a replacement copy. Presumably, a library must use another institution's copy to create its own replacement copy. Obsolescence is another tricky criterion, as the law defines a format as "obsolete" only if machines to play the format are no longer manufactured or not reasonably commercially available, a high bar that likely excludes increasingly inaccessible formats such as VHS or audiocassette.[26] Before making replacement copies, a library or archives must determine that a replacement copy is not reasonably available to purchase at a fair price. And, again, the limitation on public and off-premises circulation applies to replacement copies in digital formats.

Section 108 also allows libraries and archives to make copies for patrons in certain circumstances and to house copying technology for use by patrons. Copyright notices must be included with the copies and posted near the copying machines. Perhaps the most interesting and powerful provision in this context is Section 108(d), which allows a library or archive to provide a copy of an entire work to a patron if the library or archive has determined that a copy cannot be obtained commercially at a reasonable price and has no reason to believe that the patron's use is for any reason other than scholarship or study. Unlike the preservation provisions, however, the parts of Section 108 that permit making copies for patrons *do not apply* to musical works; pictorial, graphic, or sculptural works; or audiovisual works (e.g., motion pictures and television shows) other than news-related works. Sound recordings other than musical works are not affected by this limitation.

8.2 SPECIAL ISSUES

PRE-1972 SOUND RECORDINGS

Although musical compositions and other creative works often embodied in sound recordings have a long history of copyright protection, sound recordings themselves were not protected as a separate category by federal copyright law until 1972. Sound recordings first made before February 15, 1972,[27] continue to be exempt from federal copyright law. Instead, they are governed by state "common law" copyright and antipiracy

---

possibility of lending digital copies for scholarly study by individual researchers or for classroom use by university faculty "off premises." For an excellent guide to Section 108 in the context of video, with obvious analogies to audio, see Besser et al. 2012.

[26] Academic and research librarians have responded by taking advantage of fair use when necessary to preserve or facilitate access to these formats, as described in Principle Three of the *Code of Best Practices in Fair Use for Academic and Research Libraries*.

[27] The key event here is the initial creation of the recording, such as the creation of a master recording of a song, not the subsequent creation of a particular copy. The album version of the Stooges' song "1969" was recorded in April 1969 (appropriately), so that recording is governed by state law, even though particular pressings of the album *The Stooges* have certainly been made long after the February 15, 1972 cut-off date.

Fair Use and Sound Recordings: Lessons from Community Practice, included as Appendix A to this guide, presents strategies for reasonable application of copyright's fair use doctrine to a series of recurring situations encountered by owners of recorded sound collections:

1. Electronic access to rare/unique materials for offsite researchers/users
2. Electronic access to collected materials for affiliated students and instructors in support of teaching
3. Preservation/format-shifting
4. Collecting online materials
5. Data-mining/non-consumptive research
6. Digital exhibits and exhibits for the public
7. Transfer of copies to third parties in support of downstream fair uses

In addition to strategies tailored to each situation, we identify a series of practices we call "Indicia of good faith" that are strongly endorsed by virtually every practice community in virtually every use context. In addition to this core material, we provide a more detailed introduction to copyright and fair use as those doctrines apply to recorded sound, and a short selected bibliography of community statements on fair use.

statutes—and will be until 2067, when they will enter the public domain.

As this guide goes to press, the status of these recordings is the subject of debate in courts and in some parts of the federal government. Library groups and experts have differing opinions as to whether state law is preferable to federal law in regard to preservation and other memory institution functions. Critics of state law cite the lack of a single, consistent federal regime, as well as the absence of statutorily defined exceptions like Section 108. They point out that older sound recordings are kept out of the public domain much longer than they might be under federal law. State law may also allow copyright holders to take defendants into state courts where they do not reside when Internet uses are at issue, a less likely outcome under federal law. A series of lawsuits brought by members of the musical group The Turtles is generating renewed concern about the scope and unpredictability of state copyright protection, as trial courts in New York and California have given state law much broader scope than legal scholars had expected.[28]

On the other hand, some observers have pointed out that state law is generally more limited in scope than federal law in important respects. Most state laws single out commercial activity for regulation, leaving nonprofit uses largely untouched.[29] Some version of the broad and flexible fair use doctrine is almost certainly available and has already been applied in one high-profile state law copyright case.[30] Perhaps most important, state law does not provide for statutory damages awards, which are untethered from actual harm to the copyright holder. A nonprofit or academic user can thus be more confident that they will not face the kinds of stiff penalties associated with commercial piracy. Federal law, by contrast, provides for up to $150,000 in damages per work infringed, regardless of harm.

In any case, professionals working with pre-1972 sound recordings should work with their general counsel's office to learn more about the state laws that apply to the use of their recordings, and they must recognize that applicable state laws may include not only those of the state where the collection resides, but also those of the state where the rights

---

[28] For a good summary of the issues and stakes of these lawsuits, see Ochoa 2014.

[29] For a representative survey of 10 state law regimes, see Jaszi 2009.

[30] When Yoko Ono and the EMI record label sued the makers of a documentary film promoting creationism over critical use of the song "Imagine," the judge declared that "fair use is available as a defense in the context of sound recordings," and consulted federal case law as a guide on the scope of fair use protection against state common law copyright claims. EMI Records Ltd. v. Premise Media Corp., 2008 N.Y. Misc. Lexis 7485 at *15 (N.Y. Sup. Ct. Aug. 8, 2008). The Supreme Court has said that fair use is a "built-in First Amendment accommodation" in copyright, and presumably state law would have to recognize something similar lest they be found unconstitutional. See Eldred v. Ashcroft, 537 U.S. 186, 190 (2003).

holder resides.[31] The evolving case law in New York and California may be particularly relevant for this reason. And remember: Federal protection will still be an issue for musical compositions or other works contained in these older sound recordings, so both state and federal law may apply.

LICENSES

Recorded sound collections are not always owned by the collector or collecting institution. Licensing has become an increasingly common mode of access to recorded sound, and the legal consequences of licensing are distinct from those of ownership. First, many courts have found that contractual agreements override the protections for users in the copyright law, such as fair use. If you have agreed contractually to limit your uses (as in a donor agreement or a click-through license), you may be required to follow the agreement despite the existence of a fair use right (or a Section 108 right) to the contrary.[32] The moral of the story is to read your licenses carefully and to negotiate zealously in defense of your rights under the law whenever possible.

Licensing has become an increasingly common mode of access to recorded sound, and the legal consequences of licensing are distinct from those of ownership.

One salutary development in the copyright licensing landscape is the advent of the Creative Commons (CC) licenses.[33] These licenses, developed and supported by the Creative Commons organization, provide authors who share works on the Internet with a relatively simple way to ensure that others can use their works freely in a variety of ways without having to seek permission. Because a CC license is a grant of permission based on ownership of a copyright, only a copyright holder can attach a CC license to a work. Many creators of sound recordings posted online use CC licenses to encourage the reuse of their works. Various CC licenses are available to choose from, and each license carries a series of conditions on reuse, such as requiring attribution, barring modification, or requiring that any adapted versions be made available under the same CC license. Sound recording collectors can take advantage of CC-licensed materials to enhance their collections, can encourage donors who hold copyrights to attach CC licenses to their donated collections, and can use CC licenses to encourage sharing and reuse of the works in their collections for which they own the copyrights.

---

[31] The U.S. Copyright Office (2011) has published a report on pre-1972 sound recordings, recommending that they be incorporated into the federal scheme. Helpfully, the Office has also published two compilations showing the various state laws that apply to sound recordings. They are available at http://www.copyright.gov/docs/sound/.

[32] One particularly troubling variety of contractual limitation on use of recorded sound is the End User License Agreement or Terms of Use that govern online music markets like the iTunes Store and the Amazon MP3 Store. Music librarians have raised significant concerns about the seeming inconsistency of such licenses with library acquisition and use. See, e.g., Sound Recording Collecting in Crisis, available at http://guides.lib.washington.edu/imls2014. And, of course, these licenses are not subject to negotiation.

[33] More information about Creative Commons and the various licenses that they have developed is available at http://www.creativecommons.org.

BOOTLEGS

Some recorded sound collections may include recordings of live performances made without the consent of the performers, colloquially known as bootleg recordings.[34] Since 1994, there has been a federal prohibition on making and distributing bootlegs of musical performances.[35] These statutes mirror copyright law in the scope of activities that they cover (e.g., reproduction, distribution, rental, sale), and federal law gives performers the same civil remedies that copyright holders have, including statutory damages. Federal law does not create a claim for mere possession of a copy, although some state laws may cover possession with intent to sell, rent, and the like.[36]

Nevertheless, these legal protections for performers are not technically copyright laws because they protect performances that have not yet been fixed into (an authorized) tangible medium and they do not have a limited term. The bootleg provisions also do not have any express exemption for fair use or other protected First Amendment activities. However, there is good reason to believe that fair use (at least) is available as a defense to a claim under the bootlegging statute, suggesting that bootleg recordings can be used fairly just as ordinary recordings can.[37] Despite their inconsistency with core constitutional requirements for copyright laws, these statutes have survived constitutional challenges.[38]

---

[34] See, for example, California's antibootlegging provision, which criminalizes "[a]ny person who transports or causes to be transported for monetary or other consideration within this state, any article containing sounds of a live performance with the knowledge that the sounds thereon have been recorded or mastered without the consent of the owner of the sounds of the live performance." Cal. Penal Code § 653s (West). Unlike the federal law, California's law, applies to all performances, not just musical ones. Also, such recordings are, presumably, made without the consent of the copyright holder of any underlying work, such as a musical or literary work being performed, and copies of such recordings therefore will not be "lawfully made" for purposes of the first sale doctrine. As mentioned above, the first sale doctrine allows lending and resale only of lawfully made copies.

[35] See 17 U.S.C. § 1101 (civil cause of action) and 18 U.S.C. § 2319A(a). The criminal provision requires that the recording be made or distributed "for purposes of commercial advantage or private financial gain."

[36] California's law applies to "[e]very person who offers for sale or resale, or sells or resells, or causes the sale or resale, or rents, or possesses *for these purposes* [bootleg recordings]." Cal. Penal Code § 653s (West).

[37] William Patry observes that "there is no reason courts cannot, as with the pre-1976 statutes, read in…limitations" and points to the President's statement, endorsed by Congress as part of the passage of the antibootlegging law, that "[i]t is intended that neither civil nor criminal liability will arise in cases where First Amendment principles are implicated, such as where small portions of an unauthorized fixation are used without permission in a news broadcast or for other purposes of comment or criticism." 7 Patry on Copyright § 24:12. See also Dallon 2011, who says, "Strong historical precedent supports a fair use defense [against an anti-bootlegging claim]" (319).

[38] United States v. Martignon, 492 F.3d 140 (2d Cir. 2007), which upheld criminal provisions; Kiss Catalog, Ltd. v. Passport Int'l Prods., Inc., 405 F. Supp. 2d 1169 (C.D. Cal. 2005), which upheld civil provisions.

8.3 CONTROL AND RESPONSIBILITY FOR DOWNSTREAM USE OF WORKS

Many archives and institutions seek to control the downstream use of materials from their collections. For example, archives and special collections often require scholars to sign agreements stating that they will credit the collection as the source of an archival image if the image is reprinted in a published work, such as a book or journal article. Others require scholars who obtain access to collection materials to seek additional permission before republishing even excerpts from the materials. Sometimes these usage conditions result from donor agreements or informal understandings with donors that materials will not be made available beyond certain limited contexts.

Leaving aside the question of whether exercising this control is in line with professional norms,[39] it is important to understand the limited legal bases for exercising control over such uses. For example, collectors of sound recordings may not, in fact, own the copyrights in the works they collect, or the works may not be subject to copyright at all. In such cases, it is inappropriate to cite copyright as a source of authority for control of downstream uses of collection materials. For works in the public domain or those for which the collector does not hold copyright, control is more likely to be grounded in contract law. If a researcher does not sign an agreement with the collector or collecting institution, and the collector or institution does not own the copyright in the work, it is unlikely that the collector or the institution has any power at all to control downstream use.

By the same token, memory institutions often worry that they could be liable for others' downstream uses when they provide access to works in their collections. For example, if a patron obtains a copy of a recording in your collection and then posts the recording to social media, would you be liable if the posting constitutes copyright infringement? Put simply, it is almost impossible for an institution or an employee of an institution to be held responsible for the bad acts of others who abuse their access to copyrighted materials. Legal doctrines of secondary liability require substantial control over the infringing activity, knowing encouragement of the activity, or direct profit from the activity, none of which is likely to apply to downstream uses of materials made available for free or at cost for presumably scholarly or research purposes. For libraries and archives, there are additional protections against liability for unsupervised use of library copying equipment and for copies provided on request to patrons, so long as appropriate warnings are posted or attached to the relevant copies.[40]

---

[39] Peter Hirtle (2014) has written persuasively that such controls are often inconsistent with the norms of the archivist community. His argument revolves around the use of sound recordings from a university archive.

[40] See 17 U.S.C. § 108.

8.4 DONOR AGREEMENTS

A carefully drafted donor agreement can anticipate and solve almost any copyright-related problem for a sound recording collection (or any other collection), while a poorly or narrowly drafted agreement can leave those responsible for the collection worse off than if there were no agreement at all. Because owning a copy of a work is not the same as owning the copyrights in that work, a donor agreement can be a crucial tool for ensuring that a work can be used and preserved flexibly in the future. The following are a few things to keep in mind when negotiating donor agreements:

A poorly or narrowly drafted donor agreement can leave those responsible for the collection worse off than if there were no agreement at all.

- **Get the broadest possible grant of rights**, preferably a full transfer of the copyright in the donated works—but at a minimum, a broad license not only for the collection owners' uses, but also for uses by patrons.
- **Preserve your default rights.** It is possible to sign away legal rights such as the first sale right to freely lend or the Section 108 right to make replacement copies. Be wary of a donor agreement that leaves you worse off than if you had simply bought a copy of the recording online or at an estate sale. If possible, avoid agreements that specifically enumerate a closed list of permissible uses that the collecting institution may make of the donated work. Make sure that any restrictions apply only for a defined term not exceeding the copyright term.
- **Know the limits of what your donor can give you.** Some donors may not be copyright holders, or they may hold only part of the rights embedded in a recording. In these cases, even if the donors transfer all their copyrights to the institution, you may still need to seek permission, or else employ a statutory exception like fair use, to make certain uses of a recording. On the other hand, in cases involving joint authors of a single work (a common scenario for sound recordings), any co-author of a work can grant non-exclusive licenses without permission or consultation with other authors so long as all co-authors get appropriate shares of any profits. So, for example, any one co-author of a musical composition can grant a non-exclusive license to use the composition, but the separate copyright in the sound recording may still bar use of the recording unless the holder of that right also grants permission.

There are many model acquisition agreements available online. The Association of Research Libraries (ARL) has collected a variety of excellent model agreements in the June 2012 issue of *Research Library Issues*. These models include clauses consistent with each of the broad considerations that have been described. One clause in the ARL models that is not always present in other models is an express acknowledgment that the receiving institution reserves its full range of legal rights under fair use, notwithstanding any other provisions in the agreement. Institutions are increasingly conscious of the importance of retaining their fair use rights, and these clauses are likely to become more common, as they should.

REFERENCES

All URLs are current as of May 1, 2015

Association of Research Libraries. 2012. "A Quarterly Report from ARL, CNI, and SPARC." *Research Library Issues*. Special Issue on Special Collections and Archives in the Digital Age. Available at http://publications.arl.org/rli279.

Association of Research Libraries and American University. 2012. *Code of Best Practices in Fair Use for Academic and Research Libraries.* Washington, DC: Association of Research Libraries; Center for Social Media, School of Communication, American University; and Program on Information Justice and Intellectual Property, Washington College of Law, American University. Available at http://www.arl.org/storage/documents/publications/code-of-best-practices-fair-use.pdf.

Aufderheide, Patricia, and Peter Jaszi. 2011. *Reclaiming Fair Use: How to Put Balance Back in Copyright.* Chicago: University of Chicago Press.

Band, Jonathan. 2012. "The Impact of Substantial Compliance with Copyright Exceptions on Fair Use." *Journal of the Copyright Society of The U.S.A.* 59:453.

Besser, Howard, Melissa Brown, Robert Clarida, Walter Forsberg, Mark Righter, and Michael Stoller. 2012. *Video at Risk: Strategies for Preserving Commercial Video Collections in Libraries. Section 108 Guidelines.* New York: New York University Libraries. Available at http://www.nyu.edu/tisch/preservation/research/video-risk/VideoAtRisk_SECTION108_Guidelines_2013.pdf.

Center for Media & Social Impact. 2014. *Statement of Best Practices in Fair Use of Collections Containing Orphan Works for Libraries, Archives, and Other Memory Institutions.* Coordinated by The Program on Information Justice and Intellectual Property, Washington College of Law, American University; Center for Media & Social Impact, School of Communication, American University; and The Berkeley Digital Library Copyright Project, University of California, Berkeley, School of Law. Available at http://www.cmsimpact.org/sites/default/files/documents/orphanworks-dec14.pdf.

Dallon, Craig. 2011. "The Anti-Bootlegging Provisions: Congressional Power and Constitutional Limitations." *Vanderbilt Journal of Entertainment & Technology Law* 13(2):255–321. Available at http://www.jetlaw.org/wp-content/uploads/2011/05/Dallon-FINAL.pdf.

Dickson, Maggie. 2010. "Due Diligence, Futile Effort: Copyright and the Digitization of the Thomas E. Watson Papers." *American Archivist* 73:618, 619.

Hirtle, Peter. 2015. *Copyright Term and the Public Domain in the United States.* Available at https://copyright.cornell.edu/resources/publicdomain.cfm.

Hirtle, Peter. 2014. "What the University of Arkansas Controversy Can Teach us About Archival Permission Practices." LibraryLaw Blog, July 24, 2014. Available at http://blog.librarylaw.com/librarylaw/2014/07/arkansas-and-archival-permission-practices.html.

Jaszi, Peter. 2009. *Protection for Pre-1972 Sound Recordings Under State Law and its Impact on Use by Nonprofit Institutions: A 10-State Analysis*. Prepared by the Program on Information Justice and Intellectual Property, Washington College of Law, American University, under the supervision of Peter Jaszi with the assistance of Nick Lewis. Washington, D.C.: Council on Library and Information Resources and Library of Congress. Available at http://www.clir.org/pubs/abstract/reports/pub146.

Mannapperuma, Menesha, Brianna Schofield, Andrea K. Yankovsky, Lila Bailey, and Jennifer M. Urban. 2014. *Is It in the Public Domain? A Handbook for Evaluating the Copyright Status of a Work Created in the United States Between January 1, 1923 and December 31, 1977*. Available at https://www.law.berkeley.edu/files/FINAL_PublicDomain_Handbook_FINAL(1).pdf.

Ochoa, Tyler. 2014. *A Seismic Ruling On Pre-1972 Sound Recordings and State Copyright Law Flo & Eddie v. Sirius XM Radio*. Technology & Marketing Law Blog, October 1, 2014. Available at http://blog.ericgoldman.org/archives/2014/10/a-seismic-ruling-on-pre-1972-sound-recordings-and-state-copyright-law-flo-eddie-v-sirius-xm-radio-guest-blog-post.htm.

Rapold, Nicolas. 2014. "Even Good Films May Go to Purgatory—Old Films Fall Into Public Domain Under Copyright Law." *New York Times*, February 14. Available at http://www.nytimes.com/2014/02/16/movies/old-films-fall-into-public-domain-under-copyright-law.html?_r=0.

Ringer, Barbara A. 1961. "Renewal of Copyright." In *Copyright Law Revision: Studies Prepared for the Subcommittee on Patents, Trademarks, and Copyrights of the Committee on the Judiciary, United States Senate, Studies 29–31*, 105–225. Washington, D.C.: U.S. Government Printing Office. Available at http://www.copyright.gov/history/studies/study31.pdf.

U.S. Copyright Office. 2011. *Federal Copyright Protection for Pre-1972 Sound Recordings*. Available at http://copyright.gov/docs/sound/pre-72-report.pdf.

ADDITIONAL RESOURCES

Besek, June M. 2005. *Copyright Issues Relevant to Digital Preservation and Dissemination of Pre-1972 Commercial Sound Recordings by Libraries and Archives*. Commissioned for and sponsored by the National Recording Preservation Board, Library of Congress. Washington, D.C.: Council on Library and Information Resources and Library of Congress. Available at http://www.clir.org/pubs/abstract/reports/pub135.

Besek, June M. 2009. *Copyright and Related Issues Relevant to Digital Preservation and Dissemination of Unpublished Pre-1972 Sound Recordings by Libraries and Archives*. Commissioned for and sponsored by the National Recording Preservation Board, Library of Congress. Washington, D.C.: Council on Library and Information Resources and Library of Congress. Available at http://www.clir.org/pubs/abstract/reports/pub144.

CHAPTER 9

Disaster Prevention, Preparedness, and Response

By Kara Van Malssen

This chapter outlines some basic elements of disaster prevention, preparedness, and recovery for audio collections. It also includes a disaster recovery case study, which highlights many of the issues discussed throughout the chapter: how a recovery was organized and conducted to ensure long-term damage was minimized, how the disaster could have been mitigated, and what preparedness steps would have made the recovery more efficient.

The pages that follow focus on disaster preparedness and response for physical collections: discs, reels, and cassettes that occupy shelves and boxes. However, one thread that runs throughout this chapter is the need for digitization and digital preservation for disaster preparedness purposes. The need for digitization of many physical formats is urgent as media deteriorate, as equipment and expertise become more scarce and expensive, and as access demands for digital content are more pressing. Disaster prevention and recovery should represent yet another motivation for digitization and proper digital preservation. If managed correctly, through proper backup and geographic separation, recovery of digital data from an offsite copy will be a relatively painless, simple, and lossless process, compared with the difficult recovery and almost certain degree of loss if a flood or fire affects physical media.

Collection managers should identify the most important materials in their collections and set priorities for their digitization and management, but this will not happen overnight. In the meantime, taking measures to protect collections will help to ensure that their contents will be accessible over time.

Disaster preparedness is an ongoing process. Once one risk is addressed, another can emerge unnoticed. To be effective, preparedness must be an integral part of collection management.

9.1 DISASTER PREVENTION AND MITIGATION

Measures to help prevent disaster can also minimize the effects when one does occur. Ensuring proper building and collection security, repairing faulty or exposed wiring, and installing storm shutters will all reduce the likelihood of theft, electrical fires, and storm damage. Good storage, staff training, and collection knowledge can prevent a host of potential disasters, especially disasters in which damage builds over time, for example, as a result of continual mishandling and tape deterioration.

The activities outlined here and in the section on disaster preparedness are not mutually exclusive, nor should they be thought of as sequential. Preventive actions and preparedness measures can be tackled in parallel. Start with a risk assessment to identify areas of priority, and begin to address preventive measures, such as fixing a leaky roof, while simultaneously performing preparedness actions, such as gathering supplies in case a storm should make the damage worse before repairs are complete.

ASSESS AND REDUCE RISK

Disasters come in all shapes and sizes. A leaking pipe that goes unnoticed for a few months, resulting in mold growth, is not the same as a category five hurricane or a fire. Some risks may not be obvious. Performing a risk assessment survey will help you prepare for the threats most likely to affect your collection.

The Canadian Conservation Institute (CCI) and the International Centre for the Study of the Preservation and Restoration of Cultural Property (ICCROM) have developed a useful model for managing and reducing risks to cultural collections: (1) establish the context, (2) identify risks, (3) analyze risks, (4) evaluate risks, (5) treat risks, and (6) communicate.[1] This simple structure provides a framework for approaching risk management for recorded sound or any other type of collection. Following this approach, collection managers can begin to address and subsequently treat potential large- and small-scale disaster risks to collections. The first five phases can be described as follows.

1. Establish the context. Perform a valuation, or appraisal, of the collection by looking at the organizational context. Are all items valued equally? Do you place higher value on original recordings than you do on commercial recordings? Value may be determined by national significance, high historical or cultural value, or other attributes that best fit the institution's mission. Some items may be assigned high value because there are no duplicates of that content. Appraising audio materials is a subjective task that requires collection and subject matter expertise. In large institutions, appraisal is likely to require the input of many staff members; in small institutions or individual collections, there may be only one person who can perform appraisal. Chapter 3 provides more criteria

---

[1] See details on ICCROM's Reducing Risks to Collections program at http://www.iccrom.org/courses/reducing-risks-to-collections/. Additional information about the risk management cycle is available at http://www.iccrom.org/ifrcdn/eng/prog_en/01coll_en/archive-preven_en/2007_06risks_infodoc_en.pdf.

to consider when making appraisal decisions. At a minimum, determine a rough sense of the priority of items or collections. Although appraisal may be difficult at this stage, it is important for preparedness planning and critical during a disaster recovery operation.

2. Identify risks. Among the possible risks are rare events (e.g., flood, fire, earthquake, war) and cumulative events (e.g., water leaks). Identify risks to your region, city, building, and collection. Review the history of disasters. Look at possible risks and think through prospective scenarios that may cause damage. Write simple sentences that describe such scenarios. Sometimes the biggest threats are not obvious, so be sure to look carefully at all levels of risk. For example, you may not think much about the aging electrical system in the building, but it can be an enormous fire hazard. Once you have identified risks, take steps to minimize them.

3. Analyze risks. Categorize risks by their frequency and likely impact. For each one, determine how often the event is likely to occur and how much value would be lost in each item, as well as for the collection as a whole, if the event did occur. For instance, scratches on an LP caused by a collapsed shelving unit are not likely to damage the entire disc and, in many circumstances, can be repaired. However, the same collapsed shelf could permanently destroy lacquer and other fragile disc formats, and affect a large percentage of the value of each affected item.

4. Evaluate risks. Based on your analysis, rate risks according to probability of occurrence and impact. Is a flood likely to happen in your area in the next 10 years? Is it likely to cause major damage to collections? If so, planning for a flood should be a high priority. Is poor labeling and tracking likely to cause important items in the collection to become lost within the next year? If so, improving the labeling and tracking systems is also a high priority. Measures to prevent risks that are less likely to occur frequently, or will have lesser impact, are lower priorities.

5. Treat risks. Take steps to minimize or reduce identified risks. Although you may want to address the biggest risks first, they may also be the most challenging. Do not let the biggest tasks keep you from taking steps to treat risks for the lower priority items, especially if the latter are easy to address.

RISK TREATMENT

The following areas commonly need attention to reduce risk to collections. This list is not exhaustive, but is intended to trigger ideas about potential risk areas, including those that may be easily overlooked.

Building Structure and Systems. The building that houses a collection is the first, and at times the only, line of defense against long- and short-term disasters. Yet the building itself, or weakness within it, often poses the greatest threat to audio collections. Leaking pipes and electrical fires are frequently the cause of disasters.

When possible, work with the building's maintenance and facilities staff to identify and correct potential hazards. Incorporate preventive actions into the maintenance activities scheduled for your collection and building,[2] such as regular cleaning of the work and storage areas, inspection of the facilities, and maintenance of the plumbing. If the collection is at a very small institution or in your home, do a thorough inspection of the building. Seek help from professionals, friends, or acquaintances who have experience with building construction, renovation, or maintenance.

Take steps to ensure that the building can protect collections from external threats. For example, if you are in a hurricane-prone area, fit shutters on your windows. If dust storms are common in your area, you may need to use heavy curtains or seal cracks in walls and windows.

For the safety of collections and staff, fire detection and suppression systems should be installed.[3] There are a variety of systems to choose from, including fire extinguishers, wet and dry sprinklers, gas suppression systems, and smoke and heat detectors. Equipment should be frequently inspected and maintained. In particular, fire extinguishers need replacement, and gas suppression systems need recharging at regular intervals. All staff members should know where detection and suppression systems are located in the building and should be trained in their operation.

Proper Storage. The following recommendations will help reduce the effects of any disaster on audio materials and increase the chances of a complete recovery in the event of damage.

- **Keep tapes wound.** If a tape is damaged, the exposed area may need to be removed. It is much better to lose the leader at the beginning or end than important content in the middle of the tape.
- **Store collections in areas least prone to water damage.** Store master materials off the floor, and not in a basement or directly under a roof.

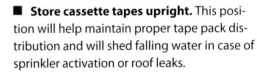

- **Store cassette tapes upright.** This position will help maintain proper tape pack distribution and will shed falling water in case of sprinkler activation or roof leaks.
- **Be sure all items are in some type of enclosure.** Plastic cases and containers are preferred. The enclosure will be the final point of defense before the carrier itself is damaged.
- **Strive for proper climate control.** As explained in chapter 4, storing media in a climate-controlled environment will greatly increase their life expectancy by reducing the risk of long-term damage, such as binder degradation, vinegar syndrome (in acetate open reel tapes), and mold growth. Climate control

Cassette tapes should be stored upright, in boxes or drawers.

---

[2] For an extensive checklist of housekeeping and maintenance activities, see Wellseiser and Scott 2002, 53–61.

[3] Granting agencies often require that institutions have fire detection and suppression systems in place before they will fund preservation projects.

is not always possible, but at least do not store valuable materials in areas where climate fluctuates, such as attics. Try to keep them in an insulated environment.

- **Keep a complete inventory of all materials offsite.** In a disaster, databases and other electronic records are likely to be unavailable. Having a paper inventory with identifiers will help greatly with identification, prioritization, and recovery.
- **Digitize collections as soon as possible.** Technological obsolescence and physical disasters pose enormous threats to the longevity of audio content. Digitization is a step toward protecting recordings from these threats, while also making them more widely accessible.
- **Back up and geographically separate digital collections.** Ensure that there is at least one geographically separate copy of all digital content. Geographic separation means that the backup is far enough away that immediate risks to the primary copy are not also threats to the backup copy. The greater the distance of separation, the better, but even keeping the copy in another building is better than keeping backups next to primary copies.

Knowing your collection is the single most important factor in successful recovery.

Collection Profiling. Collection managers who have been through a disaster say that knowing your collection is the single most important factor in successful recovery. It is almost impossible to set priorities for recovering collections that are unfamiliar, unprocessed, or have no identification. Having a broad overview of the collection enables you to identify how many items need to be stored in specific environmental conditions, to classify items by vulnerability to water or fire, and to identify the number of items that may need to be treated by an external service provider in an emergency.

Start by completing a collection profile that identifies the number and format of items in the collection. Begin with broad categories. When feasible, further categorize the items into specific audio formats (e.g., LP, ¼-inch open reel).

Inventory and Labeling. Create or update collection records and labels. Adequate identification will be critical in a disaster. Recovering audio materials is expensive and time-consuming. If you are unable to identify badly damaged items, you may clean or send to a lab something that is not of high priority or something that has an undamaged duplicate stored elsewhere, instead of items that are of high value or irreplaceable. Also, labs need information about the items they are recovering to give accurate pricing and to perform the correct procedures for the carrier.

Item labels should include at least a title or brief description and an identifier. The identifiers should correspond to those in your inventory. Ideally, item labels should also include a total running time and record date.

Chapter 5 offers guidance in creating an item-level inventory of a collection. The inventory can have more detail than the label, but in many ways, it serves as a cross reference. Include the format, date, associated collection, and description. For formats such as ¼-inch open reel, it is helpful to note on the label whether the tape is full, half, or quarter track, and the recording speed. Inventories should specify the role and generation of the item: Is it unique? Is it a duplicate? Is there a master recording stored elsewhere? Is this just an access copy?

Photographic documentation has also been suggested as a useful supplementary inventory resource in recovering from a disaster. One owner of a collection of master recordings of studio sessions has created a comprehensive set of digital photographs of his holdings. The photographs include both wide shots of media on shelves and images of labels of individual items. Images such as these may also be of value in making insurance claims for lost materials that have a specific market value, such as rare disc recordings.

Deaccessioning. In a disaster, materials tend to get knocked over, mixed together, and removed from their original storage locations. Sometimes, media are separated from their containers because of the force of water or impact, and labels can become smudged or removed. Consequently, it can be difficult to identify which items are which, and which are the most important. Precious time may be spent recovering low- or no-value items at the expense of the highest priority materials. A commitment to deaccessioning and discarding items that have been determined not to be of value, or are intended to be removed from the collection, can go a long way toward ensuring that only the important items receive the critical care that they need in a recovery operation.

Care and Handling. Small disasters are often the result of mishandling. They can be prevented by ensuring that staff and caretakers are well trained to handle collections with care, are observant of problems, and are able to record accurate information about an item's condition.

To mitigate problems caused by mishandling, staff working with collections should have the following minimal training:

- **Format identification:** All staff should be familiar with formats found in the collection (see chapter 2 for descriptions of recorded sound formats). They should be able to distinguish different types of discs (e.g., LP, shellac, transcription) and tapes (e.g., ¼-inch reels, ½-inch reels). Ideally, staff should be able to recognize the difference between audio and video formats when they look similar (e.g., MiniDV and digital audio tape).
- **Handling:** Training in handling should cover proper transport, inspection techniques, machine threading, and rewinding. (See chapter 4 for guidance on proper handling of recorded sound formats.)
- **Condition reporting:** Staff should learn to keep up-to-date, accurate records about items in the collection, as the records will be a priceless resource in setting priorities in a disaster recovery.
- **Storage preparation:** Ensure that staff members wind tapes and secure open reel tape ends to the reel before an item is returned to storage.

9.2 DISASTER PLANNING

Disaster planning is more than the creation of a written disaster plan. Although such plans are extremely valuable, they are truly effective only when collection caretakers are trained in their use and take part in their creation and maintenance. The value of disaster planning is the process itself—training, familiarization, and practice—so that when a disaster strikes, all staff or stewards are prepared. For individual collectors and artists in particular, a written plan is not nearly as important as taking appropriate steps to be prepared in an emergency.

Disaster preparedness planning has two goals:

1. Ensuring that the appropriate policies and procedures are in place so that staff know how and when to react to an emergency warning if such a warning is issued
2. Enabling effective response in case of damage

PREPAREDNESS POLICIES AND PROCEDURES

Not all emergencies are preceded by warnings. When they are, preparedness steps are taken to prevent an emergency from turning into a disaster. This is not the time to go to the store, start fixing the hole in the roof, or put cassettes in new cases. Time is of the essence. A well-researched and tested disaster preparedness plan will allow you to take swift action at these moments.

Disaster preparedness actions are by nature contextual. Hurricanes or typhoons, dust storms, flash floods, tornadoes, fires, or civil unrest warnings each require very different preparedness steps. Localized threats, arising when pipes have aged or electrical wiring is faulty and the building itself is the threat, require a different set of preparedness steps. The way each threat is addressed depends on the location of the building (e.g., on high or low ground, or near water) and its structural materials, and where and how collections are stored.

Each line of defense for the collection should be considered. Think of these defenses as layers, akin to a Russian *matryoshka*, or nesting, doll: The outermost provides protection for the next, which protects the one inside it, and so on. Start with the outermost layer, typically the building. Whenever possible, collaborate with people who know the structure well, such as the building manager or owner. Conduct research and talk to others in the region who work in buildings of a similar structure and material to find out what precautions they take when emergency warnings are issued. Factor in structural vulnerabilities that may need to be addressed.

Additional defensive lines may need to be strengthened. Depending on the anticipated risks (e.g., roof leaks, flooding, structural collapse), preparedness procedures may include covering shelves and boxes with plastic sheeting, moving collections off the floor and onto higher shelves, moving collections from one room to another, and the like.

All individuals responsible for the collection should be involved in establishing preparedness procedures. The team should work together to decide when, after warnings are issued, the planned procedures should go into effect, bearing in mind individuals' personal needs in emergency situations. If people need time to secure their own homes or evacuate the area, this should be accommodated in the preparedness procedures.

STAFF TRAINING AND SIMULATION

Once a disaster strikes, the availability of individuals to help with recovery will vary greatly, depending on their personal circumstances. Therefore, preparedness should be as inclusive as possible; anyone who might be available to help in a disaster should undergo training. Simulation training is highly recommended, as it helps people become familiar with preparedness actions and the process of disaster recovery. It addresses the confusion and anxiety that arise during disasters, while simultaneously exposing how the constraints and urgency of a recovery scenario can influence disaster preparedness steps.

Two types of staff training should be conducted:

1. *Disaster preparedness drills:* These drills should prepare staff to react when a disaster alert has been issued and the preparedness procedures must be put into place (see Preparedness Procedures and Policies in this chapter). The more often these drills are rehearsed, the more efficiently they can be enacted when the time comes.
2. *Disaster recovery training:* This training places staff in a post-emergency situation and allows them to work through a recovery operation.

Simulated disaster recovery training involves setting up a small, isolated "collection" of materials that have been affected by some type of disaster. The collection should include a mix of materials (both of type and value): audio formats found in the collection, paper records, and artifacts. Because nearly all disasters involve water, this is a good damage agent to use during recovery simulations.

The experience should force participants to think through the disaster recovery process and inform the preparedness process by raising questions: Who is our insurance company? How do you set priorities when media items are unlabeled? Are these commercial LPs really valuable? How do you clean a ¼-inch open reel tape? An experienced and trained professional should guide the training, but should leave the operation of the recovery and the discovery of lessons learned largely to the participants. Training activities include verifying that the area is safe to enter, surveying and documenting the damage site, establishing roles and responsibilities, gathering and managing supplies, performing triage, handling materials, establishing and mantaining workflow, documentation, and cleaning and drying. The outcomes of this type of training are likely to reveal steps that can be factored into preparedness planning procedures.

Additional suggestions for emergency kit inventories can be found at the following resources:

American Library Association, *"Beyond Words": Prepare an Emergency Kit.* http://www.ala.org/aasl/sites/ala.org.aasl/files/content/aaslawards/beyondwords/beyondwordstoolkit.pdf.

The Getty Conservation Institute, *Building an Emergency Plan: A Guide for Museums and Other Cultural Institutions.* Supply inventories may be found on pp. 132–33, 165–66, and 198-99. http://www.getty.edu/conservation/publications_resources/pdf_publications/pdf/emergency_plan.pdf.

Syracuse University Libraries Disaster Recovery Manual: Library Emergency Supply List. http://library.syr.edu/about/departments/preservation/recovery/.

EQUIPMENT AND SUPPLIES

In an area-wide emergency, supplies will be hard to come by; at first, you will probably have to work only with what is immediately available. Even in the case of a small, localized disaster (such as a burst pipe), it is much easier to protect collections from damage if basic supplies, such as plastic sheeting, are already on hand. Keeping a stock of emergency supplies will facilitate an effective recovery.

Use your knowledge of the area and the building to determine which supplies and equipment will be essential after a disaster. For example, if interruptions in electricity are common, an uninterruptable power supply or a small power generator might be a wise investment. If your area is earthquake-prone, having emergency lighting, or at least an adequate supply of flashlights and batteries, will be critical.

Keep emergency supplies in a watertight plastic container, in an easily accessible place (e.g., near building entrances, in your car), and if possible, in multiple locations. A basic list of supplies you might want to have on hand includes the following:

- A few gallons of distilled water
- Nitrile gloves (latex and powder-free)
- N95 face masks
- Trash bags, both large and small
- Tape: paper, masking, duct
- Plastic sheeting (to cover surfaces)
- Rolls of paper (to cover surfaces for drying)
- Paper towels
- Permanent felt markers, pencils, pens
- Flat trays or bins (for moving items)
- Flashlights, headlamps, and batteries
- Notepads and clipboards
- Microfiber towels or other lint-free cloths
- Isopropyl alcohol
- Cotton swabs
- Buckets

PRIORITIZATION AND IDENTIFICATION

Think about which items in the collection should receive priority for evacuation or recovery if damaged in a disaster. This is where the appraisal process discussed earlier becomes very important. Make sure that these items are well identified. Consider storing priority collections in a separate area that can be easily found in the dark (in case of a power outage). Organizations have used various approaches to ensure that these items can be quickly found and retrieved in an emergency. Two approaches are identifying storage locations on building diagrams and using glow-in-the-dark stickers for marking shelves.

DISASTER PLAN DOCUMENTATION

A written disaster plan is an invaluable resource in an emergency. It can be a quick reference for telephone numbers and email addresses of staff and external resources (e.g., labs). It should also contain information about preparedness steps for the building and collections, including floor plans and the location of emergency exits, shut-off valves, electrical breakers and outlets, priority materials, and details of salvage procedures.

It is not necessary for a written disaster plan to be long or overly detailed. It should be succinct, clear, and easy to use. Sections of the plan should be tabbed so they can be easily located. Lists, diagrams, and bold text will be most useful in an emergency. The document should be available in both print and electronic form.

A disaster plan should include the following:

- **Pre-disaster action steps and evacuation instructions**: Outline the steps to be taken in emergencies for which warnings are issued (e.g., hurricane, typhoon, or forest fire). Describe evacuation procedures and the location of alarms. Make sure that this information is easy to find and simple to understand.
- **Internal communication information**: For each staff member, make a list of all telephone numbers (e.g., home, mobile, partner's mobile), email addresses (including personal in case work servers go down), Twitter handles, etc. Do not assume that telephone networks (landline and cellular) or the Internet will be available and reliable in the aftermath of a major disaster. Some methods of communication may work, while others do not, and the situation may vary over the course of several days. As part of your planning, make sure that you have access to and are familiar with other options, such as short message service (SMS) text messaging and Twitter. You might consider creating a Google or Facebook group to keep everyone informed in times of emergency, as it allows updates to be sent out to all staff members simultaneously.
- **Contact information:** Make a complete list of service providers that includes insurance companies, labs, recovery experts, full recovery services, conservators, roofers, plumbers, electricians, transportation and storage services, rental facilities, drying facilities, the police and fire station, and other local emergency management response agencies. Also, talk to sister institutions or other professionals in your area that may be able to help in an emergency. Come to an agreement about what services or assistance may be provided (such as storing evacuated priority collections). Be sure to offer reciprocal assistance. Include contact information for point persons at these organizations.
- **Building floor plan:** Include the location of water shut-off valves, electrical switches, disaster equipment and supplies, and all collections.
- **Priority collections list and location**: Identify these items in the floor plan as well as in a separate inventory.

■ **Response structure and job assignments:** Identify who is in charge of the response effort and include that person's contact information. Include a backup in case the first person is not available. Be sure that anyone put in charge has the authority to spend funds. List the names and contact information of staff members who have been trained for various aspects of disaster response and recovery.

■ **Basic salvage instructions:** These instructions will vary according to the materials in the collection.

Most importantly, be sure that the disaster plan is reviewed and updated regularly and that staff training is conducted at regular intervals.

9.3 FIRST RESPONSE STEPS

Preventive actions and preparedness steps will likely eliminate or reduce damage to collections. However, a disaster can sometimes damage even the best-prepared collection. Although recovery is a highly specialized task, best left in the hands of experts, there are steps that you can take right away to help salvage valuable recordings. If funds are not immediately available for professional help, taking proper first steps can often buy time while funds are raised. Nonetheless, the earlier experts can be contacted, the better.

The basic recovery steps should focus both on human safety and on reducing further risk to collections. The recovery process itself is full of risks: mishandling, losing/dissociating materials from labels or cases, lack of documentation, and lack of efficiency leading to mold growth or other damage. Seeing your valuable collection lying under a pile of debris or submerged under water induces a sense of panic. Being well prepared will help alleviate permanent damage.

The case study near the end of this chapter illustrates how these processes were set into motion after Superstorm Sandy hit New York City in the fall of 2012.

RECOVERY TIPS

Do not give up hope. In "Disaster Recovery for Tapes in Flooded Areas," Peter Brothers (n.d.) notes that it is often assumed that water-damaged tapes are ruined and unsalvageable. In fact, this is often not the case. Experts have been able to recover tapes that have been submerged even for extended periods of time. Brothers writes that no matter how bad they may look, "most wet tapes can now be saved and restored if they are treated properly."[4]

Call the experts and authorities as early as possible. The disaster plan should contain contact information for authorities and experts, including insurance companies, disaster recovery services (for clearing water out

---

[4] See also Brothers (2012).

of the building), labs, and conservation professionals, as well as local and federal disaster recovery agencies. As soon as damage is identified, contact these groups.

Always put human safety first. Human safety should always trump the desire to get inside and rescue valuable recordings. The first step in recovery must be to ensure that the area is safe to enter. Live wires, contaminated standing water, and damaged structures can pose enormous risks to humans. Have an authority or expert inspect and clear the building for entry before proceeding and handling media.

Stop or minimize damage. If the threat is ongoing, do what you can to reduce risks to people and collections. Shut off valves, electricity, and climate systems. Cover collections with plastic sheeting if water or debris is falling. Move collections out of the hazardous space as quickly and safely as possible.

Act quickly, but responsibly. The literature about disaster recovery for collecting institutions often states that materials must be rescued within 72 hours to be fully recovered. Although it is ideal to salvage media within this time period, it is not always possible. Often entire areas are cordoned off for days or weeks because of hazardous conditions. Even after you gain entry to the space, it may be several hours or days before a recovery plan can be put in place. Salvage should be conducted quickly, but carefully, at this stage. In some cases, damage increases the longer the media sit under a pile of rubble or under water, but in other cases this may not be true at all. Create a plan of action to avoid additional threats.

Do not attempt to play wet media. Under no circumstances should you try to play wet or contaminated media. Such an action can lead to damage not only of the media, but also the playback equipment, both valuable resources. Wet or contaminated media will likely need to be cleaned in distilled water and dried before any content recovery can be attempted.

Identify damage agents. It is important to identify the types of contaminants that may be affecting media items. If collections are submerged in water, try to identify the types of contaminants that may be in the water (e.g., salt, chlorine, sewage). This will help determine what actions need to be taken. For instance, items submerged in salt water need to be cleaned in distilled water as soon as possible, as the salt is highly corrosive and will quickly damage any metal parts (e.g., rollers, layers in optical discs).

Develop a recovery operation. Before diving into salvage and recovery, develop a comprehensive plan. The plan should factor in the following:

- ■ **Space**: Identify a clean and well-ventilated space for cleaning and drying. Remember that drying space must accommodate media items, their cases/covers, and potentially labels and inserts. Ensure that there is enough surface area.
- ■ **Supplies**: There will be an immediate need for gloves, cleaning supplies, flat surfaces for transport, paper towels, and the like. Make a list of your needs, assemble what is available around

you, and send someone out to find the rest. In an area-wide disaster, this can be particularly challenging. Be creative, but start trying to find the necessary supplies as quickly as possible.

■ **Roles and responsibilities**: As many institutions have reported, "too many cooks in the kitchen" can be a problem in an emergency situation. Identify at least one person who has the authority to spend funds. Quickly identify a coordinator who can establish needed roles and begin to fill them. These roles will change as the operation progresses; for example, people who start by moving media to the recovery space may later become responsible for cleaning or documentation. Responsibilities in an emergency are likely to include coordination, documentation, cleaning, transport, security, and external communication. Some responsibilities will require several people.

■ **Documentation**: Perhaps the most important aspect of the recovery is documentation. Begin by documenting the disaster area. Photographic and written documentation of the damage is critical for insurance claims. Ensure that damages to the building and collections are thoroughly documented. Next, make sure that salvage and recovery procedures are well documented and accessible to everyone participating in the operation. Finally, make documentation an integral part of all aspects of the recovery: what cassette goes with what insert, what day/time drying started, who were the day's volunteers, and how can the volunteers be contacted. A lack of documentation, particularly associations between media items and their cases/labels, is one of the biggest risks to the successful recovery of audio items.

■ **Training and knowledge transfer**: Everyone who participates in the recovery needs to be trained in the specifics of the workflow and procedures. If staff and volunteers are coming and going according to their availability, make sure that procedural knowledge is passed between people or documented as they cycle through.

Identifiers on media and cases

Perform triage and set priorities. Separate wet from dry items. Separate items by degree of damage. Try to identify the most valued items and make them the first priority. Peter Brothers (2012) has provided a comprehensive list of triage steps on the Association of Moving Image Archivists website.

MEDIA-SPECIFIC SALVAGE

The following first aid strategies for salvaging damaged audio items focus on the most common types of damage (water, contaminants, and debris) to formats commonly found in audio collections. *These instructions are limited to salvage and stabilization only.* They are not equivalent to recovery or restoration. They are intended to stop or slow down ongoing damage and buy time until the contents can be transferred from the media. After they are cleaned and dried, it may still be necessary to send the damaged items to a lab for full restoration and transfer.

All items

- Remove media from containers, cases, or sleeves.
- Remove wet inserts from cases.
- Ensure that all pieces of the item are labeled with a common identifier so that they can be brought back together after drying. Discard any containers that can easily be replaced (e.g., CD jewel cases). If containers must be cleaned, be careful not to smear or remove label information.
- Use distilled water for cleaning. The mineral contents of tap water and even filtered water can be very harmful to the media.
- Leave all items that have been cleaned in water to dry for at least 48 hours before placing them back inside containers. Wait longer if the relative humidity is high in the drying area or if the item is severely water logged.

Optical discs (CD, DVD)

- Do not freeze optical media.
- Rinse contaminated or water-damaged discs in clean, distilled water. Do not submerge discs that are not already wet or have not been compromised through debris or contamination.
- Using a lint-free (e.g., microfiber) towel, dry the data side of the disc by wiping from the center out, in a sun-ray motion.
- If any residue remains, clean the disc with a cotton swab dipped in a solution of ⅓ isopropyl and ⅔ distilled water.
- Blot the label side only. Wiping may remove or smudge labels.
- Dry in a new, clean jewel case with the data side down, the jewel case open like a book, standing upright. If jewel cases are not available immediately, lay the disc flat on a clean, dry surface with the label side down.

Optical discs set out to dry

- If necessary, label the disc with a felt tip marker on the (usually clear) inner plastic ring.

Analog magnetic tape

- Do not freeze magnetic tape.
- Do not try to rewind wet or damaged tapes.
- Unless advised to do so by an expert, do not take cassettes apart, unwind them, or unspool open reels, as these actions can do more damage. Even when a tape is fully submerged, it is likely that only the exposed parts have been contaminated.
- Submerge tapes and reels only if they are still wet or have been damaged by contaminated water. Rinse in clean distilled water. Otherwise, allow them to dry in a well-ventilated area.
- If submerging, carefully ensure that the tape does not come un-spooled in the water. Submerge briefly, giving the tape a slight shake. Dispel dirty water into a separate bin or bucket so as to not further contaminate the water in which media are being rinsed.
- Remove any residue on the outside of the cassettes using a cotton swab dipped in a solution of ⅓ isopropyl and ⅔ distilled water, and taking care not to smudge or smear the label.
- Remove any residue on the outside of dry open reel tapes using a lint-free cloth.
- Lay cassettes upright to dry, with the exposed portion of the tape facing up. Lay open reel tapes flat. Ensure good, but not direct, air circulation.

Digital audio tape (DAT)

- Do not freeze magnetic tape.
- Do not unspool tapes.
- Do not submerge in water under any circumstances.
- Clean the outside of the cassette using a cotton swab dipped in a solution of ⅓ isopropyl and ⅔ distilled water.
- Lay upright to dry, with the exposed portion of the tape facing up.

Lacquer discs

- Do not submerge in water under any circumstances.
- If wet, dry the disc off immediately by laying the disc on a clean dry flat surface and using a soft, nonshedding, nonabrasive cloth. If possible, lay on soft surface to help avoid scratching the disc.
- Avoid flexing the disc. Lacquer discs may have a glass base that can break. Flexing may also promote delamination if there are already problems with the disc.
- If packing the disc, place it in a sleeve and pack with clean, flat cardboard spacers in between each disc. Pack discs upright and snug, making sure there is no lateral movement, but do not pack them so tight that they are stressed.

Shellac discs

- Do not submerge in water.
- Clean the disc in a solution of distilled water and a few drops of a mild dishwashing detergent.
- Using a microfiber or other lint-free cloth, wipe discs using a circular motion (following the direction of the grooves).
- Rinse in clean, distilled water.
- Wipe again in a circular motion with a dry lint-free cloth.
- Lay flat to dry.
- Place in a clean sleeve.

Vinyl discs

- Clean the disc in a solution of distilled water and a few drops of a mild dishwashing detergent.
- Using a microfiber or other lint-free cloth, wipe the disc using a circular motion (following the direction of the grooves).
- Rinse in clean, distilled water.
- Wipe again in a circular motion with a dry lint-free cloth.
- Lay flat to dry.
- Place in a clean sleeve.

Cylinders

- Do not submerge in water.
- Gently dry with a lint-free, nonabrasive cloth. Too much pressure may crack the cylinder or alter the grooves in a soft wax cylinder.

9.4 CASE STUDY

This case study describes the recovery of 1,300 flooded media items (tapes and discs) at Eyebeam Art+Technology Center in New York City following Superstorm Sandy in October 2012. Other organizations can learn from the disaster recovery experience of this group and, it is hoped, become better prepared when faced with a future disaster.[5]

THE DISASTER

0 hours

On October 29, 2012, Superstorm Sandy took aim at the New York City region. Despite urgent warnings from local and national government, mandatory evacuations, and the closing of the subway system, personal and institutional disaster plans were put into effect only sporadically, and many people even chose to ride out the storm in their coastal homes.

Sandy made landfall on the shore at the exact hour of high tide on the night of a full moon. The storm surge topped the city's barriers, inundating many neighborhoods, including the gallery district of West Chelsea in Manhattan, where Eyebeam Art+Technology Center was located at the time.

---

[5] A longer version of this case study can be found at http://www.avpreserve.com/wp-content/uploads/2013/05/RecoveringTheEyebeamCollection.pdf.

12 hours

Eyebeam Art+Technology Center is a nonprofit organization dedicated to "exposing broad and diverse audiences to new technologies and media arts."[6] Eyebeam hosts residencies and fellowships for artists and technology experts to create and exhibit their work, collaborate, and learn from master classes and from each other.

Eyebeam sat between 10th and 11th Avenues on West 21st Street, about one block from the Hudson River. Knowing that they were in a flood-prone area, staff, residents, and fellows made some minimal preparations; they covered equipment with plastic sheeting and moved computers off the floor. Unfortunately, these efforts were not enough. Three feet of a toxic mixture of saltwater, sewage, and other contaminants submerged everything on the ground floor of the building. More than $250,000 worth of equipment—computers, lighting, servers—was destroyed.

Among the damaged property was most of Eyebeam's media archive, a collection of work produced at the organization over 15 years, including optical media, vinyl discs, videotape, and computer disks containing artworks, documentation of events, and even server backups—essentially Eyebeam's entire legacy. Altogether, about 1,300 items had been submerged and were in urgent need of decontamination for eventual recovery.

FIRST RESPONSE

72 hours

On Thursday, November 1, three days after the flood, Marko Tandefelt, Eyebeam's director of technology and research, sent out an urgent plea for assistance via Twitter that read: "Need volunteers to help save archive, all formats (VHS, CHD, Mini-Disc, etc.). Experts needed to help restore," followed by his telephone number.

With lower Manhattan still without power and public transit, Erik Piil, digital archivist at Anthology Film Archives, traveled by bicycle to Manhattan's West Side on Thursday afternoon to assess the situation. The need for immediate action was obvious, as building restoration crews were preparing to demolish dry wall and power wash the floors, and the media collections were still exposed. Erik notified AVPreserve, and Chris Lacinak, Josh Ranger, and I arranged to meet him at Eyebeam the next morning.

96 hours

When we arrived Friday morning, having traveled several miles by bicycle with gloves, masks, and a few other supplies in hand, the demolition crews were already at work. Eyebeam was still without running water or power and the only lights, powered by generators, were for construction crews. Plaster chunks and other particulate matter were raining down on exposed tapes and disks. A large room on the second floor was identified as a safe (albeit not well ventilated) holding space that could be used for

---

[6] See http://www.eyebeam.org/about.

State of the collection on Friday morning

storage. Tables, desks, and shelves were cleared, cleaned, and covered with plastic to make way for the wet media objects. With the help of a few more volunteers who had arrived, within an hour, all 1,300 media items had been moved.

PLANNING CLEANING AND STABILIZATION

To stabilize the still-wet media objects quickly and effectively, a large-scale recovery operation was necessary. More help was required, and calls for volunteers were put out on social media, along with emails to the New York University Moving Image Archiving and Preservation (MIAP) and Eyebeam alumni lists. Volunteers began to trickle in. With Eyebeam staff busy dealing with other pressing tasks, the volunteer archival recovery team, led by AVPreserve and Erik Piil, set to work designing a scalable and adaptable workflow that could accommodate any number of available volunteers.

Supplies. Without traffic lights, public transit, or open shops, Manhattan below 34th Street was an eerie post-apocalyptic ghost town. Obtaining necessary supplies required a time-consuming journey to the nearest hardware store, several miles away. Marko Tandefelt was willing to make the trip and had the authority and means to buy the necessary supplies—a critical component to initiating recovery. We quickly assembled an order, which included gloves, masks, paper towels, microfiber towels, isopropyl alcohol, distilled water, lidded plastic bins, jewel cases, cotton swabs, notepads, flip-chart paper, garbage bags, buckets, permanent markers, pens, paper tape, gaffer tape, and more.

A dirty optical disc in need of cleaning

Marko returned several hours later with everything except the most crucial element: distilled water. None could be found. In total, we had only 4 gallons, certainly not enough for the whole effort. It quickly became clear that finding distilled water where there is a water shortage is very challenging.

We managed to get by with the water we had and asked volunteers to each bring a gallon on their way to Eyebeam, if possible. Fortunately, the next day, Chris Lacinak drove 24 gallons in from Brooklyn, which lasted through the cleanup operation.

Designing the Cleaning Process. Media items were still wet with floodwater and needed to be cleaned as quickly as possible. Corrosion from salt was already visible on metallic parts. The diversity of media types meant that different processes had to be developed for groups of media with shared physical characteristics. Given the number of items and resources available, there was no way to do detailed work on each item in the initial effort. The goal was to prevent further damage from contamination by removing the water from the media and associated containers, and air-drying them. It was necessary to design processes that would maximize the impact of treatment per item and could be administered by volunteers with mixed levels of knowledge of conservation and media handling.

The processes were documented on large flip-chart paper and taped to the wall for easy reference. Throughout the operation, we conducted tests, modified methodologies, and updated these posters based on test results.

Space. Eyebeam made a number of rooms in the second floor office space available for the recovery operation. The five rooms in use each had a specific function:

■ **Cleaning rooms**: Three cleaning rooms were equipped with a clean water container for washing and a separate container for expelling water and dirt after items were submerged in the clean water. Clean water containers were frequently emptied and refilled with fresh distilled water. Items that needed cleaning were delivered in "dirty" bins and removed in "clean" bins (each labeled as such). The three cleaning rooms were divided into the following areas:

— Central space: The largest cleaning area, the central space was used for nearly all formats.

— MiniDV room: Another space was devoted to the detail-oriented work of cleaning MiniDV tapes.

— Optical disc room: When there were enough volunteers, an additional space was devoted specifically to optical discs, greatly increasing productivity.

■ **Supplies room**: One office was allocated to supplies, making them easier to find. This arrangement also allowed us to monitor inventory and prevent loss.

■ **Media storage room (waiting/drying room):** The largest room served as the media storage room for items waiting to be cleaned and those being returned from washing. Once the power and heat were restored to the building, we set the thermostat to 57°F to prevent expansion and contractions of the magnetic tape, and to avoid mold growth in the damp environment. We also kept a dehumidifier/air purifier running in this room to remove excess moisture and help remove particulate matter.

Workflow. Cleaning proceeded table by table in the media storage room. Tables typically contained a mix of media types, with no intellectual or technical groupings. Items from a table were loaded up into a "dirty" bin and taken to the cleaning rooms. Volunteers cleaned the media according to their type. Once the "clean" bin was full, the media were taken back to the storage room to be set out to dry.

Overall workflow poster

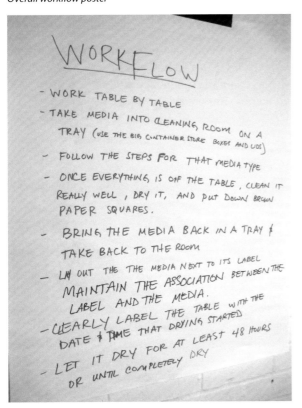

Meanwhile, the table was cleaned and prepared for the media's return. Tables and shelves were given names based on the NATO Phonetic Alphabet. After all the dirty items were removed from a table, the plastic sheeting was removed, the table cleaned, and brown craft paper laid down. The paper was labeled with the table name and the time that drying began (e.g., Charlie Nov. 4 1:30 p.m.). The media were given at least 48 hours for air drying.

Table names also provided identifiers for media items, associated cases, and label inserts. The naming convention started with the first letter of the table name followed by a number (e.g., C14). Numbers were assigned sequentially and carefully documented to avoid duplication. The identifier was applied to each component of an item with multiple pieces so they could be easily put back together after drying. For example, if a CD was labeled A2, you could be certain the case was on the Alpha table. Rigid adherence to this identifier system was among the most important aspects of the effort. As tapes, cases, and paper inserts were necessarily separated from one another for drying, identifiers were needed to bind them back together; otherwise, no one could know what was on a particular media item and whether it should be given priority for preservation.

ROLES AND TEAMS

Cleaning and drying of 1,300 media objects of various formats and their associated containers can quickly and easily become chaos. At Eyebeam, volunteers came and went as they could, and there was little consistency from day to day or even between morning and afternoon of the same day. The transport, cleaning, and drying process had to be efficient and consistent; a clear understanding of designated roles and their associated responsibilities was of utmost importance for success.

The following roles, which are essential in any recovery operation of this type, were put in place:

- **Overall coordinator**: Responsible for oversight of the entire operation, this person could unlock/lock the door, make decisions about priorities or communicate with content experts, and authorize use of space. Eyebeam resident Jonathan Minard filled this role.
- **Operations coordinator**: This person was responsible for placing volunteers into the right positions and training supervisors so that they could delegate to and train others. This was the "go-to" role for any questions about the recovery process and any media-specific issues. With the support of Chris Lacinak, I filled this role.
- **Transport crew**: This group was in charge of cleaning and preparing tables, transporting dirty and clean media, and setting media out to dry. A team supervisor was instrumental in managing the naming conventions and keeping track of what media were moved and to where. We tried to have about three people in this group when operating at full capacity.
- **Documentation crew**: This group was responsible for labeling media and related labels, inserts, and cases that had been separated from the media for drying. One documentation person per cleaning station was required at all times.
- **Cleaning crew**: The largest group, these people were responsible for cleaning the media and their cases according to specific instructions for each media type. These volunteers had to be patient and able to perform detail-oriented, but monotonous tasks.
- **Content experts**: Current and former staff who could identify high-priority materials filled the role of content expert. Fortunately, a few of them were able to stop by on the second and third days of cleaning to help set priorities and identify duplicate and commercial items.
- **Media conservation experts**: Conservators designed the cleaning procedures for each media type, tested results, modified the process as needed, and oversaw the cleaning of various media types. Erik Piil and Chris Lacinak provided critical guidance in this area.

■ **Quality assurance and control**: Although several of the roles described involve quality assurance and control, it is important enough to identify as a distinct need. Emphasizing this function across roles helped in managing the constantly revolving door of volunteers.

An important factor in the success of the Eyebeam effort was the lack of ego among the recovery crew. Recovery of archival material after a flood is not a glamorous operation. Tasks were tedious and repetitive, and the conditions were dirty. There was no working bathroom and no power the first day. The constant turnover of people required volunteers to be extremely flexible and patient.

MANAGING RISKS

In view of the context and the presence of a volunteer workforce with limited knowledge of the organization and often no expertise in the process, it is remarkable that there was minimal negative impact on the media. We were mindful of a number of ongoing risks and worked to mitigate them:

■ **Dissociation between media and label information**: As mentioned previously, one of the great risks to the intellectual value of an item arises when a tape is separated from its container or label. In our recovery effort, separation often happened in a matter of seconds, as items were moved down the cleaning assembly line. The assignment of a documentation person to keep a hawklike eye over the cleaning process was essential to avoiding constant dissociation.

■ **Lack of knowledge transfer**: It was common for an entirely new workforce to appear each day. Critical knowledge would leave with outgoing volunteers, often without being transferred to incoming volunteers. If only a few volunteers returned, training and overseeing an entirely new group of people took a great deal of time, posed a fresh set of risks, and reduced productivity.

■ **Lack of supervision**: When there is no supervision, supplies are lost, tapes are cleaned incorrectly, labels and media items are dissociated, and identifiers are repeated. We quickly found that each area—transport, cleaning, and documentation—needed a supervisor who understood the process well, was organized, and could train and delegate to others. Volunteers who filled the supervisory roles on numerous days were instrumental to the effort's overall success.

■ **Not enough people**: Having too few volunteers greatly reduces productivity and efficiency, as one person then must perform multiple tasks. Most mistakes were made when there were fewer volunteers, especially in the absence of a crew dedicated to documentation.

■ **Loss of morale**: With so much work to do in less than optimal conditions, it is important to make sure that people take breaks, eat, and drink. Free pizza provided by Eyebeam on our second and third day of work helped tremendously.

■ **Passage of time**: By day three, media left out to dry—exposed tape media, optical discs without cases—were getting dusty. On the few VHS tapes that did not have cotton buds placed between the tape and parts of the housing, contaminant deposits began to form around the tape edges (see photo) and needed to be brushed off.

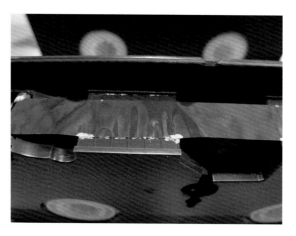

■ **Accidental or intentional loss of materials**: It is crucial that the cleaning and storage room(s) be safe and secure. Much activity occurs after a disaster, and many people come and go. Some level of security is essential to ensure things do not go missing, accidentally or intentionally.

■ **Lack of supplies**: Gloves and masks are essential items for working with this kind of contamination, and we were constantly running out of them. Distilled water became a precious commodity. Supplies had to be carefully monitored so that, when necessary, someone could make the long trek to the store to buy more.

■ **Mold growth**: Maintaining a cool, dry temperature and good ventilation is of utmost importance. The lack of ventilation, combined with the restoration of the building's heating system and wet tapes, could easily have created a fertile breeding ground for mold, causing damage to tapes and exposing volunteers to health and safety hazards. To mitigate this risk, we kept the storage room at approximately 57°F and continuously ran a dehumidifier.

PREPAREDNESS TAKEAWAYS

When working to recover valuable collections from a disaster, the trained archivist cannot help but think of the essential principles of the profession and how these could be applied in the future to better prepare collections to withstand the next threat. The following are just a few of the things that stood out to us during the recovery at Eyebeam.

Storage. Media should not be stored in basements, directly under a roof, or near windows; they should not be positioned directly below leak-prone areas, such as a bathroom or kitchen. Understand the building and geographic surroundings. If you are near a body of water, as Eyebeam was, do not store valuable collections on the ground floor, especially not in basements. If you are in a hurricane or typhoon-prone area, ensure that your roof is sound.

Intellectual Control. Maintaining an item-level inventory of a collection is helpful for a variety of day-to-day operations, but it becomes a critical tool for identifying items and setting priorities in a disaster. It is also important for insurance purposes. Without intellectual control, it is difficult to effectively allocate limited resources to salvaging the most important parts of the collection. The recovery team may be working with something of no value while overlooking the most important item.

Eyebeam did not have an inventory of its archival holdings before Superstorm Sandy. An accessible inventory (as there was no power or Internet during the first few days, a printed, laminated inventory would have been necessary) that indicated priority items would have been priceless and would have allowed us to identify those requiring immediate attention.

Deaccessioning. Disasters drive home the fact that deaccessioning duplicate and out-of-scope recordings is a good thing. When confronted with 10 copies of what appeared to be a commercial DVD, our recovery team had no choice but to treat each one as if it were unique. Volunteers could not judge whether these were simply replaceable, commercial items or art objects. Most likely, they were simply overstock that could have been thrown away. Getting rid of items can be a challenge, but devoting resources to cleaning and rehousing things that do not need to be is an even bigger one.

Labeling. For media such as audio and data tape, which are machine-dependent and have multiple parts, labels with identifiers on all components are critical. Dissociation of media and their labels could be inadvertent, such as when the water tosses the media off their shelves, or intentional, such as when things have been laid out to dry after cleaning. Although we established an identifier system during recovery at Eyebeam, identifiers that had been placed on the tape, case, and insert previously saved time and greatly simplified the recombination of separate parts.

Communications. Disaster planning guides nearly always call for the creation of a telephone tree. This concept needs to be updated for contemporary communications, as you never know which communication system may be down in an emergency. Telephone numbers (including mobile numbers for text messaging), email addresses (all associated with a person, as the company mail server could be down, but Gmail could still be functioning), and Facebook, Twitter, and other social media accounts for all critical staff and support personnel should be reviewed and updated periodically. During Superstorm Sandy, we found that text messaging and Twitter worked well, while telephone and many mail servers were out of commission.

9.5 CONCLUSION

Small, localized emergencies and large-scale disasters occur with alarming frequency and impact. Additionally, the potential for mistakes, negligence, and crime is ever present. Disaster preparedness must be a concern for all individuals and institutions that create or collect content with long-term value. The impact of disasters can be devastating, with potential total loss of material. Even the simplest response or recovery plan can be highly effective if it is practiced and understood by all stakeholders. Doing something is always better than doing nothing when it comes to emergency preparedness.

The many emergency preparedness and response basics that have been tried, tested, and improved by those experienced with disaster response and recovery of audio and other media over the years provide general guidelines. Always remember that the cause, circumstances, and context of each disaster vary greatly. Guides provide a general playbook, but cannot answer every question. Again, it is critical to have contact details for emergency response agencies (e.g., the Federal Emergency Management Agency [FEMA]), experts, insurance, and others, so that you can contact these groups as early as possible and they can guide you through the dos and don'ts of your particular situation.

Finally, as has been noted several places in this chapter, the digitization of valuable audio heritage and proper management of digital collections are among the most important disaster preparedness steps you can take. A well-managed digital archive, with proper intellectual control, backup, and geographic separation, will always fare better in a disaster than will unique analog materials. An added benefit is that digitization, already necessary for most analog formats today, will place the collection in the best position for long-term preservation and improved access.

REFERENCES

All URLs are current as of May 1, 2015

Association of Moving Image Archivists website: http://www.amianet.org/.

Brothers, Peter. 2012. *Disaster–First Actions: First Actions for Film, Tape and Discs.* Association of Moving Image Archivists. Available at http://www.amianet.org/sites/all/files/Disaster_first_steps_1.pdf.

Brothers, Peter. n.d. *Disaster Recovery for Tapes in Flooded Areas.* Association of Moving Image Archivists. Available at http://www.amianet.org/sites/all/files/Disaster%20Recovery%20for%20Tapes%20in%20Flooded%20Areas%20by%20Peter%20Brothers.pdf.

Wellseiser, Johanna, and Jude Scott. 2002. *An Ounce of Prevention: Integrated Disaster Planning for Libraries, Archives, and Record Centres,* 2d ed. Lanham, MD: The Scarecrow Press.

ADDITIONAL RESOURCES

AVPreserve. 2012. Disaster Response Information and Assistance. Available at http://www.avpreserve.com/blog/.disaster-response-information-assistance/. Includes links to audiovisual specific resources, support/assistance contacts.

Heritage Preservation. 2006. Heritage Preservation Emergency National Task Force, 2006. *Field Guide to Emergency Response.*

Heritage Preservation. n.d. Heritage Emergency National Task Force website. Available at http://www.heritagepreservation.org/PROGRAMS/TASKFER.HTM. Links and downloads for emergency response funding, recovery procedures, guidelines, etc.

Metropolitan New York Library Association. 2012. *Disaster Recovery Resources.* Available at http://metro.org/articles/disaster-recovery-resources/. Includes links to disaster assistance hotlines, resource pages, grants and funding.

National Film and Sound Archive of Australia. n.d. *First aid for fire damage.* Available at http://www.nfsa.gov.au/preservation/care/first-aid-fire-damaged-audiovisual-materials/.

National Film and Sound Archive of Australia. n.d. *First aid for water damage.* Available at http://www.nfsa.gov.au/preservation/care/stabilising-audiovisual-after-floods/.

APPENDIX A

Fair Use and Sound Recordings: Lessons from Community Practice

By Brandon Butler and Peter Jaszi

EXECUTIVE SUMMARY

This report presents strategies for reasonable application of copyright's fair use doctrine to a series of recurring situations encountered by recorded sound collections.[1] The situations were derived from detailed telephone interviews with professionals working with recorded sound collections. The strategies are based on existing best practices developed and published by related curatorial communities as well as the latest fair use case law. The following recurring situations are treated in this report:

- Electronic access to rare/unique materials for off-site researchers/users
- Electronic access to collected materials for affiliated students and instructors in support of teaching
- Preservation/format-shifting
- Collecting online materials
- Data-mining/non-consumptive research
- Digital exhibits and exhibits for the public
- Transfer of copies to third parties in support of downstream fair uses

---

[1] Throughout this report, we use "recorded sound collections" to include both individual and institutional collectors. While some institutions benefit from additional protections not available to individuals (for example, libraries and archives benefit from Section 108 in addition to their fair use rights), the contours of fair use should be the same for individuals and institutions, so long as the nature and purpose of the use is the same. The only concrete difference in the law is that there is an additional buffer zone for employees of non-profit educational institutions and broadcasters, who are exempt from statutory damages awards whenever they have a *reasonable belief* that their use is a fair use—even if the court decides that they were mistaken and the use was infringing. See 17 U.S.C. § 504(c)(2). Individual collectors in such circumstances are not entitled to this protection, though courts may still limit damages against users whose mistakes were made in good faith if they believe it is appropriate.

In addition to strategies tailored to each situation, we identify a series of practices we call "indicia of good faith" that are strongly endorsed by virtually every practice community in virtually every use context. In addition to this core material, we provide a basic introduction to copyright and fair use as those doctrines apply to recorded sound, and a short selected bibliography of community statements on fair use.

INTRODUCTION

Recorded sound collections have a mission to protect and foster access to some of the most powerful documents of our collective culture. The Association for Recorded Sound Collections (ARSC) reflects this mission in its bylaws, which provide that the association's purposes include the following:

- To foster recognition and use of sound recordings as sources of information by students and research scholars,
- To develop standards of bibliographic control and access to co-operating sound recordings collections assembled for research or instructional purposes, and
- To foster improvement of techniques for the reproduction, storage and preservation of sound recordings (ARSC 2014).

Recorded sound collections share these core purposes with a variety of research, teaching, and cultural memory institutions. Research libraries, museums, and archives, for example, are all dedicated to the same fundamental purposes.[2] Today, however, fulfilling this mission while observing copyright is not without its difficulties.

Indeed, recorded sound collections present a striking mix of opportunities and challenges. The opportunities presented by digital technology are obvious. And while the related challenges that derive from copyright law can be substantial, the public's interest in access to these collections is undeniable. In some contexts, the law seems to be working fairly well despite (or even perhaps because of) its complexity. In the realm of contemporary commercial music, for example, while some participants in the market may wish for higher profits or lower prices in this or that circumstance, in general a consumer who wants music can get it at a price that she can afford, and a musician who wants to monetize her music can do so in a wide variety of channels.

In other contexts, however, the law may seem to do more harm than good. Many recordings (musical and otherwise) that are long past their commercial life, or that never had a commercial life, seem to be in a kind of no man's land. Collectors, scholars, and other enthusiasts are finding new kinds of cultural value in these old recordings; while owners may

---

[2] See, e.g., Association of Research Libraries, *Code of Best Practices in Fair Use for Academic and Research Libraries* 1 (2010) ("Libraries' Code") ("The mission of academic and research librarians is to enable teaching, learning, and research.")

see no upside in making these recordings publicly available,[3] the owners' legal rights cast a pall over others' efforts to make socially beneficial uses of them. Fair use exists to resolve the tension when the tangle of copyright laws thwarts the public interest they are supposed to serve. The flexible character of the user's right of fair use is especially important in the realm of recorded sound, where both legal complexity and social engagement are at their peak.

Before we describe the particular challenges faced by recorded sound collections, it is worth noting the remarkable complexity of copyright as it relates to recorded sound.[4] Unlike the content of books, copyright's historical paradigm case, the content of most phonorecords[5] is subject to multiple layers of copyright protection, with both authorship and ownership divided across a diverse cast of characters. For example, a commercial music compact disc embodies at least two separate kinds of copyrightable works: the musical compositions (i.e., the words and music of each song as they might be written in a musical score) and the sound recordings (the songs as performed, mixed or modified, and encoded on the disc). Each of those two works may have multiple authors: the musical composition may have both a lyricist and a composer, and the sound recording may be authored by multiple primary and back-up performers, as well as a producer, sound engineers, and other artist-technicians. These authors frequently assign their rights to third parties: publishers, record labels, broadcast networks, and others who take ownership of copyrights in exchange for investment in production, promotion, and a share of the profits. And whether or not the copyright "work for hire" doctrine applies is often a subject of dispute. As a result, ownership of copyrights in a given phonorecord will frequently be a complex, divided affair, and will only rarely coincide with the ownership of a particular copy.

This legal complexity, together with other common traits of sound recordings, leads to the extremely common phenomenon of "orphaned" works in recorded sound collections. Artists, performers, and interview subjects disappear without a trace. The business interests involved (recording companies, radio networks, music publishers) are routinely bought, sold, and go out of business. Many of the parties involved keep

---

[3] In many cases, owners are not aware that they have rights in older or more obscure works. When works are made in noncommercial contexts, or their ownership is shrouded in the mist of time, owners can easily lose track of their works. When owners do not know which works are theirs, collections and users are even more at sea.

[4] For a broader discussion of copyright and recorded sound, see chapter 8 of this volume.

[5] With some reluctance, we have decided to use legal terminology in this context to untangle several distinct, but closely related, concepts. We will use "phonorecord" to refer to any physical object on which sounds are fixed and from which the sounds can be perceived; for example, a vinyl record, a compact disc, and a segment of a computer hard drive can all be phonorecords. A "sound recording" is the copyrighted work that results from the fixation of a series of musical, spoken, or other sounds on any tangible medium. One sound recording can be reproduced on multiple phonorecords in multiple formats. So, while it may be natural to use "sound recordings" to refer to the physical objects collected by institutions and individuals, we will use that term in its technical legal sense to refer to the intangible "works" that are the subjects of copyright protection and are embodied in phonorecords, which are the actual physical objects collected. We will use "recorded sound collections" to refer to the institutions and individuals who share the mission described in the ARSC bylaws, to assemble, preserve, and encourage various socially beneficial uses of recorded sound.

incomplete records. And, like all human enterprises, the affairs of authors and rightsholders are subject to all manner of catastrophe. The proliferation of rights and authors, together with the vicissitudes of life and commerce, very frequently make the identity or the location of relevant rightsholders difficult or impossible to ascertain. Tracing rights in ephemeral and noncommercial sound recordings presents additional challenges.

To this perfect storm of complexity we can add the extraordinary circumstance that different legal regimes apply to different sound recordings depending on the date they were first recorded. While recordings made on or after February 15, 1972, are subject to federal copyright law—and only to federal law—recordings made before February 15, 1972, are subject to state protection (even though rights in their contents, like music, are federally regulated). The patchwork of relevant state laws can be intimidating[6] and their exact boundaries are still being defined on a case-by-case basis in high-stakes litigation in New York and California, among other places.[7]

Finally, anyone considering action that may implicate copyright in sound recordings cannot help but take note of the fearsome litigation history of some of the rightsholders in this area. The Recording Industry Association of America (RIAA) has pursued and obtained some of the most widely publicized, wildly disproportionate damages awards in the history of copyright. Their campaign of litigation against peer-to-peer file sharing may have come to an end, but the extraordinary penalties the record labels obtained—for example, one jury awarded the labels over $2 million against one defendant who shared barely two-dozen songs (the judge later reduced the award, calling it excessive)—have certainly had a deterrent effect (McBride and Smith 2008; Kravets 2013).

The chill that copyright casts on sound recording collections' uses of recordings is worth overcoming, however, given the extraordinary opportunities presented by new technology for storing, sharing, manipulating, and analyzing recorded sound. It is possible to migrate recordings stored on fragile media to digital file formats that can be copied redundantly and securely across servers in disparate geographic locations, ensuring there will never be another mass destruction of unique pieces of cultural heritage like the burning of the Library of Alexandria. (Unique physical objects will remain unique, of course, but the underlying works can be preserved in redundant copies.)

---

[6] Studies have revealed patterns that make these state laws less intimidating. For example, most state statutes and many common law tort claims deal with commercial record piracy, unfair competition, and related commercial activity, and few states have laws with the same scope as federal copyright law. See, e.g., Jaszi 2009. The Copyright Office has published a useful chart of state criminal law provisions governing sound recordings at http://copyright.gov/docs/sound/20111212_survey_state_criminal_laws_ARL_CO_v2.pdf, as well as the text of relevant state laws at http://copyright.gov/docs/sound/20110705_state_law_texts.pdf.

[7] See, e.g., Capitol Records, Inc. v. Naxos of America, Inc., 830 N.E.2d 250 (N.Y. 2005) (finding state common law protection applies to pre-1972 sound recordings); EMI Records Ltd. v. Premise Media Corp., 2008 N.Y. Misc. Lexis 7485 (N.Y. Sup. Ct. Aug. 8, 2008) (applying fair use to state common law copyright); Flo & Eddie, Inc. v. Sirius XM Radio, Inc. et al, No. 1:13-cv-05784 (S.D.N.Y. 2013) (suit involving public performance of pre-1972 sound recordings by digital broadcaster).

Access to sound recordings is subject to the same revolutionizing effects that the Internet has had for other kinds of works. Recordings that have languished unused or underused in collections to which few users could afford to travel can be brought online and made accessible worldwide, instantaneously, to anyone with a connected device. The promise of such access is significant. It could go a long way to erasing the gap that separates rich and poor students, researchers, institutions, and even countries. Education could be enriched, forgotten works rediscovered, startling juxtapositions created, and so on. Some of the opportunities discussed in more detail below include the following:

- Providing remote streaming access to collections materials for interested researchers, students, teachers, and others
- Creating new kinds of online exhibits and other curated learning experiences
- Facilitating data mining and other modes of computer-assisted research
- Providing copies to interested users for reuse in a wide variety of downstream projects.

Recorded sound collections exist in a variety of contexts. Libraries and other research institutions collect phonorecords alongside other materials in support of their missions. Museums and galleries collect rare or unique recordings as part of their curatorial efforts. Private collectors play a major role, with some of the most fascinating and valuable holdings in their hands. Finally, corporate entities may have archives of phonorecords directly and indirectly related to their businesses, which can run the gamut from radio interviews to taped board meetings.

If copyright sometimes is perceived as an impediment to making such collections accessible, the copyright doctrine of fair use is a crucial tool for making the vast array of recorded sound collections available for socially valuable uses. When a use is fair, the tangled web of ownership becomes irrelevant; you do not need to seek permission from anyone, since (by definition) fair use is "not infringement."[8] With a clear fair use argument, a user need not fear an angry copyright holder, who will be more likely to negotiate than to sue. Fair use is a right, on which recorded sound collections can rely openly to fulfill their mission. Perhaps most importantly, given how conscientious most managers of recorded sound collections are about following the law, fair use is not merely tolerated or excused; it is encouraged and justified. Fair use is one of copyright's "built in First Amendment accommodations,"[9] and the courts have said clearly that fair uses are to be welcomed. In describing some of the common scenarios where this right can apply to activities involving recorded sound collections, we hope to encourage the robust and responsible exercise of fair use.

---

[8] 17 U.S.C. § 107.

[9] Eldred v. Ashcroft, 537 U.S. 186, 190 (2003).

COPYRIGHT AND FAIR USE TODAY

COPYRIGHT AND FAIR USE GENERALLY

The purpose of copyright is specified in the constitution: "to promote the Progress of Science," a term which at the time meant learning and culture generally. As Justice O'Connor wrote for the Supreme Court majority in the landmark *Feist* decision, "The primary objective of copyright is not to reward the labor of authors, but '[t]o promote the Progress of Science and useful Arts.'"[10] As we have already seen, sometimes the copyright bargain breaks down and the statutory monopoly undermines the very progress it is meant to promote. Fair use trumps copyright protection in these circumstances.

Based on years of judge-made law, Congress codified the fair use doctrine using four non-exclusive factors that judges (and others) are directed to consider:

1. The purpose and character of the use, including whether the use is commercial or for nonprofit, educational purposes
2. The nature of the work used
3. The amount and substantiality of the portion of the work used
4. The effect of the use on the market value of the work

Courts are to weigh these factors together in light of the purposes of copyright.

Courts today routinely look to a powerful concept known as transformative use as a key part of the fair use determination. The idea of transformative use was first articulated in 1990 by a federal judge named Pierre N. Leval,[11] and it was strongly endorsed shortly afterward by the Supreme Court, which called transformative uses "the heart of fair use."[12] A use is transformative if it takes existing copyrighted material and uses it for new, socially beneficial purposes. While some transformative uses involve altering or editing the underlying works, courts have also endorsed uses where entire works are used without alteration for dramatically new purposes. Search engines, for example, often require copying millions of works to create a useful search index.[13] Books about historical subjects sometimes reproduce full images to illuminate their subject.[14] When a use is for a transformative purpose, courts ask whether the amount of the original work used is appropriate to that purpose. Courts overwhelmingly find uses fair where they find the purpose is transformative and the amount taken is appropriate to the purpose.[15]

---

[10] Feist Pubs., Inc. v. Rural Tel. Svc. Co., Inc., 499 U.S. 340, 349 (1991).

[11] See Leval 1990.

[12] Campbell v. Acuff-Rose, 510 U.S. 569, 579 (1994).

[13] See, e.g., Authors Guild v. HathiTrust, 755 F.3d 87 (2d Cir. 2014).

[14] See, e.g., Bill Graham Archives v. Dorling Kindersley Ltd., 448 F.3d 605 (2d Cir. 2006) (reproducing full color concert posters and tickets as part of Grateful Dead timeline was fair use); Warren Pub. Co. v. Spurlock, 645 F.Supp.2d 402 (E.D. Pa. 2009) (reproducing complete magazine covers in biography of artist was fair use).

[15] The ascendance and present dominance of the transformative use framework is explained in detail in Netanel 2011.

Legal scholars have shown that courts tend to care about what is "normal" in a given practice community. When communities routinely acquiesce to license demands, courts may take this practice as evidence that such uses are generally not fair and that payment is therefore appropriate (Gibson 2007). On the other hand, where courts see an established norm or practice of making unlicensed uses, they may infer that such uses are fair and legitimate and pose no special threat to copyright holders.[16] Facts about custom and practice are not decisive, of course. Courts know that sometimes licenses are sought for reasons of expedience or risk management rather than genuine legal obligation,[17] and that sometimes licensing is avoided for reasons other than the user's justified entitlement. Nevertheless, evidence that a practice is broadly approved and justified in light of community mission will favor fair use in the right circumstances. This report is an effort to bring together the considered opinions of related communities about activities that recorded sound collections would like to pursue.

COMMON MYTHS AND MISUNDERSTANDINGS ABOUT FAIR USE

Before pursuing this approach, we should ask what direct guidance, if any, may be available from decided fair use cases. Certainly, court decisions help put to rest some common myths and misunderstandings that recorded sound collections, like memory institutions in general, may have about relying on fair use.

One common misunderstanding of fair use is that the key criterion for fairness is the amount of the work that is used, and that the amount must be slight to qualify as fair use. In reality, whenever courts consider the extent of unlicensed use as a component of fair use analysis, as they are directed to do by the statute, the inquiry is contextual. And, contrary to the "folk wisdom" of copyright, there is no rule that automatically bars the use of works in their entirety. Instead, where uses are transformative, courts will look to the purpose of the use to determine whether the amount is appropriate. Thus, for example, a teacher who insists that students in a course on the history of popular music listen to a selection of recordings, in their entirety, in preparation for class may have a strong fair use claim, especially if this is recognized as an appropriate instructional practice among teachers.

Another source of concern for would-be fair users is the widely held belief that unpublished works (a category that includes some musical and a larger number of non-musical recordings) have a fundamentally different and more protected status under the law than published ones. While there was some basis for this distinction years ago, when publication was a more significant legal event in the copyright system, there is very little reason to treat unpublished materials substantially differently for fair use

---

[16] See Madison 2004 and Jaszi 2007.

[17] See, e.g., Campbell, 510 U.S. at 585 n.18 (2 Live Crew's willingness to pay a license does not prove the group thought its use of "Oh Pretty Woman" was not fair, and may instead have simply been a "good faith effort to avoid this litigation").

purposes today.[18] The key, as always, is the relationship between the nature of the work and the user's purpose. A work's unpublished status may weigh against fair use if the purpose is purely exploitative or frivolous (so that the author's interest in keeping the work obscure is not outweighed by the user's or the public's interest in publication). It may favor fair use if the purpose is scholarly or critical and the public interest in learning from new information trumps the author's decision to keep information hidden.

Likewise, there is no basis in fact for the proposition that because many recordings were originally produced for entertainment purposes, they are somehow shielded from fair use. While courts do consider whether a work is primarily factual or creative, the key is context. If the user is "covering" a copyrighted song discovered on an old record, the fact that both the original and the ultimate purpose of the use were for entertainment may be highly relevant. By contrast, a scholar using a historical popular song to make points about cultural history has little to be concerned about on this score.[19] And it is worth noting that when considerations such as whether the work is unpublished or creative in nature do come up, it typically is in connection with the second statutory factor ("The nature of the work used"), which is typically marginal in its effect on the final outcomes of fair use cases.[20]

Finally, memory institutions often worry needlessly that they could be liable for others' downstream uses when they provide access to works in their collections. For example, if someone obtains a copy of a recording from a sound recording collection under false pretenses then sells CDs of it on eBay, would the collection be liable somehow if the sales constitute copyright infringement? Put simply, it is almost impossible that a collector, an institution, or an employee of an institution could be held responsible for the bad acts of others who abuse their access to copyrighted materials. Legal doctrines of secondary liability require control over the infringing activity, knowing encouragement of the activity, or direct profit from the activity, none of which is likely to apply to downstream uses of materials made available for free or at cost under a defensible fair use rationale.

WHAT THE CASELAW TELLS US

Unfortunately, the courts have little direct guidance to offer on the specific question of the scope of fair use for recorded sound. Certainly, federal judges have heard a variety of cases regarding use and reuse of sound

---

[18] Following a series of court decisions suggesting fair use may never apply to unpublished works, Congress amended the fair use provision of the Copyright Act to add the savings clause: "The fact that a work is unpublished shall not itself bar a finding of fair use if such finding is made upon consideration of all the above factors."

[19] See, e.g., Sag 2012 (observing that cases involving "creativity shift"—"where the plaintiff's work is creative and the defendant's is informational, or vice versa"—are very likely to be ruled fair).

[20] For more on the oft-overlooked second fair use factor, see Kasunic 2008. Kasunic argues persuasively that the second factor could play a more compelling role in fair use decisions if courts explored the nature of the work with more nuance, but so far the courts have not taken his advice.

recordings, but the vast majority of these cases have to do with commercial infringement by competing musicians, commercial "pirates," or online platforms. In most of these cases, fair use has not been a serious issue. The most that a recorded sound collection can learn from them is that it is not fair use to copy and distribute musical recordings in ways that serve general consumer interest in commercial recordings in direct competition with copyright holders.

On the other hand, it is clear that contemporary trends in fair use jurisprudence do apply, with full force, where sound recordings are concerned. Thus, a recent decision from the Second Circuit Court of Appeals, which is widely respected as an "expert" circuit on copyright matters, found that a financial news agency had wide fair use rights to distribute the full recorded audio of a newsworthy earnings call, even though the copyright owner had expressly forbidden redistribution.[21]

Such cases "on point," however, are few and far between. The guidance the courts have to offer is substantial, but largely indirect. Another way for recorded sound collections to understand how fair use will apply to their activities is to look at analogous uses by similar groups of similar materials. Thus, in what follows, we will discuss analogies derived from judicial caselaw in the context of best practices statements formulated by curatorial communities with which recorded sound collections share interests and concerns.

One question remains: Does fair use, a doctrine developed in federal court, apply to claims relating to the use of pre-1972 sound recordings in potential violation of state law? Only one court has considered this question explicitly, but the affirmative answer it gave was definite enough to command respect.[22] Moreover, the logic of the decision seems inevitable: the Supreme Court has said that fair use is a limit on copyright that is required by the First Amendment of the U.S. Constitution.[23] Since no state law can trump the Constitution, a court hearing a state copyright dispute should apply some version of the fair use exception as a limitation to state law just as it would in a case involving federal copyright law. Indeed, courts applied fair use as a judge-made limitation to copyright for more than a century before the doctrine was expressly codified in federal law in 1976. State courts currently apply a similar "transformative use" test as a First Amendment defense against state law right of publicity claims.[24] They should apply the fair use doctrine to pre-1972 sound recordings in the same way, and with an eye to the way federal courts have done so.

WHAT THIS REPORT IS

The method of this report is fairly straightforward. Through a series of interviews with professionals working with recorded sound collections, we

---

[21] Swatch Grp. Mgmt. Servs. Ltd. v. Bloomberg L.P., 756 F.3d 73 (2d Cir. 2014).

[22] EMI Records Ltd. v. Premise Media Corp., 2008 N.Y. Misc. Lexis 7485 (N.Y. Sup. Ct. Aug. 8, 2008) (applying fair use to state common law copyright).

[23] See Eldred, 537 U.S. at 190.

[24] See Bartholomew and Tehranian 2013.

have identified some of the core recurring situations where copyright law creates uncertainty for recorded sound collections that fair use could potentially resolve. This much of the process is shared in common with the series of fair use best practices that we and our colleague Patricia Aufderheide at American University have helped facilitate in collaboration with various communities of practice over the past decade.[25]

The interviews revealed that recorded sound collections have a remarkable amount in common with other communities that have developed fair use best practices documents—teachers, scholars, archivists, and librarians. The overlap was so extensive that we chose to proceed by distilling the lessons of the existing literature as they apply to the recurring copyright challenges faced by recorded sound collections. We believe the time is right for such an approach because of the overlapping and mutually reinforcing quality of the existing best practices documents, especially those that treat academic and research activities. From a corpus that now encompasses more than a dozen statements and codes, trend lines are becoming clear and a kind of meta-consensus across various fields is emerging. Crucially, most of the professionals who deal with recorded sound collections on a regular basis are also members of communities that have already described best practices in fair use for themselves—librarians, archivists, scholars, and artists. For all these reasons, it should be possible to apply existing fair use norms to the analogous use scenarios that are most frequently faced by recorded sound collections. In the following pages, we will summarize the growing cross-disciplinary consensus on fair use as it applies to each recurring scenario, with reference to specific principles from existing statements for readers who would like to explore the source material more deeply.

WHAT THIS REPORT ISN'T

Like the fair use best practices documents it references, this report describes norms grounded in the values and priorities of practice communities. It does not reflect a negotiated agreement with copyright holders. Such agreements typically have little to do with the law and policy of fair use and are mostly grounded in perceived political and financial power. They describe "safe harbor" behaviors that copyright holders say they will tolerate, but are often subsequently invoked as quantitative and normative outer limits of the law.[26] Courts have recently declined to give them much weight,[27] as have the affected communities.[28]

---

[25] These documents are collected by the Center for Media and Social Impact at http://www. cmsimpact.org/fair-use/best-practices. Their history and theory are explained at length in Jaszi and Aufderheide 2011.

[26] See Crews 2001.

[27] Cambridge Univ. Press v. Patton, 769 F.3d 1232 (11th Cir. 2014).

[28] Consortium of College and University Media Centers, *CCUMC Adopts Code of Best Practices in Fair Use for Academic and Research Libraries*, http://www.ccumc.org/ blogpost/1054055/174940/CCUMC-Adopts-Code-of-Best-Practices-in-Fair-Use-for-Academic-and-Research-Libraries, Dec. 5, 2013 (retiring the *Fair Use Guidelines for Educational Multimedia*, which CCUMC had helped to negotiate, and replacing them with the Libraries' Code).

Neither is this report a summary of all the features of the Copyright Act that may enable uses of recorded sound collection holdings. Besides fair use, the Act has other built-in exceptions that allow socially valuable uses without permission. These exceptions describe certain narrowly defined circumstances where the copyright monopoly does not apply, typically to certain favored users such as libraries or teachers when they engage in specific activities within specified limits, such as preservation or face-to-face teaching. For more on the relevant exceptions, please consult chapter 8 of this volume. These exceptions can be powerful where they apply, but they have been carefully negotiated by the affected industries, resulting in some arbitrary and unwieldy limitations to their application. Fortunately, fair use may be available to supplement specific exceptions in circumstances where they fall short,[29] and may actually be strengthened by its proximity to a use Congress has specifically condoned.[30]

It is impossible to exhaust the field of potential future fair uses of sound recordings, or otherwise to exclude or cast doubt on the lawfulness of existing institutional practices that are not described below. Managers of recorded sound collections that encounter circumstances not described here, or circumstances that differ in crucial ways from the ones we describe, should feel free to use their best judgment to exercise their rights. Fair use is a broad, flexible doctrine that can adapt to new, unforeseen, or unusual circumstances. The goal of this report is to make a start.

This report does not attempt to provide bright quantitative lines—we do not give "rules of thumb," such as "not more than 30 seconds can be used under fair use" or "nothing can be used for more than one semester without permission." While such fixed metrics may go a long way toward making fair use decisions "easy," they do little to make such decisions accurate. We offer a different kind of guidance here: a guide to reasoning, not an alternative to reasoning. You will still need to use your own judgment to know whether your use is appropriate.

Institutions and individuals will make different choices about fair use depending on a variety of external considerations, all equally valid depending on context. Donor relations, funding availability, opportunities for collaboration, local strategic plans and priorities, and a host of other factors will shape decisions about when and how to use recorded sound collections. It is our conviction, however, that any meaningful exercise in institutional risk management should begin with a clear understanding of applicable legal rights and responsibilities.

The pages that follow describe broadly shared norms for fair use where copyright would otherwise require permission. In a host of situations, however, no permission will be necessary regardless of fair use. This is true for works in the public domain, for example. Works can enter the public domain when the term of their copyrights expires, or, in the case of works of the U.S. government, they may never be protected by copyright

---

[29] Indeed, the peaceful coexistence of Section 108 and fair use is made explicit in Section 108(f)(4): "Nothing in this section… in any way affects the right of fair use as provided by section 107."

[30] See Band 2012.

in the first place.[31] Copyright holders can also use mechanisms such as the Creative Commons licenses to announce in advance that they grant members of the public permission freely to use their works in certain ways.[32]

Copyright law is territorial, meaning that, generally, the law that applies to a given act is the law of the country where the act takes place. Fair use is an aspect of U.S. copyright law, and its precise contours are the result of U.S. court opinions. Thus, the norms described below apply to any copyrighted work used in the United States, regardless of whether the work originated outside the country. The reasoning described in this report does not apply to reproductions, distributions, performances, and other uses outside the United States, including web-based uses specifically targeted toward other countries, to which those countries' laws may apply.

Last but certainly not least, the norms of fair use do not necessarily apply to licensed resources and materials subject to deeds of gift and other contractual arrangements. Many courts have treated contractual agreements as overriding the protections of fair use. Where you have agreed contractually to limit your uses (as in a donor agreement or a click-through license), you may be required to follow the agreement despite the existence of a fair use right to the contrary.[33] The moral of the story, here, is to read your licenses carefully and to negotiate zealously in defense of your rights under the law.

FAIR USE APPROACHES TO COMMON PROBLEMS

SOME GENERAL CONSIDERATIONS—INDICIA OF GOOD FAITH

Before exploring fair use considerations that are particular to specific recurring situations, we would like to highlight a suite of core fair use best practices that recur across a range of situations. These practices can be characterized broadly as practices indicative of good faith. Some courts have made much of this notion where would-be fair users are seen to have "unclean hands" because their activity involved some other wrongdoing,[34] but more recent cases have been less concerned with this consideration.[35] Nevertheless, communities of practice that develop their

---

[31] For a useful resource for calculating likely copyright terms for any given work, see Hirtle 2015.

[32] For more about Creative Commons, see http://www.creativecommons.org.

[33] One particularly troubling variety of contractual limitation on use of recorded sound is the End User License Agreement or Terms of Use that govern online music markets such as the iTunes Store and the Amazon MP3 Store. Music librarians have raised significant concerns about the seeming inconsistency of such licenses with library acquisition and use. See, e.g., Sound Recording Collecting in Crisis, http://guides.lib.washington.edu/imls2014.

[34] See, e.g., Harper & Row v. The Nation Enters., Inc., 471 U.S. 539 (1985).

[35] See Campbell, 510 U.S. at 585 n. 18 (leaving the relevance of good faith an open issue). Academics have argued that good faith is irrelevant to fair use. See, e.g., Leval 1990, 1126 ("The [fair use] inquiry should focus not on the morality of the secondary user, but on whether her creation claiming the benefits of the doctrine is of the type that should receive those benefits."); Frankel and Kellog 2013.

own standards of good practice in fair use have repeatedly emphasized the importance of acting in good faith as an aspect of satisfying professional norms. Accordingly, many of the best practices documents include requirements or strong recommendations that fair users engage in a series of good faith practices when fair use is invoked to make copyrighted materials available to all or some members of the public.

The first of these practices is that, wherever possible, **materials used fairly should be properly attributed**, according to conventions of the field. We see this articulated in virtually every context and by virtually every community, from libraries to online video makers to documentary filmmakers to poets. The practice of attribution shows good faith by giving credit, directing interested parties to source material, fostering future scholarship and reuse, and helping to put creators themselves on notice when their works are incorporated in new uses. Research also shows that "creators are willing to sacrifice significant economic payments in favor of receiving attribution for their work" (Sprigman et al. 2013). Attribution thus helps ensure that the fair use bargain is not entirely one-sided by giving creators a genuine and valuable benefit.[36]

Another very common practice across communities is to **show due consideration to concerns about privacy and other potential harm to vulnerable third parties** who may be affected by a planned use. Previously unpublished or obscure materials may contain information that could be damaging if revealed, and many fair uses can go forward without making unnecessary disclosure of this kind of information. Archivists, librarians, scholars, and teachers have all agreed that, where possible, materials that are made public on the basis of fair use should be screened to avoid unnecessary harm of this kind.[37]

A third common practice is to provide a **mechanism to get feedback** from interested parties (copyright holders, performers, subjects, family members, and so on). This need not be a "notice-and-takedown" mechanism,[38] per se, and in fact many communities have found that this engagement is just as likely to be positive (yielding expressions of appreciation for the project, offers to provide related materials) as it is to be negative (takedown requests, privacy concerns, and the like). The important thing is to make it easy for anyone with questions or concerns about a given project to communicate with someone on the project team.

A fourth general practice is to **provide users with some basic**

---

[36] Of course, for some orphaned works full attribution will be difficult or impossible; all that is required is that the user make reasonable effort.

[37] An example that came up more than once in our conversations with recorded sound collections professionals was ethnographic recordings of spiritual rites and similar culturally sensitive materials.

[38] A part of the Digital Millennium Copyright Act requires certain online intermediaries to follow very strict "notice-and-takedown" procedures in order to avoid liability for the acts of their users. To comply with these procedures, a service provider must immediately disable access to user-posted material when they receive a compliant notice. These provisions, codified at 17 U.S.C. § 512, do not apply to recorded sound collections and others who use materials themselves, but many have adapted analogous procedures as a safety valve to give third parties a way to register concern without resorting to more formal, high-stakes measures.

information about copyright and fair use as they apply to the kinds of uses you intend to foster (for example, teaching, scholarship, or study) by making materials available. This typically includes notice that **users are responsible for their own downstream uses** of materials. These notices and educational efforts help foster a healthy respect for copyright as well as awareness of the purpose and value of fair use.

ELECTRONIC ACCESS TO RARE/UNIQUE MATERIALS FOR OFF-SITE RESEARCHERS/USERS

Interviewees from recorded sound collections told us repeatedly that one of the most important things they could do to better advance their various institutional or personal missions would be to make the rare or unique items in their collections more readily available to remote users and researchers. Practical barriers to this activity are lower than ever thanks to the growth and power of the Internet, together with the explosion of service and technology providers catering to storage and streaming of even large, high-quality files. The connection to mission is clear, as recorded sound collections exist to provide access to culture.

The legal barriers, however, can seem daunting at first glance. More than any other activity, provision of access to remote users may seem at first to resemble high-profile cases involving online file sharing. On closer inspection, however, the superficial resemblance dissolves.

First, the courts have made it clear that large-scale file sharing is a disfavored activity, and that fair use cannot be invoked to justify it. By contrast, however, the Copyright Act actively favors the provision of research copies to students and scholars. Sections 108(d) and (e) of the Copyright Act allow libraries to provide patrons with copies of works where the library reasonably believes unused copies of the work are no longer commercially available at a "fair price." While these provisions are helpful where they apply, their application is limited: they exclude musical works, for example, and they only apply to libraries whose collections are open to researchers in general. Still, the existence of this exception shows that Congress looks favorably upon provision of copies for research in appropriate circumstances. This, in turn, supports claims of fair use.[39] Courts have blessed similar claims in the context of unpublished manuscripts,[40] and should be equally open to fair use claims for recorded sound materials.

Second, and crucially, the sound recordings that our interviewees seek to make available are almost by definition materials that have no commercial value, and may never have been commercial objects. These recordings are sufficiently old, rare, ephemeral, personal, technical, arcane, and so on, that no appreciable segment of consumers is interested in paying for access to them, and consequently no market actor has an interest in making them available for a reasonable price. Academic studies show

---

[39] See Band 2012.

[40] Sundeman v. Seajay Soc'y, Inc., 142 F.3d 194 (4th Cir. 1998) (finding fair use where collector provided a copy of the full text of an unpublished manuscript to a scholar in order to facilitate scholarship without endangering the fragile original).

that even for music that was at one time popular, the vast majority of sound recordings quickly become unavailable from commercial outlets.[41] As several interviewees told us, it is in these circumstances, where commercial markets have truly failed, that the imperative to provide access to researchers is strongest.

The provision of copies to remote individual users for research and study, considered as a possible fair use, has been a recurrent topic of best practices codes over the last decade. Principle Four of the *Code of Best Practices in Fair Use for Academic and Research Libraries* ("Libraries' Code") provides that, "It is fair use to create digital versions of a library's special collections and archives and to make these versions electronically accessible in appropriate contexts" (20). The *Statement Of Best Practices In Fair Use Of Collections Containing Orphan Works For Libraries, Archives, And Other Memory Institutions* ("Orphan Works Statement") states that "providing access to their collections [is] the ultimate goal of all [memory institution] activities" and that "fair use [is] available to them for this purpose" (27). It goes on to describe a series of detailed best practices for providing access to collections materials, addressing acquisition, seeking clearances, and more. The *Statement of Best Practices in Fair Use of Dance-Related Materials* ("Dance Heritage Statement") provides that "Furthermore, where Dance Collections can assist academic efforts from afar by making scarce, one-of-a-kind, or out-of-print resources available through secure electronic, streamed, or other digital technology, or conventional models of information delivery, these efforts fall within fair use" (14–15).

The strongly positive community norms around this activity share several key characteristics. One is that the fair use case will be much stronger where **the works are not commercially available** or were never intended for commercial exploitation. For example, the Libraries' Code cautions that, "Providing access to published works that are available in unused copies on the commercial market at reasonable prices should be undertaken only with careful consideration, if at all" (20). Wise **use of technology to shape access**, while not always required, was recommended as a way to ensure that access is commensurate with a legitimate purpose. Streaming might be preferred to downloading, for example, or lower quality downloads over higher, depending on context.

ELECTRONIC ACCESS TO COLLECTED MATERIALS FOR AFFILIATED STUDENTS AND INSTRUCTORS IN SUPPORT OF TEACHING

In addition to supporting research and promoting interest in collections using themed exhibits, interviewees expressed interest in finding ways to support teaching by making collected recordings available to students in relevant classes at educational institutions. For example, university libraries frequently support courses by placing professor-selected collections of recordings on electronic reserve sites available only to authenticated

---

[41] See Brooks 2005 (finding that "On average, rights owners have made available 14 percent of the historic recordings that they control" for a sample of recordings released between 1890 and 1964).

enrolled students. This functionality was seen as a natural part of a library's traditional mission to support teaching and learning by collecting materials that would be useful to students as a complement to textbooks and other materials that students traditionally purchase for class. While interviewees showed particular enthusiasm for making rare or unique holdings available for this purpose, there was also interest in making items from the broader collection available in support of teaching (as, for example, documentation of trends in popular music).

Section 110(1) of the Copyright Act substantially immunizes the use of copyrighted materials in connection with live classroom teaching from copyright liability. Many other teaching practices that recorded sound collections can support, especially those enabled by new technology, are not covered, however. Fortunately, "Teaching" is one of the examples of a core fair use that is mentioned in the preamble to Section 107, and courts have cited the importance of educational use as a compelling "purpose" in fair use analysis. Indeed, its centrality is so widely assumed that—in practice—rights holders seldom challenge educational uses.

Recently, however, courts have had a chance to weigh in on fair use in this context in two cases, *AIME v. UCLA*[42] and *Cambridge Univ. Press v. Patton* (the Georgia State e-reserves case),[43] both with relatively positive outcomes for educators that were consistent with the best practices. In the *UCLA* case, an association of video vendors sued the university for copyright infringement in connection with its practice of making films available securely online to authenticated students, via a streaming media server, when their professors had assigned those films for class. The case was not decided on fair use grounds because the films at issue had been licensed to UCLA in a way that the court found allowed streaming, but along the way the court did acknowledge that there was at least a reasonable argument to be made that streaming the films was fair use.

The decision in *Cambridge Univ. Press* is much more detailed, and focuses almost exclusively on fair use. The very specificity of its focus, however, limits its value as a source of general guidance. On one hand, the question of whether the particular uses involved (excerpts from scholarly monographs posted for students at instructors' direction) are fair is discussed in extensive detail—hundreds of pages across the district court and appellate court decisions. However, both decisions depend to a large extent on the finding that while these materials may have been written and published with an "academic market" in mind, as a practical matter, no mechanism existed by which most of the actual uses involved in the case could be licensed. Although the district court opinion found the majority of Georgia State University's uses were fair, the appellate decision was much more ambivalent, announcing an intentionally vague set of standards that gives little indication of how lower courts should evaluate similar cases in the future. Be that as it may, much of the reasoning was entirely consistent with that of the best practices documents insofar as

---

[42] Assoc. Info. & Media Equip. v. Regents of the Univ. of Cal., 2012 WL 7683452 (C.D. Cal. 2012).
[43] Cambridge Univ. Press v. Patton, 769 F.3d 1232 (11th Cir. 2014).

the court urged caution where educational materials are being used for educational purposes. As of this writing, the case has been sent back to the district court for a second round of fair use evaluation.

Many of the communities that have devised fair use best practices have a strong direct or indirect interest in enabling teaching from primary sources. Thus, because research libraries support the teaching missions of their institutions, the Libraries' Code clearly favors this practice, subject to important qualifications and limitations.[44] The *Code of Best Practices in Fair Use for Media Literacy Education* ("Media Literacy Code"), which deals primarily with the K-12 classroom, also expresses strong support for exercising fair use to make all kinds of media "available to learners, in class, in workshops, in informal mentoring and teaching settings, and on school-related Web sites" (10) and affirms that, "Under fair use, educators…can integrate copyrighted material into curriculum materials, including books, workbooks, podcasts, DVD compilations, videos, Web sites, and other materials designed for learning" (11). The OCW [Open CourseWare] Code describes several contexts in which teachers can use copyrighted works online in support of teaching. The Dance Heritage Statement also affirms that providing electronic access in support of teaching is a fair use (14–15). The *Society for Cinema and Media Studies' Statement of Best Practices for Fair Use in Teaching for Film and Media Educators* (SCMS Teaching Statement) includes a general recognition that "Educators engaged in distance education teaching may rely on the general protection afforded under the fair use doctrine…to create an educational experience for online students that is comparable to that of their face-to-face classroom counterparts" (161). The Poetry Code provides that, "Under fair use, instructors at all levels who devote class time to teaching examples of published poetry may reproduce those poems fully or partially in their teaching materials and make them available to students using the conventional educational technologies most appropriate for their instructional purposes" (11). Last, but certainly not least, the Music Library Association has issued a *Statement on the Digital Transmission of Audio Reserves* that is largely consistent with these best practices documents (Music Library Association 2010).

These communities of librarians, educators, and collectors have identified several best practices for sharing materials in support of education. First, musical materials **made or marketed expressly for use in support of teaching**, such as CDs designed to complement specific textbooks or anthologies compiled for teaching, should be used in this context only with great caution, if at all. The extent of the work used should of course be **justified in relation to the teacher's pedagogical purpose**; where excerpts will serve just as well as entire works, excerpts are preferred. Relatedly, **access should be carefully managed** so that only enrolled students can obtain relevant materials, and only for the duration of the course.

The good news for recorded sound collections is that the materials they hold are seldom intended solely for educational use, nor are they being actively licensed for that purpose. It also should be noted that

---

[44] Libraries' Code, 14 ("It is fair use to make appropriately tailored course-related content available to enrolled students via digital networks.").

the appellate court in *Cambridge Univ. Press* specifically acknowledged the applicability of transformative use arguments in the educational context,[45] so the logic of the best practices concerning the use of non-educational materials to support teaching is still very much available to educators and their allies. Indeed, the *Cambridge Univ. Press* courts endorsed some of the same considerations identified in the best practices, such as the importance of choosing an amount that is justified by educational purpose, limiting access to students currently enrolled in the relevant class, and providing information about fair use to teachers and students so that they can make responsible decisions about using the material.

PRESERVATION/FORMAT-SHIFTING

Most interviewees saw digitizing and other reformatting of sound recordings in support of preservation as a high-priority and low-risk fair use activity. Several studies have shown the pressing need for mass-scale reformatting of sound recordings trapped in fragile and outdated formats, but the scope of Section 108's express provision for preservation is widely seen as narrow and burdensome.[46] In particular, the idea that a particular copy must already be damaged or deteriorating before it can be preserved has been criticized as tantamount to requiring preservation "malfeasance."[47] Another source of frustration with Section 108 is the narrow definition of "obsolete format," which rules out any format where compatible equipment is available on the market, regardless of whether the equipment is scarce, expensive, or adequate to professional needs. Fair use is clearly available as a supplement to permit preservation where 108 stops short. The text[48] and legislative history[49] of the Copyright Act are both explicit on this point, and community best practices agree.

Courts have considered preservation in at least two cases, finding fair use explicitly in one case and implicitly in the other. In *Sundeman v. Seajay Society*, an author's estate brought suit against the owner of a copy of an unpublished manuscript for making and distributing copies of the manuscript to a scholar and to the University of Florida. While there were several uses at issue in the case, the Fourth Circuit ruled that it was fair use for the Seajay Society to make and distribute copies of the manuscript for the scholar and the university as a form of preservation, in order to minimize the risk of harm to the rare and fragile original manuscript. In the *HathiTrust* case, the Second Circuit did not expressly find that

---

[45] *Cambridge* at 1263 n.21.

[46] See, e.g., Council on Library and Information Resources and Library of Congress 2010, 120-21 ("Section 108…has failed to keep pace with best practices currently followed by the audio engineering and the federally and privately funded restoration communities."); Association for Recorded Sound Collections 2005 ("Regarding preservation, the Association believes that current copyright laws and regulation should be modified to eliminate many of the restrictions present in the law.")

[47] See Loughney 2011 ("To deliberately delay preserving a culturally, historically or aesthetically important sound recording until it is in a deteriorated condition is a foolhardy practice that could constitute malfeasance on the part of a professional librarian or archivist.")

[48] See 17 U.S.C. 108(f)(4).

[49] See H.R. Rep. No. 94-1476 ("[T]he making of duplicate copies for purposes of archival preservation certainly falls within the scope of 'fair use.'").

preservation, in itself, justified digitizing millions of books—ruling instead that facilitating search was a sufficient independent basis. However, in the district court, Judge Baer had ruled that preservation was an eligible fair use,[50] a ruling that was not reversed on appeal. Judge Chin's district court opinion in the related *Authors Guild v. Google* case also signaled approval for preservation as a legitimate fair use purpose.[51]

Some of the community statements that have endorsed fair use for preservation include the Libraries' Code (17ff.), the Orphan Works Statement (26), the Dance Heritage Statement (8ff.), the Visual Resources Association *Statement on the Fair Use of Images for Teaching, Research and Study* ("VRA Statement"),[52] and the Online Video Code (7). These communities agreed that preservation is highly socially beneficial and (when separated from questions of access) poses no threat to the market prerogatives of copyright holders. Libraries and memory institutions agreed that preservation was a core mission that should not be unduly hindered by copyright concerns. At the same time, these institutions agreed that copying for preservation was **unnecessary when a particular copy was not unique and a suitable replacement was readily available at a reasonable price**. Statements also suggested that **originals and preservation surrogates should not circulate simultaneously**, lest the preservation function become a pretext for multiplying usable copies when no other fair use justification is available. When preservation surrogates are created to facilitate access (and fragile originals are taken out of circulation), the Libraries' Code suggests **limiting general circulation of preservation copies** to "authenticated members of the library's patron community."[53]

COLLECTING ONLINE MATERIALS

While the situations discussed so far have involved materials already acquired, interviewees also described encountering copyright uncertainty in connection with building their collections. Most of this uncertainty had to do with acquiring materials that are (or may be) available only online, including various kinds of ephemera. For some of the works in question, such as musical recordings sold (or, perhaps, "licensed") exclusively through online stores such as iTunes or Amazon, the purchase is made subject to "Terms of Use" or an "End User License Agreement" (EULA) that often include terms that preclude lending, preservation, and other

---

[50] The appellate court did not comment on this ruling, so Judge Baer's ruling appears to be the last word on the issue.

[51] See 954 F.Supp.2d 282, 293 (2013) (lauding the Google Books scanning project because, "It preserves books, in particular out-of-print and old books that have been forgotten in the bowels of libraries….").

[52] VRA Statement,10. Note that the VRA Statement was not developed using the usual process of interviews and small group discussions with community members, nor was it facilitated by any of the usual team at American University. Rather, it was authored by a committee of the Visual Resources Association with input from a panel of distinguished IP experts. Nevertheless, the principles described in the VRA Statement are consistent with the norms identified by the various American University-facilitated statements.

[53] Section 108(c) and (d) bar off-premises circulation of digital preservation copies "to the public." Some commentators have suggested that allowing off-premises circulation to a subset of users, such as faculty, students, or affiliate researchers would not constitute circulation "to the public."

activities typical of an institutional collector. As discussed in the introductory material, courts have generally allowed agreed-upon contractual terms to trump fair use rights, even where the contracts are seemingly one-sided, take-it-or-leave-it affairs, as EULAs and other electronic licenses generally are.[54] Accordingly, the existing best practices literature can do little to assist a user who is bound by hostile contract terms, at least as the law currently seems to stand.

Not surprisingly, neither the statute nor the caselaw addressed the acquisition of electronic content by memory institutions. But fair use certainly is available for materials posted or distributed online without a contractual limitation on use, and communities have described some useful ways to think about collecting and using materials from the web and other born-digital works. First, the Libraries' Code has said that it is fair use to "create topically based collections of websites and other material from the Internet and to make them available for scholarly use" (27). The ICA [International Communications Association] Code found that it is fair use for individual scholars to assemble personal research collections that include material from the Internet, reasoning that, "The materials in question, generally topical or even ephemeral in character, are transformed by collection or organization into a research corpus, which exists for a new and fundamentally different purpose" (12).

Norms for collecting materials in this way are fairly straightforward. The Libraries' Code counsels that collectors **represent any captured materials accurately** in the way they would have appeared online, and include information about when and how the material was captured from the web. **Attribution** should be provided not only for the creator of captured material (as discussed above) but also for the proprietor of the website— or, by extension, any other online source. While not required, the Libraries' Code suggests that having a **clear and consistent policy about bot exclusion headers**[55] will bolster a fair use case, as will an effort to **collect as comprehensively as possible** within a given topic, theme, or other collecting rationale.

While the ICA Code was written by and for individual researchers, the limitations on its personal archiving principle may also be instructive. Collections should be reasonably **related to a specific research or collecting interest** of the collecting institution or individual; for example, a state university might reasonably try to collect sound recordings posted online

---

[54] A leading case is Bowers v. Baystate Techs., Inc., 320 F.3d 1317 (Fed. Cir. 2003), in which the court found that a shrink-wrap license barring reverse engineering trumped the established rule that reverse engineering software is fair use. Judge Dyk's dissent in the case is instructive, and, we think, the better view.

[55] Typically stored in a file called "robots.txt," a bot exclusion header allows website proprietors to signal their preference that their site not be automatically copied or indexed by companies like Google. Requests for exclusion can be motivated by a variety of concerns, often having to do with audience, bandwidth, and server capacity rather than copyright. Research institutions have found that uncritically following the instructions of every robots.txt file is not a reliable way to discern the wishes of site proprietors regarding archiving. Quite often robots.txt files will exclude only parts of websites, which can result in substantial unjustified omissions from collections. See Legal Issues, International Internet Preservation Consortium (n.d.). In at least one case, the Libraries' Code has helped libraries move to more nuanced policies. See Gray and Martin 2013.

by local artists in the state. As with other collections, institutions should make clear to users that they are responsible for using materials to which they are granted access legitimately—including **use for scholarship and research.**

DATA-MINING/NON-CONSUMPTIVE RESEARCH

Exponential growth in computing power together with the shrinking cost of storage has made it increasingly feasible to create and process comprehensive databases of all kinds of media. To date, the leading use of such databases is the creation of a search engine to locate particular terms in a corpus, the way a search engine helps users find relevant websites on the Internet. As computational power grows, however, the kinds of information that can be gleaned from analysis of large corpuses grows with it. The power of "big data" seems nearly impossible to overestimate.

For recorded sound collections, the potential of digital analysis manifests itself in several ways. First, it makes possible the creation of new search tools that allow researchers anywhere to identify whether and where particular recordings or kinds of recordings can be found, based not on textual information but on the characteristics of those recordings themselves. This is the promise of digitized search. Second, technology enables the computer analysis of recordings to facilitate an increasingly common mode of research sometimes called "distant reading."[56] Interviewees described existing projects that analyze music, metadata,[57] and lyrics,[58] and expressed keen interest in exploring ways to leverage computer analysis, including providing databases for this purpose, so that scholars and students could learn more from recorded sound collections. Scholars have called uses like these "non-consumptive" or "non-expressive."[59] The use is "non-consumptive" because the works are searched or analyzed—usually in large quantities—by a computer, rather than being "consumed" (i.e., read or heard) by a human being in a way that might implicate the market prerogatives of a copyright holder. The outputs of a computer analysis are "non-expressive," i.e., they are facts about a work or a corpus—the frequency and proximity of particular words, phrases, notes, and so on.

The courts have been quite clear in their endorsement of fair use for search engines and similar uses. Early cases were about mass market Internet search engines run by companies like Google and Amazon, but later cases have considered uses in more specialized contexts such as

---

[56] See, e.g., Moretti 2013.

[57] Scholars interested in this issue have created The International Society for Music Information Retrieval, a group that hosts an email list and annual conferences for presentation of research. See http://ismir.net. Work in this area is spread across many leading research institutions and funded by groups including the National Science Foundation in the United States and JISC in the United Kingdom. See Byrd and Fingerhut 2002.

[58] One example that came up several times was Tahir Hemphill's "Hip Hop Word Count" project, a Kickstarter-funded database of rap lyrics that has since become part of an educational project called the Rap Research Lab. For more information, see Hemphill's website, http://staplecrops.com. Information about his Kickstarter campaign is at https://www.kickstarter.com/projects/1801076626/the-hip-hop-word-count-a-searchable-rap-almanac.

[59] See, e.g., Sag 2009.

plagiarism detection tools[60] and, most recently, in the *Authors Guild v. HathiTrust* case, search and text mining for scholarly use. While the most familiar search engines deal primarily with text, courts have also applied the fair use doctrine to search engines that scan images and display "thumbnail" images as results,[61] as well as search services that crawl television programming.[62] Extending the logic of these cases to cover sound recordings poses no particular conceptual challenge.

The Libraries' Code addresses these uses directly and finds that it is fair use "to develop and facilitate the development of digital databases of collection items to enable non-consumptive analysis across the collection for both scholarly and reference purposes" (25). The principle is grounded in a strong community consensus that such uses are well within the realm of what libraries and memory institutions have always done to add value to their collections—extracting factual information about items in the collection that helps researchers and users understand collections and locate material that will best serve their research needs.

Best practices that impose limitations on such uses are mainly directed to ensuring that materials digitized and collected for non-consumptive purposes are not repurposed without independent justification. For example, while non-consumptive research may be sufficient to justify mass digitization and computer analysis of a collection of sound recordings, **a new and separate fair use argument** (or a statutory justification, or a license) would be required before making the same works individually available for listening. Also, when creating a public-facing search or research tool, it is important that any portions of text displayed as search results (often called "snippets") are carefully chosen to ensure they **serve the research purpose and do not unduly intrude on the ordinary market for access to the works**.

DIGITAL EXHIBITS AND EXHIBITS FOR THE PUBLIC

A distinct but related recurring use scenario, as significant for other cultural institutions as it is for recorded sound collections, involves the assembly of a group of recordings into a curated collection or exhibit available on the open web and designed to facilitate exploration of a particular theme, such as a genre, an era, a performer, or a geographic region. Interviewees suggested that recorded sound collections could facilitate teaching in formal settings such as public school classrooms or informally by reaching individuals via the Internet. Ideally, such collections will include rich metadata and contextual information as well as the collected recordings, giving instructors or individual browsers some of the information they need to make sense of the recordings and to derive value from the collection.

Although the courts have not addressed the fair use status of virtual (or,

---

[60] A.V. ex rel Vanderheye v. iParadigms, LLC, 562 F.3d 630 (4th Cir. 2009).

[61] Perfect 10 v. Amazon.com, 508 F.3d 1146 (9th Cir. 2007)

[62] Fox News Network, LLC v. TVEyes, Inc., No. 13 CIV. 5315 AKH, 2014 WL 4444043 (S.D.N.Y. Sept. 9, 2014).

for that matter, physical) exhibits, it is widely assumed that such uses should be considered a form of privileged public education, to which fair use applies with full force. Not only is the inclusion of copyrighted material in the context of an exhibit an obvious example of transformative use, but also such exhibits pose little or no threat to the copyright owners' legitimate interest in commercializing their intellectual property.[63]

Almost every relevant community that has undertaken to articulate best practices in fair use has described some version of this practice as a legitimate exercise of fair use rights. Both the Libraries' Code and the Orphan Works Statement address this type of use. Principle Four of the Libraries' Code, which addresses digitizing special collections, is also relevant here, but Principle Two deals more specifically with the creation of exhibits, both online and in physical space. Principle Two provides that, "It is fair use for a library to use appropriate selections from collection materials to increase public awareness and engagement with these collections and to promote new scholarship drawing on them" (16). Similar principles occur in the *Code Of Best Practices In Fair Use For Poetry* (Poetry Code),[64] the *Set of Principles in Fair Use for Journalism* (Journalism Principles),[65] the Dance Heritage Statement,[66] The *Code of Best Practices in Fair Use for OpenCourse-Ware* ("OCW Code"),[67] and the *Code of Best Practices in Fair Use for Online Video* (Online Video Code).[68]

These statements share several key characteristics. They **emphasize the value added** by informed curation as well as additional information and commentary posted along with collected materials. Most communities require some minimal information (attribution, clear indication of the theme or purpose of the exhibit) as a threshold matter, and agree that providing more information (historical context, critique, etc.) will strengthen any fair use claim.[69] Second, the statements indicate that the amount of any given work posted should be **appropriate to the educational purpose** of the exhibit or collection. Where excerpts of works will

---

[63] In this sense, the exhibitor is in the same position as the publisher of a book surveying the history of the Grateful Dead, which the court found had no (negative) effect on the commercial efforts of concert promoters whose posters were reproduced in the book. See Bill Graham Archives v. Dorling Kindersley Ltd., 448 F.3d 605, 614 (2d Cir. 2006).

[64] Poetry Code, 13 (Principle Six: "Under fair use, an online resource (such as a blog or web site) may make examples of selected published poetry electronically available to the public, provided that the site also includes substantial additional cultural resources, including but not limited to critique or commentary, that contextualize or otherwise add value to the selections.").

[65] Journalism Principles, 14 (Situation Six: "The use of copyrighted material to promote public discussion and analysis can qualify as fair use.").

[66] Dance Heritage Statement, 10 (Situation 2, Exhibits: "Given the significant cultural and educational function provided by Dance Collection exhibitions and displays, fair use should apply in instances of this kind, both for the materials on display and for the items used for ancillary materials."); 15 (Situation 5, Digital Information Exchange: "Creating web-based resources and engaging in digital delivery of selected materials can be an appropriate way to extend the Dance Collections' mandate to deliver their culturally valuable materials.")

[67] OCW Code, 11–14 (describing fair use of copyrighted materials in online course materials known as "OpenCourseWare" for purposes of criticism, commentary, and illustration.).

[68] Online Video Code, 7 ("Four: Reproducing, Reposting, Or Quoting In Order To Memorialize, Preserve, Or Rescue An Experience, An Event, Or A Cultural Phenomenon.")

[69] See, e.g., Dance Heritage Statement, 17 ("the less extensive the indications of significant added value are, the weaker the fair use claim will be.").

suffice as illustrations of a given theme, posting of entire works will tend to weaken a fair use argument. Indeed, the Libraries' Code suggests, "[U]se of a work (other than a single image) in its entirety is likely to require a special level of justification." Third, several statements suggest that **provision of additional tools** to allow for engagement with the collection will strengthen a fair use case.[70] Fourth, **the absence of commercial availability** is again a factor that some communities have found relevant in deciding what materials to include.

TRANSFER OF COPIES TO THIRD PARTIES IN SUPPORT OF DOWNSTREAM FAIR USES

Many interviewees described receiving requests from a variety of users—e.g., musicians, documentarians, journalists, artists, writers—who sought copies of sound recordings for use in their own creative cultural activities that go beyond research, study, or teaching. While supporting academic and educational uses is certainly a core part of what many libraries and memory institutions do, they also have a mission to provide points of cultural reference for the current generation of creators. Indeed, one of the principal reasons for the fair use doctrine is the necessity that successive generations of creators incorporate material from existing works.[71] For these users, a stream or other technologically limited mode of access would not suffice, nor (in some cases) would a partial copy. Professionals charged with managing recorded sound collections generally have a mission to support fair and legitimate use of collections materials, which can go beyond mere provision of access in many contexts. The legitimacy and importance of these uses have been recognized not only in the statute but also in the variety of best practices statements that have been created to date.

Notably, criticism and commentary are mentioned expressly in the Copyright Act as the kinds of uses that often qualify as fair,[72] and the courts have made it clear that intermediate uses of copyrighted material that enable or facilitate ultimate legitimate uses can be considered fair in appropriate circumstances. One notable example is the copying of large amounts of computer code in order to engage in lawful "reverse engineering;"[73] another is the unauthorized reproduction of millions of student papers to fuel a digital engine for detecting plagiarism.[74] The same principle can and should be applied to uses in the cultural sector.

Indeed, there are compelling arguments in favor of providing copies in good faith to would-be fair users. This situation is susceptible to some of

---

[70] See, e.g., Journalism Principles, 14 ("The journalist (or outlet) should make available tools and forums designed to encourage participation by news consumers."); Orphan Works Statement, 32 ("provide users with specialized search tools");

[71] See, e.g., Leval 1990, 1109 ("First, all intellectual creative activity is in part derivative. There is no such thing as a wholly original thought or invention. Each advance stands on building blocks fashioned by prior thinkers.").

[72] 17 USC 107 ("fair use…for purposes such as criticism, comment… is not an infringement of copyright.").

[73] See Sega Enters. Ltd. v. Accolade, 977 F.2d 1510 (9th Cir. 1993).

[74] See A.V. ex rel Vanderheye v. iParadigms, LLC, 562 F.3d 630 (4th Cir. 2009).

the same arguments that apply where remote researchers seek access to rare or unique items simply for study. Section 108 provides some limited allowance for making copies that become the property of the requesting user, and there is good reason to believe that fair use could apply where Section 108 leaves off (to musical works, for example). Section 108 also shields libraries from liability for patrons' use of on-site copying equipment, a measure that helps to facilitate unsupervised patron copying. Also, in many cases the materials that users request are rare or unique, meaning they are subject to compelling arguments about lack of market harm: no market exists and commercial exploitation may not have played a role in their creation.

The variety of fair uses that might be made of sound recordings is virtually limitless, but practice communities have identified several recurring varieties of fair use in their domains that also exist where recorded sound collections are concerned, and these creator communities recognize such uses as fair in all of their best practices statements.[75] Reproducing portions of copyrighted works as **evidence, illustration, or documentation, as well as objects of commentary,** is a recurring fair use activity across multiple best practices statements.[76]

Educators have described scenarios when fair use allows incorporation of copyrighted material in their lectures and curriculum materials,[77] as well as when students should employ fair use as part of their coursework.[78] Users present these arguments to sound recording collectors, and request access to collections materials to facilitate fair uses. Community practices associated with providing copies to users for research as well as creating online exhibits could easily be adapted to apply here. For example, recorded sound collections should follow the general practice of including information about copyright and fair use with each copy, and signifying clearly that the user is solely responsible for their own uses of copyrighted materials. A click-through **acknowledgment of the user's responsibility to comply with copyright** is a related practice recommended in the Orphan Works Statement. If possible, the **nature and quality of the**

---

[75] See, e.g., the *Documentary Filmmakers' Statement of Best Practices in Fair Use* ("Documentary Statement"), 4 ("Employing Copyrighted Material As The Object Of Social, Political, Or Cultural Critique"); Poetry Code, 11 ("Under fair use, a critic discussing a published poem or body of poetry may quote freely as justified by the critical purpose; likewise, a commentator may quote to exemplify or illuminate a cultural/historical phenomenon, and a visual artist may incorporate relevant quotations into his or her work."); Journalism Principles, 11 ("When Copyrighted Material Is Used In Cultural Reporting And Criticism"); Online Video Code, 5 ("Commenting On Or Critiquing Of Copyrighted Material").

[76] See, e.g., Documentary Statement, 4 ff. ("Quoting Copyrighted Works Of Popular Culture To Illustrate An Argument Or Point"); Journalism Principles, 11 ("Use Of Copyrighted Material As Proof Or Substantiation In News Reporting Or Analysis"), 12 ("When Copyrighted Material Is Used As Illustration In News Reporting Or Analysis"); Online Video Code, 7 ("Reproducing, Reposting, Or Quoting In Order To Memorialize, Preserve, Or Rescue An Experience, An Event, Or A Cultural Phenomenon"); *Code Of Best Practices In Fair Use For Scholarly Research In Communication* ("ICA Code"), 10 ("Scholars may invoke fair use to reproduce copyrighted material where it serves to explain or illustrate their scholarly insights or conclusions about communications in relation to social, cultural, political, or economic phenomena.").

[77] See, e.g., Poetry Code, 10–11; Dance Heritage Statement, 13-15; Media Literacy Code, 10-12; OpenCourseWare Code, 11–14; SCMS Teaching Statement, 157–61; VRA Statement, 11–12.

[78] See, e.g., Media Literacy Code, 12–13; VRA Statement, 13–14.

access provided could be limited in ways commensurate to the needs of the user, though a user who needs a downloaded copy for fair use purposes may need higher quality than a researcher.

REFERENCES

Association for Recorded Sound Collections, Inc. Bylaws. Available at http://www.arsc-audio.org/pdf/ARSCBylaws-2014-09-03.pdf.

Association for Recorded Sound Collections. 2005. *Board Statement on Copyright and Sound Recordings*. Available at http://www.arsc-audio.org/copyright-board.html.

Band, Jonathan. 2012. "The Impact of Substantial Compliance with Copyright Exceptions on Fair Use." *Journal of the Copyright Society*, U.S.A. 59: 453.

Bartholomew, Mark, and John Tehranian. 2013. "An Intersystemic View of Intellectual Property and Free Speech." *The George Washington Law Review* 81(1). Available at http://www.gwlr.org/wp-content/uploads/2013/01/Bartholomew_81_1.pdf.

Brooks, Tim. 2005. *Survey of Reissues of U.S. Recordings*. Washington, D.C.: Council on Library and Information Resources and Library of Congress. Available at http://www.clir.org/pubs/abstract/reports/pub133.

Byrd, Donald, and Michael Fingerhut. 2002. "The History of ISMIR—A Short Happy Tale." *D-Lib Magazine* 8(11). Available at http://www.dlib.org/dlib/november02/11inbrief.html.

Council on Library and Information Resources and Library of Congress. 2010. *The State of Recorded Sound Preservation in the United States: A National Legacy at Risk in the Digital Age*. Washington, D.C.: Council on Library and Information Resources and Library of Congress. Available at http://www.clir.org/pubs/abstract/reports/pub148.

Crews, Kenneth D. 2001. *The Law of Fair Use and the Illusion of Fair-Use Guidelines. Ohio State Law Journal* 62: 602–664.

Frankel, Simon, and Matt Kellogg. 2013. *Bad Faith and Fair Use, Journal of the Copyright Society of the USA* 60. Available at http://papers.ssrn.com/sol3/papers.cfm?abstract_id=2165468.

Gibson, James. 2007. "Risk Aversion and Rights Accretion in Intellectual Property Law." *Yale Law Journal* 116: 882–951. Available at http://www.yalelawjournal.org/article/risk-aversion-and-rights-accretion-in-intellectual-property-law.

Gray, Gabriella, and Scott Martin. 2013. "Choosing a Sustainable Web Archiving Method: A Comparison of Capture Quality." *D-Lib Magazine* 19(5/6). Available at http://www.dlib.org/dlib/may13/gray/05gray.print.html.

Hirtle, Peter. 2015. *Copyright Term and the Public Domain in the United States.* Available at https://copyright.cornell.edu/resources/publicdomain.cfm.

International Internet Preservation Consortium. n.d. "Legal Issues." Available at http://netpreserve.org/web-archiving/legal-issues#robots.

Jaszi, Peter, and Patricia Aufderheide. 2011. *Reclaiming Fair Use.* Chicago, IL: University of Chicago Press.

Jaszi, Peter. 2009. *Protection for Pre-1972 Sound Recordings Under State Law and its Impact on Use by Nonprofit Institutions: A 10-State Analysis.* Prepared by the Program on Information Justice and Intellectual Property, Washington College of Law, American University, under the supervision of Peter Jaszi with the assistance of Nick Lewis. Washington, D.C.: Council on Library and Information Resources and Library of Congress. Available at http://www.clir.org/pubs/abstract/reports/pub146.

Jaszi, Peter. 2007. "Copyright, Fair Use, and Motion Pictures." *Utah Law Review* (2007) 3: 715–740. Available at http://epubs.utah.edu/index.php/ulr/article/viewFile/23/17.

Kasunic, Robert. 2008. "Is That All There Is? Reflections On The Nature Of The Second Fair Use Factor." *Columbia Journal of Law & the Arts* 31(4): 529.

Kravets, David. 2013. "Supreme Court OKs $222K Verdict for Sharing 24 Songs." *Wired* (March 18, 2013). Available at http://www.wired.com/2013/03/scotus-jammie-thomas-rasset/.

Leval, Pierre N. 1990. "Toward a Fair Use Standard." *Harvard Law Review* 103: 1105.

Loughney, Patrick. 2011. "Library of Congress Comments in Response to: Copyright Office Notice of Inquiry Pertaining to Federal Copyright Protection of Sound Recordings Fixed Before February 15, 1972" [Docket No. 2010-4]. Available at http://www.copyright.gov/docs/sound/comments/initial/20110131-Patrick-Loughney-Library-of-Congress.pdf.

Madison, Michael. 2004. "A Pattern-Oriented Approach to Fair Use." *William & Mary Law Review* 45(4): 1525–1690. Available at http://scholarship.law.wm.edu/cgi/viewcontent.cgi?article=1333&context=wmlr.

McBride, Sarah, and Ethan Smith. 2008. "Music Industry to Abandon Mass Suits." *Wall Street Journal* (Dec. 19, 2008). Available at http://www.wsj.com/articles/SB122966038836021137.

Moretti, Franco. 2013. *Distant Reading.* Brooklyn, NY, and London: Verso.

Netanel, Neil. 2011. "Making Sense of Fair Use." *Lewis & Clark Law Review* 15(3): 715–771. Available at https://law.lclark.edu/live/files/9132-lcb153netanelpdf/.

Sag, Matthew. 2012. "Predicting Fair Use." *Ohio State Law Journal* 73(1): 47–91. Available at http://moritzlaw.osu.edu/students/groups/oslj/files/2012/05/73.1.Sag_.pdf.

Sag, Matthew. 2009. "Copyright and Copy-Reliant Technology." *Northwestern University Law Review* 103(4): 1607–1682.

Springman, Christopher, Christopher J. Buccafusco, and Zachary C. Burns. 2013. "What's a Name Worth?: Experimental Tests of the Value of Attribution in Intellectual Property." *Boston University Law Review* 93: 1389–1435. Available at http://www.bu.edu/bulawreview/files/2013/10/SPRIGMAN-Whats-a-Name.pdf.

APPENDIX:
BEST PRACTICES STATEMENTS AND RELATED DOCUMENTS

Adler, Prudence S., Patricia Aufderheide, Brandon Butler, Peter Jaszi. 2012. *Code Of Best Practices In Fair Use For Academic And Research Libraries*. Available at http://www.arl.org/fairuse.

Association of Independent Video and Filmmakers et al. 2005. *Documentary Filmmakers' Statement of Best Practices in Fair Use Electronic Media*. Available at http://www.centerforsocialmedia.org/sites/default/files/fair_use_final.pdf.

Aufderheide, Patricia, David R. Hansen, Meredith Jacob, Peter Jaszi, and Jennifer M. Urban. 2014. *Statement Of Best Practices In Fair Use Of Collections Containing Orphan Works For Libraries, Archives, And Other Memory Institutions*. Available at http://cmsimpact.org/sites/default/files/documents/orphanworks-dec14.pdf.

Aufderheide, Patricia, Katherine Coles, Peter Jaszi, and Jennifer Urban. 2011. *Code Of Best Practices In Fair Use For Poetry*. Available at http://www.cmsimpact.org/sites/default/files/documents/pages/fairusepoetrybooklet_singlepg_3.pdf.

Center for Media and Social Impact. 2013. *Set of Principles in Fair Use for Journalism*. Available at http://www.cmsimpact.org/sites/default/files/documents/pages/principles_in_fair_use_for_journalism.pdf.

Center for Media and Social Impact. 2010. *Code Of Best Practices In Fair Use For Scholarly Research In Communication*. Available at http://www.cmsimpact.org/sites/default/files/WEB_ICA_CODE.pdf.

Center for Media and Social Impact. 2009. *Code of Best Practices in Fair Use for OpenCourseWare*. Available at http://www.cmsimpact.org/sites/default/files/10-305-OCW-Oct29.pdf.

Center for Media and Social Impact. 2008. *Code of Best Practices in Fair Use for Online Video*. Available at http://www.cmsimpact.org/sites/default/files/online_best_practices_in_fair_use.pdf.

Center for Media and Social Impact. 2008. *Code of Best Practices in Fair Use for Media Literacy Education*. Available at http://mediaeducationlab.com/sites/mediaeducationlab.com/files/CodeofBestPracticesinFairUse_0.pdf.

Dance Heritage Coalition. 2009. *Statement of Best Practices in Fair Use of Dance-Related Materials*. Available at http://www.cmsimpact.org/sites/default/files/documents/pages/DHC_fair_use_statement.pdf.

Music Library Association. 2010. *Statement on the Digital Transmission of Audio Reserves*. Available at http://copyright.musiclibraryassoc.org/Resources/DigitalReserves.

Society for Cinema and Media Studies. 2008. "The Society for Cinema and Media Studies' Statement of Best Practices for Fair Use in Teaching for Film and Media Educators." *Cinema Journal* 47(2): 155-164. Available at http://c.ymcdn.com/sites/www.cmstudies.org/resource/resmgr/files/scms_teaching_statement_-_20.pdf.

Society for Cinema and Media Studies. 2009. *Society for Cinema and Media Studies' Statement of Fair Use Best Practices for Media Studies Publishing*. Available at https://c.ymcdn.com/sites/cmstudies.site-ym.com/resource/resmgr/docs/scmsbestpractices4fairuseinp.pdf.

Wagner, Gretchen, and Allan T. Kohl. 2012. Visual Resources Association: *Statement on the Fair Use of Images for Teaching, Research and Study*. Available at http://vraweb.org/wp-content/uploads/2011/01/VRA_FairUse_Statement_Pages_Links.pdf.

APPENDIX B

Glossary

AAC (Advanced Audio Coding): an audio coding standard for lossy digital audio compression. As of 2015, it is the default or standard audio format for streaming and download services such as YouTube and iTunes.

AACR2 (Anglo-American Cataloguing Rules, 2nd edition): a national cataloging code first published in 1967 by the American Library Association, Canadian Library Association, and Chartered Institute of Library and Information Professionals in the United Kingdom. AACR2 is designed for use in the construction of catalogs and other lists in general libraries of all sizes.

Access copy: a file that is optimized for playback and accessibility by users. It is commonly in the form of a compressed file, such as an MP3, for online streaming or download. An access copy may also be in a physical format, such as a CD.

Access master (also called production master, or edit master): an uncompressed BWF file from which all access copies—physical and file-based—are derived. Access masters are made from the preservation master file but may have restoration processes applied, such as editing or signal processing to reduce noise.

Acclimatization: a process for allowing archival materials to transition slowly from the temperature and humidity in which they are stored to the temperature and humidity of the processing and listening areas. This is typically done when there is more than a 10-degree difference between cold storage and working spaces in order to prevent condensation.

A/D converter (analog-to-digital converter): a device that converts a continuously variable electronic signal to discrete numerical values representing the signal's amplitude or change in amplitude.

Administrative metadata: information about provenance, technical characteristics, intellectual property rights, preservation issues and actions, and location.

Aliasing: distortion in digitally recorded sound caused by a sampling rate lower than half of the cycles of the frequency being reproduced.

Analog: a device or system that represents sound as continuously variable physical quantities.

Archival Management System (AMS): an open source, web-based tool initially developed by AVPreserve to manage records provided by stations contributing to the American Archive of Public Broadcasting.

ArchivesSpace: an open source, archival-collection management and description system for providing access to archives, manuscripts, and digital objects.

Archiving: a type of backup consisting of policies in which the target destination retains data that are deleted or altered on the original storage device.

Audio data compression: a process by which software decreases bandwidth and file size storage space needed to represent a sound recording.

AVCC (AudioVisual Collaborative Cataloging): a free, open-source web application developed by AVPreserve for item-level description of audio, video, and film collections.

AVID (Audio-Visual and Image Database): a Microsoft Access-based desktop application for managing and tracking audio, moving image, and still image materials.

Backup: the replication of data to one or more devices, and ideally, locations.

BEXT (Broadcast audio EXTension): a plain text area of a WAVE file wrapped as part of the BWF standard, providing additional embedded metadata within BWF files. See INFO chunk.

BIBFRAME (Bibliographic Framework Initiative): as of 2015, an emerging structural standard based on linked data principles and expressed through the RDF data model.

Bit depth: number of bits used for each sample. In an audio codec, each bit is equal to 6dB of dynamic range.

Bit rot: the corruption of data stored on media.

Born digital: a recording that was digitally encoded at the point of creation.

Broadcast Audio Extension: see BEXT

Broadcast Wave Format: see BWF

BWF (Broadcast Wave Format): a European Broadcasting Union standard that extends the Microsoft RIFF WAVE file standard by adding the broadcast audio extension, or BEXT, metadata chunk and restricting the types of codecs supported. The current standard is EBU 3285 v2.

BWF MetaEdit: an open source tool useful for embedding metadata in WAVE files.

Carriers: the physical component of an analog recording, e.g., 1/4-inch magnetic tape, vinyl disc, compact disc, hard drive, etc.

Cartridge tape media: magnetic tape housed and played back in a casing; examples are audiocassettes, microcassettes, and 8-track tapes.

CD-DA (Compact Discs Digital Audio standard): also known as the Red Book standard, a standard created by Sony and Phillips for encoding and manufacturing audio CDs.

CD-R (Recordable Compact Disc): also known as the Orange Book standard, a type of compact disc that can be recorded on only once.

Checksum: a small numerical value, typically 128 or 256 characters long, representing a digital file of any size. The value is generated using an algorithm of a particular type, such as MD5, SHA-256, or SHA-1. The formula is designed such that even the smallest change in a file, a single bit, will yield a vastly different output, making the change explicit. As a method of detecting errors or changes in the file it represents, checksums are used for monitoring the authenticity and integrity of data.

Chunk: a subportion of a file used for a specific function; in the audio context, chunks organize and identify data within files as part of the RIFF and WAVE file standards, such as the data (sound) chunk, the format (sometimes called header) chunk, and textual metadata chunks. See also BEXT and INFO chunk.

Cloud storage: a service model in which data are stored remotely by a service provider and made available to clients over the Internet.

Coarse groove disc: a disc with a groove width greater than 1 mil. See microgroove disc.

Codec: the packaging instructions used for encoding (during recording) and decoding (during playback) the information within a file wrapper; e.g. PCM and MP3.

Collection profiling: a means of getting an overview of your collection; specifically, number and format of the items in the collection.

CollectiveAccess: free, open source software for creating and publishing collection metadata. It is preconfigured for several descriptive standards, but may be customized for additional uses.

Compression: see Audio data compression

Creative Commons: a licensing system, developed and supported by the Creative Commons organization, which provides authors with a relatively simple means to ensure that others can use their works freely in a variety of ways without having to seek permission.

CSV (comma separated values): a common file format used to organize and structure tabular data where the data elements are separated by commas in the same way they would appear in separate cells in a table. The format is widely supported by consumer, business, and scientific applications. Among its most common uses is moving tabular data between programs that natively operate on incompatible formats.

Cupping: on magnetic tape, a condition when the binder layer that contains magnetic information shrinks or deforms at a rate different from that of the tape base, resulting in curl of the tape.

DACS (Describing Archives: A Content Standard): a set of rules for describing archives, personal papers, and manuscript collections. The descriptive standard can be used for all types of archival material.

DAT (Digital Audio Tape): a signal recording and playback medium for digital audio developed by Sony and introduced in 1987. In appearance it is similar to a compact video cassette, using 4 mm magnetic tape enclosed in a protective shell, but is roughly half the size at 73 mm × 54 mm × 10.5 mm.

Data mining: the practice of examining large databases to generate new insights undetectable in smaller data sets.

Data tape: magnetic tape used for storing digital files as an alternative to spinning disk or optical media.

Delamination: the separation of layers in a recording medium.

Derivative file: a version of an original file, often called a service, access, production, edit, delivery, viewing, or output file. Derivative files are usually compressed, smaller in size than the original files.

Descriptive metadata: basic information elements, such as creator, title, date, contents, subject, and genre, for identifying and discovering resources.

Digital provenance: describes the tools and processes used to create a digital file, the responsible entity, and when and where the process events occurred. Sometimes called "process history."

Discovery: the process of finding described resources (e.g., books, sound and video recordings, maps) through search and retrieval.

Dolby noise reduction: a form of dynamic preemphasis used during recording, plus a form of dynamic deemphasis used during playback, that work in tandem to improve the signal-to-noise ratio. It is commonly applied to tape recordings to reduce hiss.

Dublin Core: a set of 13 attributes (title, creator, date, etc.) that can be used to describe library and archival holdings, including web resources (e.g., video, images, web pages), as well as physical resources such as books or CDs, and objects such as artworks.

Dynamic range: the range from the largest to the smallest amplitudes that can be accurately reproduced.

EAC-CPF (Encoded Archival Context-Corporate Bodies, Persons and Families): a structural standard for XML encoding of authority records about persons, corporate bodies, and families relating to archival materials.

EAD (Encoded Archival Description): an opensource, XML-based structural standard for electronic finding aids, maintained by the Society of American Archivists and the Library of Congress. It was first published in 1998; EAD3 was implemented in 2015.

EGAD (Experts Group on Archival Description): appointed by the International Council on Archives in 2012 to develop a conceptual model for archival description. The model will provide a foundation for description systems that enhance access to archival resources in a linked data environment.

Embedded metadata: metadata that are stored inside the same file, or container, that also stores the essence to which the metadata refer.

Essence: the portion of a physical or file-based object representing the recorded signal.

Ethernet: the global standard for cabling computers together in a network. Standardized by the IEEE as 802.3.

Exudation: the appearance on the surface of a medium of one or several byproducts of decomposition of the medium. An example is a white powder form of palmitic acid caused by the breakdown of plasticizer in a lacquer disc.

FADGI (Federal Agencies Digitization Guidelines Initiative): a collaborative effort by the Library of Congress and other federal agencies to define common guidelines, methods, and practices for digitizing historical content. The initiative has formed working groups for still image digitization and audiovisual digitization.

Fair use: outlined in Section 107 of the U.S. copyright law, the doctrine that portions of copyrighted material may be used for purposes such as criticism, news reporting, teaching, and research, without the need for permission from or payment to the copyright holder.

File-based digital: digital information stored in files on a generic data carrier (such as hard drive, CD/DVD-ROM, data tape, etc.), as distinct from digital information stored on a format specific carrier such as CD-DA, MiniDV, DAT, etc.

Firewall: a technological barrier designed to prevent unauthorized or unwanted communications between computer networks or hosts.

First sale doctrine (also known as exhaustion): a legal principle allowing the purchaser of a lawfully made copy of a copyrighted work to sell or otherwise dispose of that copy without permission.

Fixity information: data that are generated and used to ensure that the state of a file, or collection of files, is as expected. See checksum.

FTP (file transfer protocol): a standard network protocol used to transfer computer files from one host to another host over a TCP-based network, such as the Internet.

Generation: the number of times a recording is removed from the original format.

Geographic separation: maintaining redundant copies of data in multiple locations that are physically distant from each other.

Gigabit (Gb, Gbit): one billion bits, commonly used for rating the amount of data that is transferred in a second between two points.

HTML: hypertext markup language.

HTTPS (HyperText Transport Protocol Secure): a secure method of sending and receiving data. A web server encrypts and decrypts user page requests as well as the pages that are returned by the web server.

HVAC: heating, ventilating, and air conditioning.

INFO chunk: a metadata chunk developed by Microsoft as part of the RIFF file specification that contains a list of metadata fields, each including an identifier or tag.

Instantaneous discs: discs manufactured to be played immediately after recording, without further processing. Instantaneous discs were widely used from the 1930s to the 1950s for recording and broadcast purposes. Also called lacquer discs.

IRENE 3D: A specialized scanner, developed by Carl Haber, Earl Cornell, and others at the Lawrence Berkeley National Laboratory, that uses optical scanning technology to preserve and restore sound recordings. IRENE produces a three-dimensional optical scan of the grooves in fragile or decayed recordings. Its software creates a virtual representation of a groove that may be manipulated and converted to a digital sound file.

Lacquer discs: a type of phonograph record created by using a recording lathe to cut an audio-signal-modulated groove into the surface of a special lacquer-coated blank disc. Lacquer discs are often referred to as acetate discs, even though the term misstates their composition.

Lateral-cut groove recording process: a method of creating an audio recording in which a stylus cuts side-to-side within the record groove.

Library wind: a process whereby tape is wound at a consistent speed, not fast-forward or rewind, to create a flat tape pack edge with even tension throughout. The consistent speed may be a play speed or faster, such as 120 inches per second.

Linked data: a method of exposing structured data so that it can be interlinked and become more useful through semantic links and queries.

LIST INFO: same as INFO chunk.

Lossless compression: a form of data compression in which there is no loss of data.

Lossy compression: a form of data compression that results in loss of data.

LTO (Linear Tape Open): a commonly used magnetic tape data storage technology that is an open standard. It was created by a consortium of manufacturers of hardware, software, and media. Each generation of LTO drive can read back two generations and write back one generation in order to extend access to information beyond the life cycle of one generation.

MARC (Machine-Readable Cataloging): a data structure devised in the 1960s for exchange of descriptive metadata (i.e., catalog information) among libraries and other similar institutions. The current version is known as MARC21. MARC will be replaced by BIBFRAME (based on linked data principles) in coming years.

MarcEdit: a free MARC editing utility that can be used to search, download, edit, and create new MARC records individually or in batches.

Metadata: structured information that describes, explains, locates, or otherwise makes it possible to retrieve, use, or manage an information resource. In the cultural heritage community, metadata are often broken into three classifications: administrative, structural, and descriptive.

Metadata schema: structured sets of elements intended to describe and enable exchange of information resources of specific areas of endeavor, specified sorts of material, or certain information environments. A schema may define fields, rules of entry, controlled vocabularies, structure, encoding, and other parameters.

METS (Metadata Encoding Transmission Standard): a flexible mechanism for encoding descriptive, administrative, and structural metadata for a digital library object, and for expressing the complex links between metadata, physical objects, and digital objects.

Microgroove disc: a disc with a groove width of approximately 0.7 mil. See coarse groove disc.

Migration: the act of placing the contents of a file in a new wrapper, and/or transcoding from one codec to another.

MiniDiscs: a now-obsolete consumer-based magneto-optical digital disc medium for recording released by Sony in the early 1990s. MiniDiscs use a proprietary lossy codec to record sound.

Mirroring: the process of replication between multiple devices in which the policies are set for the devices to hold the exact same data.

MODS (Metadata Object Description Schema): a simplified XML version of MARC that may be used to describe all types of material. Any content standard may be used with MODS.

MP3: a standard technology and format for compressing digital sound into a smaller, lossy file that requires less bandwidth to send or play. MP3 files may be created at a number of different compression rates.

MPEG-1, 2, 3, and 4: codecs developed for recording moving pictures and associated audio information.

NAS (Network Attached Storage): a file-system and storage device accessed over a network using Ethernet.

Nearline: a type of storage in which data are available to users with some lag time but without human intervention (e.g., magnetic tape libraries).

Non-consumptive use: a type of use in which works are searched or analyzed, usually in large quantities, by a computer, rather than being "consumed" (i.e., read or heard) by a human being.

NUMC (National Union Catalog of Manuscript Collections): a service offered by the Library of Congress wherein catalogers prepare MARC21 collection-level records for eligible U.S. repositories and include them in OCLC WorldCat.

Nyquist-Shannon sampling theorem: a correlation between sampling rate and frequency of the signal being digitized which states that the sampling rate must be at least twice that of the highest frequency being recorded.

OAI-PMH (Open Archives Initiative Protocol for Metadata Harvesting): a low-barrier mechanism for repository interoperability.

OAIS (Open Archival Information System): a model of a system for long-term preservation. Digital preservation systems that are "OAIS-compliant" conform to a recommended framework for ingest, access, data management, storage, metadata, and more.

OAIster: a retrieval service for publicly available digital library resources provided by the research library community.

Object of preservation: the result of faithful reproduction of the original recording.

Offgassing: the release of a gas that was dissolved, trapped, frozen, or absorbed in some material, or by the product of decomposition.

Offline: a type of storage in which data are kept on a piece of media in a location that requires human intervention to retrieve (e.g., an LTO tape stored in a physical storage facility that must be retrieved and placed in an LTO deck before the data can be retrieved).

Omeka: a free and open source web publishing tool for cultural heritage collections. Omeka provides publishing "themes" and add-ons that allow online access to digital collection items and their metadata.

Online: a storage environment that makes data available to users immediately (e.g., a spinning disk server).

Open Archives Initiative (OAI): develops and promotes interoperability standards that aim to facilitate the efficient dissemination of content.

Open Metadata Registry: provides services to developers and consumers of controlled vocabularies to support metadata interoperability. It is one of the first production deployments of the RDF-based Semantic Web Community's Simple Knowledge Organization System.

Optical discs: a grooveless disk on which digital data, as text, music, or pictures, is stored as tiny pits in the surface and is read or replayed by a laser beam scanning the surface.

Orphan Works Statement: developed by the Society of American Archivists' Intellectual Property Working Group, a document describing what professional archivists consider to be best practices regarding reasonable efforts to identify and locate rights holders.

Overlapping rights: a situation in which more than one party owns rights to a work. In the case of a sound recording, it is common for the underlying work (the musical or literary work performed) and the performance or recording of that work to be owned by different parties.

PBCore: an XML-based metadata schema for describing digital and analog audiovisual media, including structural relationships between elements, administrative information such as creators and rights, and technical and descriptive metadata about the elements. It was developed by the public broadcasting archival community and has been in use since 2004. The most recent version, 2.0, was released in January 2011. Version 2.1 is expected to be released in 2015.

PCM: see pulse code modulation

Performing rights organization (PRO): an organization that provides intermediary functions, particularly collection of royalties, between copyright holders and parties who wish to use copyrighted works publicly, e.g., broadcasts, performance venues, and restaurants. The three major PROs in the United States are ASCAP, BMI, and SESAC.

Physical digital: audio specific media in physical form in which the audio content is digitally encoded.

Port: 1. an application or process-specific channel of communication between systems over a network. 2. The act of moving information from one carrier or in some form or codec to another.

PREMIS (PREservation Metadata: Implementation Strategies): an international working group concerned with developing metadata for use in digital preservation, notably, the PREMIS Data Dictionary for Preservation Metadata.

Preservation master: a digital surrogate for the original recording; the preservation master accurately captures all information in the source, typically without any signal processing.

Preservation metadata: the information that supports and documents the digital preservation process. Preservation metadata includes technical details on the format, structure, and use of the digital content; the history of what has been done to preserve the digital object; authenticity information; and the responsibilities and rights information applicable to preservation actions.

Preservation reformatting: the process of transferring the essence or intellectual content of an object to another medium. Also called a "preservation transfer."

Preservation transfers: the process and product of copying the content of an existing recording to a new format, being as faithful to the original as possible.

Production master: see access master.

Public domain: the state of belonging or being available to the public as a whole, and therefore not subject to copyright.

Pulse code modulation (PCM): a method used to digitally represent sampled analog signals. At a regularly defined interval (in preservation it is most often 96,000 times per second), the amplitude of the analog signal is measured and stored (in preservation it is most often at 24 bit resolution).

RAID (Redundant Array of Independent Disks): a method of writing data across multiple disk drives for the purpose of data redundancy or performance improvements.

RDA (Resource Description and Access): a standard for descriptive cataloging initially released in June 2010. It is currently the Library of Congress-wide standard for name and title access points and authority records; however, it has not been implemented for bibliographic description in either the Motion Picture, Broadcasting, and Recorded Sound Division or the American Folklife Center, the two Library of Congress divisions that are chiefly responsible for recorded sound cataloging.

RDF (Resource Description Framework): a framework for describing metadata on a website. RDF uses "subject-predicate-object" triples to describe objects, their attributes, and their relationships. It provides interoperability between applications that exchange machine-understandable information on the web.

Recovery Point Objective: the target duration representing the greatest amount of time in which data that is not yet replicated is vulnerable to non-recoverability in case of a disaster.

Recovery Time Objective: the target duration representing the maximum amount of time in which it would take to recover data from a redundant storage location in case of a disaster.

Red Book standard: see CD-DA.

Redundancy: having multiple copies of the same data.

Refreshing: the process of copying bits that make up one or more files from one storage device to another.

Replication: the act of copying bits of data from one storage location to another.

Restoration: the process of removing imperfections or interpolating lost material in a recording to optimize its sound quality.

RIFF (Resource Interchange File Format): a tagged file structure primarily used to store multimedia resource files. The basic building block of a RIFF file is a chunk. A WAVE file is a type of RIFF file.

Sampling rate: how many times per second a continuous (analog) signal is sampled during the digitization process.

Section 108: a part of the Copyright Act that describes a series of specific scenarios in which works can be reproduced for patrons' use, for interlibrary loan, or for preservation.

Semantic Web: an extension of the current web that provides an easier way to find, share, reuse, and combine information. It is based on machine-readable information and builds on XML technology's capability to define customized tagging schemes and RDF's flexible approach to representing data.

SFTP (Secure File Transport Protocol): network protocol for secure file transfer using SSH.

Shellac disc: term used to describe pressed disc recordings of the first half of the 20th century that are made of many compounds, often including a resin from the lac beetle.

SSH (Secure Shell): a UNIX-based command interface and protocol for securely gaining access to a remote computer.

Sticky shed syndrome: a condition afflicting some polyester tape stock in which the binder on the tape stock absorbs atmospheric water (binder hydrolysis), thus weakening the bond between the substrate and the magnetic layer.

Structural metadata: information that describes the structure of a compound object, such as an album, its individual tracks, its labels, and its packaging artwork, or the components of an oral history collection.

Tails-out wind: a wind with the tape of the program's beginning at the core of the reel and the end at its outer edge.

Technical metadata: information that describes specific attributes of an audio object. For a physical source object, some of these attributes might include material composition, dimensions, audio signal characteristics, and condition. For a digital file, they might include sampling rate, bit depth, data encoding type, checksum value, and other information necessary to reproduce the information.

Track configuration: the arrangement of one or more signals on magnetic recording tape.

USID (Unique Source Identifier): a code that is assigned to BWF source sound files so that they can be identified unambiguously. The practice is defined under EBU Rec-099.

Vertical cut groove recording process: a method of creating an audio recording in which a stylus cuts up-and-down within the record groove. Also known as the "hill and dale" process, vertical cut recordings were used to record phonograph cylinder records, as well as Edison Disc records and Pathé disc records.

VIAF (Virtual International Authority File): a joint project of several national libraries and operated by OCLC, VIAF is an international authority file whose aim is to link the national authority files to a single virtual authority file. In this file, identical records from the different data sets are linked together.

Vinegar syndrome: a condition afflicting acetate tape. The acetate base film chemical decomposes with age. A byproduct of the decomposition is acetic acid, the familiar smell of household vinegar. Vinegar syndrome is characterized by a sour smell and tape shrinkage and deformation.

WAV: see WAVE

WAVE (Waveform Audio File Format): a standard for storing sound files, developed by Microsoft and IBM. It is a subtype of the Resource Interchange File Format (RIFF), using the method of storing data in chunks. Also known as WAV. See also BWF.

WMA (Windows Media Audio): an audio data compression technology developed by Microsoft. The name can be used to refer to its audio file format or its audio codecs. It is a proprietary technology that forms part of the Windows Media framework. May be used in derivatives.

Wrapper: the portion of a file that serves as the container for the essence and associated metadata.

XML (Extensible Markup Language): a commonly used language for marking up the structure and other features of electronic documents.

XSLT (Extensible Stylesheet Language Transformations): a language for transforming XML documents into other XML documents, or to other formats.

CONTRIBUTORS

CARLA ARTON works as a recorded sound processing technician at the Library of Congress in the Motion Picture, Broadcasting, and Recorded Sound Division. She holds a Master of Arts in Film Archiving from the University of East Anglia in England and a Bachelor of Arts in Film Studies from Chapman University in California. Prior to joining the Library of Congress, Arton held film archiving positions at the Wende Museum of the Cold War and Chace Audio by Deluxe. She was the 2006 recipient of the Association of Moving Image Archivists (AMIA) Kodak Fellowship and currently serves as the co-chair for the AMIA Education Committee.

HARRISON BEHL is the audiovisual specialist for the Rodgers & Hammerstein Archive of Recorded Sound of New York Public Library. He has also worked as a processing technician in the Recorded Sound Section at the National Audiovisual Conservation Center of the Library of Congress. He received a Masters in Library and Information Science from the University of Pittsburgh with a specialization in archives, preservation, and records management. Behl has extensive experience in the processing, conservation, and preservation of a wide range of audio formats and is interested in promoting increased access and exposure of archival audio collections.

BRANDON BUTLER is the practitioner-in-residence at the Glushko-Samuelson Intellectual Property Clinic at the Washington College of Law at American University in Washington, D.C. At the clinic, he supervises student attorneys who represent clients in a variety of IP matters. Before teaching law, Butler was the director of public policy initiatives at the Association of Research Libraries (ARL). While there, he worked on issues ranging from fair use to network neutrality to the PATRIOT Act. He is a co-facilitator, with Peter Jaszi and Patricia Aufderheide, of the ARL Code of Best Practices in Fair Use for Academic and Research Libraries, released in January 2012. Before coming to ARL, Butler was an associate in the Media and Information Technologies practice group at the Washington, D.C., law firm Dow Lohnes PLLC. He received his J.D. from the University of Virginia School of Law.

WILLIAM CHASE belongs to the Research, Archives and Data Strategy Group at National Public Radio, where his duties include leading audio reformatting initiatives, editorial research, and metadata creation. He has previously worked as an audio preservation engineer for the Southern Folklife Collection at the University of North Carolina at Chapel Hill, and as a sound archivist at the State Archives of Florida. He holds a B.A. in Music and M.S. in Library and Information Studies from Florida State University.

PETER JASZI is a professor of law at American University Washington College of Law, where he teaches copyright law and courses in law and cinema, as well as supervising students in the Glushko-Samuelson Intellectual Property Law Clinic, which he helped to establish, along with the Program on Intellectual Property and Information Justice. He has served as a trustee of the Copyright Society of the U.S.A. and is a member of the editorial board of its journal. In 2007, he received the American Library Association's L. Ray Patterson Copyright Award, and in 2009 the Intellectual Property Section of the District of Columbia Bar honored him as the year's Champion of Intellectual Property. He has written about copyright history and theory, and co-authored a standard copyright textbook.

CHRIS LACINAK is the president and founder of AVPreserve, a consulting and software development firm that works internationally with a focus on empowering organizations to maximize the usability of their data for education, distribution, production, research, monetization, marketing, and business intelligence. Much of his latest work has focused on strategic and business planning, as well as research and development of standards and technologies for the creation and management of digital media. Lacinak sits on the board of the Association of Moving Image Archivists, the National Recording Preservation Board Technical Task Force, and Technical Committees within ARSC and the International Association of Sound and Audiovisual Archives. He is also active in standards-forming organizations such as the Audio Engineering Society, Society of Motion Picture and Television Engineers, and the International Organization for Standardization.

MAYA LERMAN works in the Recorded Sound Section of the Library of Congress at the Packard Campus for Audiovisual Conservation. She also undertakes digital curation activities at the Library's American Folklife Center. Lerman helped build the National Jukebox Project and currently works to provide access to music and oral history collections. Her work cataloging the Studs Terkel collection led to a presentation at ARSC about Terkel's music interviews. Lerman's involvement in recorded sound and folklife archives began during a field documentation project for the 2003 Smithsonian Folklife Festival and has inspired her to work in several libraries and archives, including the Archives of Traditional Music at Indiana University and the Lilly Library. As a guitarist, singer, and songwriter, she produced and recorded her first full-length album, *Take This Song With You*, in 2012. She earned her B.A. in Anthropology from McGill University and a Master's in Library Science with an archives specialization at Indiana University.

MARSHA MAGUIRE has been processing and describing audio and multiple-format collections in library, archival, and museum settings for more than 35 years. In her work in the Motion Picture, Broadcasting, and Recorded Sound Division of the Library of Congress; the University of Washington Libraries; the Experience Music Project; the American Folklife Center at the Library of Congress; and the American Film Institute, she has not only used but often implemented metadata standards such as AACR2, RDA, DACS, MARC, EAD,

Dublin Core, METS, MODS, and PBCore. She has also written manuals, data dictionaries, and best practice documents for their use, and given classes and workshops on them at local, regional, and national events. Maguire served for two years as secretary of ARSC and chaired the Subcommittee on DACS for Archival Sound Recordings of the ARSC Cataloging Committee.

CURTIS PEOPLES, Ph.D., is an archivist at the Southwest Collection/Special Collections Library at Texas Tech University (TTU). He is a musician who has worked in the music business for three decades. He is a graduate and former instructor of the Sound Technology program at South Plains College. Peoples has worked in numerous recording studios and has been a production manager for many events. In 2001, he helped launch the Crossroads Music Archive in the Southwest Collection. He is the archivist for the collection and head of the Crossroads Recording Studio in the TTU Library. He also teaches the History of West Texas Music in the TTU Honors College. His research centers on music and place.

KARA VAN MALSSEN is senior consultant at AudioVisual Preservation Solutions, where she works with clients on digital and media asset management, metadata management, and digital preservation initiatives. She is also adjunct professor at New York University (NYU), where she teaches digital preservation for the Moving Image Archiving and Preservation (MIAP) graduate program. Van Malssen's work with disasters and audiovisual collections began in 2005 when, as a student in NYU's MIAP program and as part of her master's thesis, she conducted research and helped organizations in New Orleans whose audiovisual collections were damaged by Hurricane Katrina. In 2012, she used her experience in disaster response to manage the recovery of the media archive at Eyebeam Art+Technology Center following Superstorm Sandy. She has taught disaster preparedness and recovery workshops for Metropolitan New York Library Council, the International Centre for the Study of the Preservation and Restoration of Cultural Property (ICCROM) Sound and Image Collections Conservation programme, and for NYU MIAP.

EDITORS

SAM BRYLAWSKI is co-director of the *American Discography Project* at the University of California, Santa Barbara, and editor of UCSB's *Discography of American Historical Recordings* (adp.library.ucsb.edu). He is the former head of the Library of Congress Recorded Sound Section. Brylawski is the co-author of both the Library of Congress National Recording Preservation Board (NRPB) study on audio preservation, *The State of Recorded Sound Preservation in the United States: A National Legacy at Risk in the Digital Age*, and the *Library of Congress National Recording Preservation Plan*. He served as chair of the NRPB from 2013 to 2015.

MAYA LERMAN is profiled on page 232.

ROBIN PIKE is manager of the Digital Conversion and Media Reformatting Department at the University of Maryland, College Park Libraries. Previously, she worked as the audiovisual archivist at The Catholic University of America. She graduated in 2007 from the University of Pittsburgh with an MLIS, specializing in archives and records management. Pike chairs the Society of American Archivists Recorded Sound Roundtable, and serves on the Education and Training Committee of the Association for Recorded Sound Collections. She is also an ACA Certified Archivist and holds the Digital Archivist Specialist certificate from SAA.

KATHLIN SMITH is director of communications at the Council on Library and Information Resources. She has overseen the editing and publication of more than 70 reports, including *The State of Recorded Sound Preservation in the United States: A National Legacy at Risk in the Digital Age*, *The Library of Congress National Recording Preservation Plan*, and several others commissioned by the National Recording Preservation Board.

INDEX

A

AAC/MPEG-4 v.2 (audio file format), 3; 34
AACR2, 88; 89-90; 92; 96; 98; 99
acclimatization, 69
accompanying documentation, storage of, 65
acoustics, 10-11
acquisition criteria, 39-42
administrative metadata. *See*: metadata—
  administrative
AES, 7; 113; 114; 115
AIFF (audio file format), 33
ALAC. *See*: Apple Lossless Audio Codec
aliasing, 10
AmerTape, 31
analog-to-digital converters, 10; 71; 110; 114; 120 [fn]
Anderson, Seth, 142; 143
Apple Lossless Audio Codec (audio file format), 33
Archéophone, 1; 72
Archival Management System (AMS), 104
Archive of World Music (Harvard University), 5
Archives of Traditional Music (Indiana Unbiversity), 5
ArchivesSpace, 102
arrangement of physical media, 68
ARSC. *See*: Association for Recorded Sound Collections
Association for Recorded Sound Collections (ARSC), 7;
  71 [fn]; 195
Association of Moving Image Archivists (AMIA), 7
Audio Engineering Society. *See*: AES
audio files. *See*: digital audio file formats; storage—
  digital files
audio formats, history of, 6-7; 15-25; 28-34
Audio Interchange File Format. *See*: AIFF
audio restoration. *See*: restoration, audio
Audio-Visual and Image Database (AVID) (dedicated
  descriptive metadata tool), 82
audiocassettes. *See*: magnetic media, analog—
  cartridges and cassettes
AudioVisual Collaborative Cataloging (AVCC)
  (dedicated descriptive metadata tool), 80; 82-84

Audit and certification of trustworthy digital
  repositories, 129

B

backup (of digital files), 130; 131; 136; 143; 145; 168;
  172; 192
Berliner, Emile, 17; 99-100
Besser, Howard, 127
BEXT. *See*: metadata—embedded—BEXT
BIBFRAME, 88; 89; 90; 91; 92-93
bit depth, 10-11; 28; 29; 111; 112; 113; 114; 117; 122
  compact discs, 29; 32
  DAT, 28
  embedded metadata, inclusion in, 99; 117
  preservation files, master, 33; 112; 122
bit rot, 132
Blue Amberol cylinders. *See*: cylinders
Broadcast Wave File format. *See*: BWF
brown wax cylinders. *See*: cylinders
BWF (audio file format), 11; 33; 111; 112; 114; 116; 118;
  135
BWF MetaEdit (application), 114; 116; 117-118

C

care and maintenance, 52-74; 168-173; 178-183
cassettes. *See*: magnetic media, analog—cartridges
  and cassettes
cataloging tools, library, 93-94. *See also*: metadata—
  descriptive
cataloging, Item-level, 89
cataloging, perfectionism in, 78
CD-Rs. *See*: discs (optical)—writable
CDs. *See*: discs (optical)
checksums, 113; 121; 133. *See also*: fixity
cleaning physical media, 58-62; 180-183; 186-188
climate control. *See*: storage, physical media—
  environment
CLIR. *See:* Council on Library and Information Resources
collaboration on digital preservation (files), 129
collaboration, importance of, 5; 15

collection assessment, tools for, 44-45

collection development policies, 38-39

CollectiveAccess (dedicated descriptive metadata tool) 82; 86

compact discs. *See*: discs (optical)

compression and refraction, wave, 10

compression, file, 3; 7; 11; 32; 33-34; 42; 111-112

condition assessment, physical media, 40-41; 44-45; 54-57; 173

conservation, 52-74; 168-173; 178-183

conservation: core needs, 52; 62

copyright, 152-167; 194-222

    bootleg recordings, 163-164

    collectors and copyright, 159

    copyright notices, 155-156

    divisibility, 155

    donations, terms of, 49; 165-166

    end user license agreements, 205; 212-213

    fair use, 153; 154; 156; 157-159; 161; 194-222

        access to remote users, providing, 207-208

        attribution of copies, 206; 213; 216

        criteria, general, 157-159; 199

        data mining, 214-215

        definition, 157-159; 199

        exhibitions, use of audio in, 215-217

        good faith, indicia of, 205-206

        instruction and education, support to, 198; 199; 208-211; 217

        libraries and archives, application to, 158; 207-211; 212-214; 217-219

        myths, 157; 200-201

        online materials, harvesting, 212-214

        preservation, application to, 158-159; 211-212

        privacy, 206

        third party use of recordings, 208; 217-219

        value added, 216

    first sale doctrine, 156

    licenses, 162-163; 200; 205

    orphan works, 196; 206[fn]; 208

    overlapping rights, 154-155; 196

    pre-1972 recordings, 153-154; 155-156; 160-162; 197; 202

        copyright disposition of, 153; 197

        fair use, 160-162; 197; 202

        status, 160-162

        term of copyright, 155-156

    preservation copies, authorization to make, 159-160

    public domain, 155-156

    reproduction by libaries and archives, 160

    rights of copyright holders, 153-154

    Section 107. *See*: copyright—fair use

    Section 108, 159-160; 161; 162; 165; 204 [fn]; 207; 211; 212 [fn]; 218

        reproduction by libraries and archives, 159-160

    state laws. *See*: copyright—term of copyright

    status, researching copyright, 153[fn]

    term of copyright, 155-156; 160-161

    violations by patrons, liability for, 164-165; 217-219

Council on Library and Information Resources, 7

Creative Commons licenses. *See*: copyright—licenses

cylinders, 1; 3; 6; 15-16; 31; 43; 53; 58; 59; 63; 64[fn 10]; 66; 69; 70; 71; 72; 183

    cleaning, 59; 183

    damage and deterioration, 16

    description of types, 15

    format composition, 15; 16

    handling, 53

    history, 6; 15-16

    housing and storage, 62-63; 66; 69; 171

    overview, 15-16

    playback, 15; 16; 64 [fn 10]; 71; 72

    salvage, 183

    transporting, 70

D

DACS, 88; 93; 94; 95-96; 97; 98; 99; 102

DAT. *See*: magnetic media, digital—digital audio tape

deaccessioning, 42; 43; 173; 191

decibels, 10

delamination. *See*: discs, grooved—lacquer—damage and deterioration

derivatives, file. *See*: compression, file

descriptive metadata. *See*: metadata—descriptive

Diamond Discs, 6; 18; 20; 43; 59 [fn]

dictation belts, 31; 53; 60; 64; 73

    cleaning, 60

    description of types, 31

    handling, 53

    housing and storage, 62; 64

    playback, 73

digital audio file formats, 32-34

digital file obsolescence monitoring. *See*: obsolescence monitoring of digital files

digital files, management of, 127-151

digital provenance. *See*: metadata—technical—digital provenance

digital repositories, 129

digitization, 10-11; 42-48; 110-112; 119-123; 135

    in-house, 119-121

        equipment and facilities, 120

funding, 121
    personnel, 119-120
outsourcing, 110; 119; 121-123
    communication with vendor, 122
    cost control, 123
    quality control, 122-123
    requests-for-proposals, 121-122
    vendor selection, 121
prioritization, criteria, 42-48
    tools, 44-45
disasters, 43; 67-68; 121; 131; 136; 143; 144; 168-193
    preparedness, 43; 67-68; 121; 131; 136; 143; 144;
        172; 174-178; 190-191
        collection redundancy (deaccessioning), 43; 173;
            191
        disaster plan creation, 174-178
        equipment and supplies, 169; 175; 176; 177; 186
        knowledge of collections, 169-170; 172-173; 176;
            191
        risk assessment and treatment, 169-174
        storage, 67-68; 171-172; 190-191
        training, 174-175
    prevention, 169-174
        building and systems, 67-68; 170-171
    response and recovery, 178-192
        mold, 169; 171; 178; 187; 190. *See also*: mold
        risk management, 189-191
        salvage, 180-188; 190
        staffing, 188-189
        supplies, 176; 177; 179-180; 186; 187; 190
        workflow, 178-180; 183-191
discovery tools, 82; 86-87; 93; 98
discs, grooved, 17-21; 55; 59; 63; 73
    aluminum, 6; 21; 55; 59; 63
    cleaning, 58-59; 182-183
    composition, 17-21
    groove type,
        lateral, 17; 18; 19; 21
        microgroove, 19; 20; 21
        vertical, 6; 18; 19; 21; 31
    handling, 53
    history, 6-7; 17-21
    housing and storage, 62-68
    lacquer, 6; 17; 20; 21; 23; 43; 44; 53; 55; 58; 59; 63;
        73; 170; 182
        damage and deterioration, 20; 21; 44; 53; 55
        history, 6; 21; 23
        housing and storage, 62; 59; 63; 170
        playback, 21; 71; 73
        salvage, 182

cleaning, 58; 59; 182
    handling, 53
    shellac, 7; 17; 18; 20; 58-59; 71; 183. *See also*:
        Diamond Discs
        cleaning, 58-59; 183
        damage and deterioration, 18; 20
        history, 7; 17; 18; 20
        playback, 18; 71
        salvage, 183
    vinyl, 3; 7; 17; 19; 20; 46; 54; 55-57; 58-59; 63; 64; 68;
        71; 73; 183
        damage and deterioration, 3; 7; 17; 19; 20; 46; 54
        history, 7; 19; 20
        playback, 19; 71; 73
        salvage, 183
discs, optical, 7; 10; 20; 28-31; 53; 55; 57; 61; 64; 65; 66;
    69; 74; 112; 131; 141-142; 181-182; 185; 186; 190
    disadvantages, 4; 130
    playback, 30
    cleaning, 61; 181-182; 186
    damage and deterioration, 3; 20; 28-31; 55; 57; 181-
        182
    handling, 53
    history, 7; 28-31
    housing and storage, 62; 64; 65; 66; 69
    playback, 29-30; 74
    preservation medium, poor choice as, 3; 4; 141
    preservation reformatting, 112
    salvage, 181-182; 185; 190
    writable, 4; 7; 28; 30; 130
Dolby, 7; 23; 24
donations, tax appraisal for, 48-50
donations, terms for, 49; 165-166
Dublin Core, 78; 81; 82; 84; 88; 94; 102; 103-104; 114
duplicates copies, retention of, 43

E

EAC-CPF, 88; 102
EAD, 82; 88; 93; 94; 96; 97-102; 104
    conversion of spreadsheet data, 101; 102
    data structure, 97-98
    display of finding aids on the web, 98
    EAD listserv, 101
    tools for EAD, 99; 101-102
EADiva, 101
Edison Diamond Discs. *See*: Diamond Discs
Edison, Thomas, 6; 15
EGAD, 88; 95
Encoded Archival Description. *See*: EAD
European Broadcasting Union, 7

exhaustion. *See*: copyright—first sale doctrine

eXist (XML database), 97

exudation. *See*: discs, grooved—lacquer—damage and deterioration

F

FADGI. *See*: Federal Agencies Digitization Guidelines Initiative

Fair use. *See*: copyright—fair use

Federal Agencies Digitization Guidelines Initiative, 116; 120 [fn]

file attendance. *See*: file security—attendance

file security, 86; 130-131; 139-140; 143; 145-146
      file attendance, 133
      virus prevention, 131; 140; 146

File Transfer Protocol, 140

Filemaker Pro, 81; 82; 85; 86; 104

files, preservation. *See*: preservation file formats

finding aids, 88; 93; 95; 96; 97; 98; 99; 101; 102; 104; 115

fire suppression systems, 67; 68

first sale doctrine, 156

fixity, 130-33; 137; 145; 146; 148. *See also*: checksums

FLAC (audio file format), 11; 33

floor load capacities, 67

formats, history of, 6-7; 15-25; 28-34

FRBR, 90

Free Lossless Audio Codec. *See*: FLAC

FTP. *See*: File Transfer Protocol

Functional Requirements for Bibliographic Records. *See*: FRBR

funding, 42; 45; 46; 47; 119; 121; 124-125

G

geographic separation of digital files, 130; 131; 136; 143; 145; 146; 168; 172; 192; 197

H

handling, general, 52-54

Harvard University Archive of World Music. *See*: Archive of World Music

Hertz (Hz), 10

hill and dale groove. *See*: vertical groove

history of audio formats. *See*: audio formats, history of

housing of physical media, 62-65

I

IASA. *See*: International Association of Sound and Audiovisual Archives

in-house digitization. *See*: digitization—in-house

Indiana University Archives of Traditional Music. *See*: Archives of Traditional Music

Indiana University media preservation survey, 6

intellectual property rights. *See*: copyright—access restrictions

International Association of Sound and Audiovisual Archives (IASA), 7; 71; 112; 119; 120

International Standards Organization, 33; 128-129

inventories, item-level, 42; 43; 47; 78; 79-86; 88; 95; 97; 104; 119; 123; 172-173; 177; 191
      uses, 41; 42; 43; 47; 78; 79; 119; 123; 172-173; 191

ISO. *See*: International Standards Organization

L

labeling of physical media, 64-65

lacquer discs. *See*: discs, grooved—lacquer

laminated media, 18; 20; 29; 30; 31; 55; 59; 69; 182

laser rot, 3; 57

lateral cut groove, 17; 18; 19; 21; 31

levels of digital preservation. *See*: NDSA Levels of Digital Preservation

Library of Congress National Digital Information Preservation Program. *See*: National Digital Information Preservation Program

Library of Congress National Recording Preservation Plan. *See*: National Recording Preservation Plan

library winds, 55; 60

lossy audio files, disadvantages of, 3; 111

LP 33-1/3 discs. *See*: discs, grooved—vinyl

M

magnetic fields near storage, 67

magnetic formats, general description of, 22-28

magnetic media, analog,
      cartridges and cassettes, 3; 7; 23; 25-27; 34; 43-44; 53; 57; 61; 62; 74; 120; 171; 182
            cleaning, 60-61
            damage and deterioration, 24-25; 57; 182
            handling, 53
            history, 7; 23; 25
            housing and storage, 62; 120; 171
            playback, 25-26; 27; 74
            repairing, 61; 120
      open reel, 6-7; 22-25; 26-27; 53; 55-56; 57; 59; 60; 61; 62; 64; 73-74; 120; 171; 173; 182
            acetate from polyester, differentiating, 26
            baking, 26; 56; 60; 61
            cleaning, 59; 60-61; 182
            damage and deterioration, 24; 55-56. *See also*: sticky shed syndrome; wind problems

handling, 53

history, 6-7; 22-25

housing and storage, 61; 62; 64

playback, 24; 26-27; 73-74

salvage, 180; 182

speeds, 24

splicing, 24; 56; 59; 60; 120

sticky shed syndrome, 4; 20; 24; 54; 56; 60; 61

tape lengths/duration, 24; 26-27

tape tracks, 26-27

vinegar syndrome, 24; 56; 171

wind problems, 56

magnetic media, digital,

   digital audio tape, 4; 7; 28; 40; 43; 57; 74; 110; 112; 120; 128; 182

      damage and deterioration, 28; 57; 110; 112

      history, 4; 7; 28

      playback, 28; 74; 120

      preservation reformatting, 112

      salvage, 182

MARC, 87; 88; 89; 91; 92; 93; 94; 95; 96; 99; 100; 102; 104

MarcEdit, 94

MARCXML, 102

MarkLogic (XML database), 97

metadata,

   administrative, 79; 112-115; 131

      rights management, 115

   definition, 79

   descriptive,

      archive descriptive metadata, 94-103

      archive standards for descriptive metadata content, 95-97

      archive standards for descriptive metadata structure, 97-103

      dedicated metadata database tools, 82-86

      desktop tools, 81-82

      library standards for descriptive metadata content, 89-91

      library standards for descriptive metadata structure, 91-94

      published materials, 89

      sources, 80-81

      standards, choice of, 87-88

      uses, 77; 79

   embedded, 115-118

      BEXT (Broadcast extension chunk), 33; 116-118

      BWF file header fields, 116

      INFO chunk, 116

      Resource Interchange File Format (RIFF), 116; 118

   preservation uses, 112-118; 137-139

   structural, 79; 112; 115

   technical, 113-118

      AES-X098C, 114

      AES57-2011: Audio Engineering Society standard for audio metadata, 114

      digiProvMD, 114

      digital provenance, 114-115; 116

      schema, 114

METRO, 84

migration of digital files. *See*: refreshing and migration of digital files

MiniDiscs, 31; 43; 74; 112

mirroring and replication, 136

MODS, 89; 93; 94; 102

mold, 16; 54; 55; 57; 58; 60; 62; 169; 171; 178; 187; 190

molded cylinders. *See*: cylinders

MP3 (audio file format), 3; 7; 11; 33; 34; 111; 115; 116; 128

MPEG-1 Layer III (audio file format). *See*: MP3

MS Access (application), 44-45; 81; 82; 94

music box discs, 31

music retrieval systems, 77

N

NAS. *See*: Network Attached Storage

National Digital Information Infrastructure Preservation Program (NDIIPP), 5

National Digital Stewardship Alliance. *See*: NDSA Levels of Digital Preservation

National Recording Preservation Board, 5; 82-84

National Recording Preservation Plan, 5

NDIIPP. *See*: National Digital Information Preservation Program

NDSA Levels of Digital Preservation, 130-132; 139; 140; 143; 148

Network Attached Storage, 139; 141; 146-147

NRPB. *See*: National Recording Preservation Board

NUCMC, 96-97

Nyquist-Shannon Sampling Theorem, 10

O

OAI-PMH, 103

OAIster, 103

obsolescence monitoring of digital files, 134-135

OCLC, 89; 92; 93-94; 96-97; 98; 103

Ogg Vorbis (audio file format), 34

Omeka, 86; 103

online catalogs, 87; 89

Online Computer Library Center. See: OCLC
Open Archival Information Systems (OAIS), 129
Open Archives Initiative (OAI), 94; 129
optical soundtracks, 31
outsourcing digitization. *See*: digitization—
    outsourcing
Oxygen (application), 97

P

partnerships, preservation, 129
PBCore, 82; 84-86; 87; 88; 93; 96; 98; 99; 103; 104; 113-
    114
PBCore, tools for, 85-86; 104
PCC. *See*: Program for Cooperative Cataloging
PCM. *See*: pulse code modulation
phasing of preservation of digital files,130-132
physical media, conservation of, 52-76. *See also*:
    cleaning; housing and storage; playback; and
    salvage; *also*, disasters; shelving; and storage,
    physical media—environment
playback, 15-34; 71-74
PREMIS. *See*: Preservation Metadata: Implementation
    Strategies
preservation and restoration engineers, ARSC directory
    of audio, 71 [fn]
preservation file types, 111-112
preservation media, 4; 130
Preservation Metadata: Implementation Strategies
    (PREMIS), 85; 137
preservation phasing (files). *See*: phasing of
    preservation of digital files
preservation priorities. *See*: digitization—prioritization
preservation reformatting, 110-126
PrestoCentre, 7
process history metadata. *See*: metadata—technical—
    digital provenance
public relations, 124
pulse code modulation (PCM), 7; 10-11; 28; 29; 32; 33;
    111; 135

R

RDA, 88; 89; 90-91; 96; 98; 102
recovery point objective (RPO), 136
recovery time objective (RTO), 136
Red Book standard for compact discs, 11; 28; 29
redundance of digital files, 136; 140; 145; 146; 148; 197
reformatting. *See*: preservation reformatting
refreshing and migration of digital files, 135
repair of tapes, 24; 55-56; 60

reproduction by libaries and archives. *See*: copyright—
    Section 108—reproduction by libraries and archives
restoration, audio, 71; 110-111; 119;
restrictions, access, 41-42; 44; 45; 46; 77; 83; 95; 98; 113;
    115; 165
RIFF. *See*: metadata—embedded—Resource
    Interchange File Format
RPO. *See*: recovery point objective
RTO. *See*: recovery time objective

S

sampling rate, digital, 7; 10-11; 28; 29; 32; 99; 111; 112;
    113; 114; 117; 122
    formats, 7; 10-11; 28; 29; 32; 111; 112
    metadata, inclusion in, 99; 113; 114; 117; 122
schemas, 78
security, collection, 67; 180; 190
security, file. *See*: file security
shellac discs. *See*: discs, grooved—shellac
shelving for physical media. *See*: storage—physical
    media
Society of American Archivists, 98
Sony MiniDiscs. *See*: MiniDiscs
sound pressure level (SPL), 10
sticky shed syndrome. *See*: magnetic media, analog—
    sticky shed syndrome
storage, digital files, 130; 140-148
    cloud, 130; 140; 142-148
    comparison of options, 141-148
    cost, 147-148
    infrastucture, 140-148
    interim storage, 130
    local, 144-147
    long-term storage, 130
    media, 130; 141-145
    nearline, 141
    offline, 141
    online, 141
    scenarios, 145-148
    total cost of ownership, 142-144; 147-148
storage, physical media, 19; 20; 24; 25; 40; 52; 54-55;
    62; 65-69; 75; 121; 170-173. *See also*: housing and
    storage under specific media
    arrangement, 68
    environment, 19; 20; 24; 25; 40; 52; 54-55; 62; 67; 69;
        75; 121; 171-172
    risk prevention, 170-173
    shelving, 65-67
    structural considerations and building locations,
        67-68

streaming audio, 3; 7; 11; 42; 111-112
    preservation challenges of, 3; 42
structural metadata. *See*: metadata—structural
supplies, 59; 120; 121; 169; 175; 176; 177; 179-180; 186;
    187; 189; 190

T

tape. *See*: magnetic media
target file format for preservation, 135
tax appraisal for donations. *See*: donations, tax
    appraisal for
TCO. *See*: storage—digital files—total cost of
    ownership
transport of collections, 52; 54; 70

U

UNESCO, 7

V

vertical groove, 6; 15; 16; 18; 19; 21; 31
VIAF, 91; 96; 102
vinegar syndrome, 24; 56; 171
vinyl discs. *See*: discs, grooved—vinyl
virus prevention. *See*: file security—virus prevention
Vitaphone system, 20

W

WAVE (audio file format), 33; 111; 116. *See also*: BWF
WaveLab (application), 118
Windows Media Audio (audio file format), 3; 33; 34
wires, 6; 22; 23; 53; 59; 64; 67; 73; 84; 171-172
    cleaning, 22; 59
    composition, 22; 23
    damage and deterioration, 22
    handling, 53
    history, 6; 22; 23
    housing and storage, 62; 64; 67; 171-172
    playback, 73
WMA. *See*: Windows Media Audio

X

XML, 81; 84; 85; 86; 88; 93; 94; 96; 97; 98; 100-101; 101;
    102; 104; 114
XMLSpy, 97